At last, African women judges receive the careful scholarly attention they deserve. This work underscores the centrality of the third branch of government in democratization. The authors' careful following of a common protocol allows both valuable comparisons as well as solid introductions for the country specialist and novice alike. While the authors review no simple answers to the puzzle of significant country-to-country variation, happily, they analyze how to increase women's representation rather than replaying tired essentialist arguments about difference. Perhaps African feminists will inspire the rest of the world to demand a diverse and representative judiciary? A must read for anyone interested in comparative politics, African politics, women and politics, or judicial politics.

Sally J. Kenney, *Newcomb College, USA*

This volume offers a fascinating and timely look at the changing role and status of women in Africa's judicial systems. Covering a large and diverse collection of countries, the chapters provide deep and sophisticated analyses of the factors shaping patterns of gender representation in judiciaries, the legal, institutional and societal impacts of greater representation for women, and the ongoing challenges facing that project. The book will be of interest to those concerned with comparative judicial development, gender politics, and patterns of change and continuity in African politics and society.

Peter VonDoepp, *University of Vermont, USA*

Gender and the Judiciary in Africa

Across Africa over the last two decades, nearly two dozen women have been appointed head of the highest court in the land in a range of countries – either as chief justice in common law countries or president of the constitutional court in civil law countries. In most cases, these appointments were a 'first' in terms of the gender of the office holder. At the same time, women are being appointed in record numbers as magistrates, judges and justices across the continent. While women's increasing numbers and roles in African executives and legislatures have been addressed in a burgeoning scholarly literature, very little work has focused on women in judiciaries. This book addresses the important issue of the increasing numbers and varied roles of women judges and justices, as judiciaries evolve across the continent.

Scholars of gender and politics and African politics provide overviews of recent developments in gender and the judiciary in nine African countries that represent north, east, south and west Africa as well as a range of colonial experiences, postcolonial trajectories and legal systems, including mixes of common, civil, customary, or sharia law. In the process, each chapter seeks to address the following questions:

- What has been the historical experience of the judicial system in a given country, from before colonialism until the present?
- What is the current court structure and where are the women judges, justices, magistrates and other women located?
- What are the selection or appointment processes for joining the bench and in what ways may these help or hinder women in gaining access to courts as judges and justices?
- Once women become judges, do they promote the rights of women through their judicial powers?
- What are the challenges and obstacles facing women judges and justices in Africa?

Timely and relevant in this era in which governmental accountability and transparency are essential to the consolidation of democracy in Africa and when women are accessing significant leadership positions across the continent, this book considers the substantive and symbolic representation of women's interests by women judges and the wider implications of their presence for changing institutional norms and advancing the rule of law and human rights.

Gretchen Bauer is professor of political science and international relations at the University of Delaware, USA. Her current research focuses on women's political leadership in sub-Saharan Africa. She is the co-editor with Manon Tremblay of *Women in Executive Power: A Global Overview* (2011) and with Hannah Britton of *Women in African Parliaments* (2006).

Josephine Dawuni is an assistant professor of political science at Howard University, USA. Her current research focuses on women and the judiciary in sub-Saharan Africa.

Routledge Research in Gender and Politics

1. **The Women's Movement in Protest, Institutions and the Internet**
   Australia in transnational perspective
   Sarah Maddison and Marian Sawer

2. **The Politics of Gender Culture under State Socialism**
   An expropriated voice
   Hana Havelková and Libora Oates-Indruchova

3. **Maternal Transition**
   A North-South politics of pregnancy and childbirth
   Candace Johnson

4. **The Principles of Gender-Sensitive Parliaments**
   Lena Wängnerud

5. **Gender and the Judiciary in Africa**
   From obscurity to parity?
   Edited by Gretchen Bauer and Josephine Dawuni

Gender and the Judiciary in Africa

From Obscurity to Parity?

Edited by
Gretchen Bauer and
Josephine Dawuni

Routledge
Taylor & Francis Group
LONDON AND NEW YORK

First published 2016
by Routledge

2 Park Square, Milton Park, Abingdon, Oxfordshire OX14 4RN
711 Third Avenue, New York, NY 10017

Routledge is an imprint of the Taylor & Francis Group, an informa business

First issued in paperback 2018

Library of Congress Cataloging-in-Publication Data
Gender and the judiciary in Africa : from obscurity to parity? / edited by Gretchen Bauer and Josephine Dawuni.
pages cm. — (Routledge research in gender and politics)
Includes bibliographical references and index.
1. Women judges—Africa. I. Bauer, Gretchen, 1959– editor.
II. Dawuni, Josephine, editor.
KQC51.G46 2016
347.6'014082—dc23
2015021637

ISBN: 978-1-138-85649-3 (hbk)
ISBN: 978-0-8153-7055-0 (pbk)

Typeset in Times New Roman
by Apex CoVantage, LLC

In Memoriam

My mother, Merry Jo Bauer, who raised us to be strong
—Gretchen

The wonderful women in my life who taught me to love and persevere: my grandmother Maayi, my mother Mercy, and my sister Bernice
—Josephine

Contents

Figures

Tables

Foreword

An esteemed colleague of mine recently described the judiciary in Ghana as an ill-tolerated distant cousin of the other arms of government. I daresay the description is apt for many judiciaries in Africa. It therefore does not surprise me that the giant strides attained in the bid to attain gender balance in the composition of the bench in so many countries on the continent appear to have gone unnoticed, or at least remained unsung, until now.

Many African countries have fledgling democracies and the rule of law has, in the last decade or two, attained prominence as a benchmark of proper governance. Thus have judiciaries been recognized (albeit grudgingly) as pivotal to the attainment of true democratic governance. Yet although many judiciaries in sub-Saharan Africa have 'suffered violence' in the histories of many countries in that a change of government often meant the overthrow of the constitution and the consequent marginalization of the judiciary, many countries, former colonies of advanced countries, have had enduring legal systems—often a hybrid of received foreign law: common law, civil law, Roman-Dutch law, and local customary laws. The courts have therefore been with us for a long time. Many judicial systems are more than a century old, predating the nations spawned by the independence movements of the last century, and their constitutions that established and continued their judiciaries. Yet, while the participation of the first female High Court judge to be appointed in the British Commonwealth—Ghana's Mrs. Justice Annie Jiagge—was permitted in 1961, it is only in the last 40 years that female participation therein has been positively acknowledged, and in the last 20 years, embraced.

I joined the lower echelons of the bench in 1991 and worked my way up the ladder. I was by no means the first female member at the time, but there is no denying that our numbers were very few. Indeed, I recall that the first court I was assigned to as a magistrate was at one of the regional capitals of Ghana which had not had a female judge/magistrate for more than 10 years. It will be difficult in a few sentences to articulate my struggle, with its attendant frustrations, to be taken seriously, and to gain the acceptance and respect of the community, including the legal fraternity.

Twenty years down the line, we have a glut of female judicial appointees. No doubt as judicial officers, female judges still grapple with problems connected with adjudication, but I daresay that the quest to be accepted and to gain the respect of peers within the legal fraternity and the society at large, is no longer the challenge that it once was. I refer to my experience in Ghana.

In The Gambia where I worked as a judge on assignment from the Commonwealth Secretariat in 2004, I found that female judges, when I first joined that bench, were still somewhat of a novelty, as there were two female resident judges and two judges of the Supreme Court that sat in session. I can say without fear of contradiction that the Gambian bench is now very gender-balanced and indeed, appears to be female-dominated at the Superior Court level.

I also worked as a judge in Swaziland from 2008 until 2010. I was the second female judge to sit at the High Court of Swaziland. I had been sent there on assignment from the Commonwealth Secretariat; the other was the first female judge of Swaziland and she was appointed as recently as 2005! Today it is my information that there are more female High Court judges, a positive stride, without a doubt.

Between 2007 and 2013, four countries in West Africa alone appointed their first female chief justices. Judiciaries in many countries in Africa seem to have suddenly woken up to the fact that in many countries, women make up half (or more) of the population and now, judicial appointments regularly include women. I have often wondered at the trend, and I am persuaded that it is the result of excellent and commendable pioneering work done by the few who from the 1960s charted the narrow path that has become today's highway. The challenge of acceptance is, however, not altogether wiped out although the societies, including male members of the legal profession, are more accepting of the office and role of women judges. It is significant that a number of African judiciaries still use the male form of address for female judges, and there is at present a struggle in some countries for women judges to be addressed as 'My Lady' or 'Her Ladyship,' instead of the traditional 'My Lord' or 'Your Lordship.' Even so, there is no denying that women judges have come a long way in determining the course of, and indeed in shaping policy for, adjudication in a number of African countries.

But what benefit have we, as a region, obtained from this expansion of the judicial net to include female members of the legal fraternity (or perhaps I should more accurately describe it as the legal sorority)? Many tout this trend as a benefit to gender equality and to the more engaged, understanding and compassionate handling of cases in our courts, especially where women's issues are under consideration or at stake. Many perceive an agenda to achieve the promotion of women's rights, in that a court manned by a woman judge may probably produce judgments and rulings that have regard to real-world implications in their impact on the lives of female members of our communities.

Speaking for myself, while I will not debate the widely held view that female judicial appointments promote gender equality and female rights, I hold the view that just as the iconic Lady Justice, female in image, is reputed to be blind, the gender of the adjudicator ought not to favor any particular segment of society. The entire society, in my view, is enriched by the inclusion of a moiety of its citizenry hitherto ignored for the most part.

But whatever the reason, and whatever the perceived impact or benefit to women's rights in particular and the society in general, there is no gainsaying that many African judiciaries are achieving a good gender balance and the trend continues in a profession that has been seen as a province of the male and was male-dominated until recently.

This book, which focuses on the presence, purpose and product of women members of the bench in Africa, is timely and relevant as a tool for advocacy regarding female participation in governance generally. It is a must-read for all persons who seek to follow the development of female participation in adjudication in fledgling democracies in Africa. The research has unearthed the challenges, past and present, and points the way forward in the continued struggle for gender parity. The scholarly assessment of the impact of the increased numbers of women on the bench will no doubt raise the stakes in the debate on the contribution of women not only in the judiciary but in various sectors of governance. Lastly, it will undoubtedly ignite a discussion on whether the appointments, seen by many as a plus for the promotion of women's rights, have affected impartiality, a *sine qua non* for the exercise of judicial independence. This last is a thorny issue, and while I wish I could say an emphatic no to it, I cannot in all good conscience do so. This is because people have their motivations for what they do or permit. I have seen serious gender activists go on to become judges. Would it not be simplistic, and perhaps naive, to expect them to drop their prejudices just because they find themselves in judicial robes? The hope is that they will appreciate their new role of arbiter and do so. Nor would I lightly discount the perception held by many that a number of female judges are partial to female issues and causes. What I can say is that a judge with any kind or form of bias undermines the very essence of being and I should hope that our inclusion maintains, rather than undermines, judicial independence.

Mabel Agyemang
Judge of the Court of Appeal, Ghana
Former Commonwealth Expert Judge

1 Gender and the Judiciary in Africa

An Introduction

Josephine Dawuni

Between 2000 and 2015, women ascended to the top of judiciaries across Africa, most notably as chief justices of Supreme Courts in common law countries like Ghana, Nigeria, Sierra Leone, Gambia, Malawi, Lesotho and Zambia, but also as presidents of Constitutional Courts in civil law countries such as Benin, Burundi, Gabon, Niger and Senegal (Dawuni & Kang, 2014). Most of these appointments were a 'first' for a woman chief justice or Constitutional Court president. At the same time, women gained appointments in record numbers as magistrates, judges and justices across the continent. What do these appointments tell us about women's access to judiciaries and the changing nature of judiciaries across Africa? What roles are women judges and justices playing in promoting democracy in their countries and what impacts are they having in terms of promoting women's rights? These questions form the basis for this book. Women have constituted an increasing presence in legislatures and executives in many African countries since the early 1990s, a development that has received significant scholarly attention (see Bauer, 2012; Bauer & Okpotor, 2013). The role of women in African judiciaries, by contrast, remains largely underinvestigated, with a few notable, mostly South African, exceptions (Bonthuys, 2013; Cowan, 2006, 2013; Johnson, 2014; Kamau, 2013).

The remarkable trend of women rising to the top of some judiciaries across Africa warrants closer scrutiny. In unearthing this debate, however, this volume is not limited to the pinnacle of the judiciary, but focuses across a range of higher courts, less so on the lower courts. This volume provides an in-depth exploration of the presence, or lack thereof, of women on the bench in select African countries. The book seeks to open the door for further research, debate and discussion on the role of women judges across the continent, an area that has long been overlooked. Collectively, the country case studies in this volume set the context for understanding that in Africa gender issues within the judiciary are context specific—bound by rich legal traditions and histories which require nuanced study. Collectively, the chapters lay out a blueprint for understanding the similarities and differences in gender and judiciaries across the continent. Finally, the chapters in this book provide a lens through which to better compare questions driving the research on gender and judging in Africa with the same in the global north.

A Renewed Focus on Judiciaries

The third wave of democracy, which swept across Africa beginning in the late 1980s, unleashed dramatic changes in the political landscape of the continent. A significant body of research chronicled these changes, focusing on the unfolding of democratic transitions and the challenges of democratic consolidation (Bratton & Van de Walle, 1997; Gros, 1998; Joseph, 1999; Villalon & VonDoepp, 2005). Many of these studies investigated the actions of specific actors in the transitions—political leaders, foreign donors, civil society organizations and social movements. Other studies privileged the institutional context—the power of executives over the other two branches of government, the practice of appointments to cabinets, the rules for selecting members of parliament, the functions and outputs of members of cabinet and parliament, and so on.

In these analyses of reviving democratic institutions in Africa, the judiciary has often been ignored, although outside of Africa a rich scholarship on women and the judiciary has emerged during the last decade or so (Malleson & Russell, 2006; Kenney, 2013; Lee, 2011; Rackley, 2013; Shultz & Shaw, 2003b, 2012b, 2013b). For Africa, this volume provides the first comprehensive examination of women and the judiciary. The book is organized around three underlying themes that run through each of the chapters—the *presence, purpose and product* of women on the bench in Africa. By *presence*, it compares the number of women on the bench to their male counterparts; more importantly, it seeks to evaluate the processes by which women gain access to the bench. By *purpose*, it seeks to engage questions about why gender matters on the bench, what difference women judges might make for judicial legitimacy, and democratic principles like equality. Lastly, by *product*, the goal is to assess the extent to which the number of women on the bench impacts the judiciary as an institution, women's rights and democratic values.

In an attempt to provide a harmonized discussion of the broad array of issues within the literature on gender and judging, each chapter in this volume provides an in-depth exploration of specific sets of questions. First, as important context, what are the major historical developments and legal traditions in the country? Second, what is the structure and organization of the courts and what is the gendered representation and composition within each rung of the court structure? Third, what are the processes and methods for appointing judges and the implications of selection and appointment methods for women relative to men? Fourth, can we identify certain impacts that women judges are having? Fifth, what are some ongoing challenges and obstacles faced by women judges? Through these general questions, some similarities and differences facing one diverse set of countries on the continent become apparent.

This volume as a whole is guided by two central theoretical approaches, though others may be in evidence in individual chapters. First, using historical institutionalism, we examine the development of the judiciary as an independent branch in postcolonial Africa. This approach is essential in establishing the context for vital processes within judiciaries, such as judicial appointments.

Historical institutionalism allows us to draw out some of the key developmental trajectories of African judiciaries from the precolonial period up to the present. Second, we rely upon critical mass theory, which posits that once there is a critical mass of a minority group, members of the group can begin to have an impact (Dahlerup, 2006). This approach is relevant in analyzing gender and representation on the bench, just as in legislatures and executives. This approach, and a corollary that suggests that critical acts and actors may be just as important as critical mass, or more so (Childs & Krook, 2006), sets the context for understanding the extent to which gains in women's presence on the bench may have a corresponding impact on women's rights and gender issues more broadly. These two approaches underline the analysis in the country cases in this volume.

Historical Context and Legal Traditions Across Africa

Contextualizing contemporary judiciaries in Africa cannot be accomplished without a detour into the historical archives of judicial growth and legal pluralism on the continent. Precolonial African systems of governance relied upon chiefs and other traditional leaders as the arbiters of laws and courts. These legal systems belong to the chthonic legal tradition, often characterized by the interpretation and application of the law with the aim of promoting reconciliation and communal harmony (Glenn, 2014). As a result, the law was viewed as less adversarial. Women's roles within traditional African legal systems varied widely. In many precolonial societies, such as in Botswana and Rwanda, women could and did act as regents on behalf of male relatives. In other places, especially in West Africa, but also in other parts such as in Rwanda, women held the important role of Queen Mother (Amadiume, 1997). Steady (2011), in her discussion on women leaders in precolonial Africa, makes a strong claim for the relative autonomy and authority women enjoyed within precolonial legal and judicial systems. She stresses the role of African women in 'mothering the nation' (p. 4) and the need for analyses of women's leadership in Africa to utilize an African perspective and not depend heavily on Western standards of womanhood. Heeding this call, we consider what became of traditional legal systems in Africa that may have accorded women some power vis-à-vis men within the legal and judicial systems of communities. With colonialism came the introduction of legal systems modeled along those of the imperial powers, resulting in some usurpation or at least modification of the powers and roles of traditional leaders, including women and, importantly, in the plural legal systems that exist across the continent today.

Today, African judicial systems are marked by legal pluralism, characterized by different legal systems and traditions constituting the sources of law applied in the adjudication of cases in the courts. In many cases, the onset of colonialism marked at least a modification of African systems of governance—including judicial systems in which women may have played discrete roles. British, French, Belgian and Portuguese colonial rule brought forms of governance to the colonies that were modeled on their own. Women's roles as chiefs, religious leaders and warriors were subsumed under the patriarchal systems of governance of the colonial powers. For instance, laws that limited the rights of women through family codes in some civil law countries were the result of a direct inheritance from the Belgian laws at that time. Additionally, laws in common law countries justifying marital rape were introduced into family law from the British laws as observed in England at the time. A defining characteristic of the colonial legal and judicial systems was the division of law between the 'natives' and those from the colonial mother countries. As Mamdani (1996) notes, the result was the application of a set of rules and norms on the 'native' inhabitants, which was often very harsh and punitive, resulting in the native subjects being viewed as passive subjects. The result was the development of a two-tiered judicial system—one belonging to the natives and one belonging to the colonizers.

As a result, what we see across the continent today is a mix of common law traditions inherited from Britain, on the one hand, and civil law traditions inherited from countries of continental Europe on the other. In a few countries such as South Africa (and by extension Botswana), which was colonized at different times by the British and Dutch, we witness a hybrid legal tradition that combines civil and common law traditions. Indeed, the postcolonial judicial systems of Africa are often plural legal systems, combining the inherited legal tradition of the colonizing powers with customary laws existing before colonization and, in some cases, sharia law. Thus African countries today may be categorized as largely common law countries, civil law countries or hybrid systems that combine civil law and common law. In some countries across the continent, we also witness a combination of customary and sharia influences as well.

Customary laws may be defined as laws that existed before the imposition of colonial rule, and once colonial rule was consolidated, were applied only to the 'native' population. As LeVine (1964) has pointed out, 'native' or 'customary' laws were still largely determined by the colonial forces and often administered by special courts created by the colonial administration. Sharia law—laws derived from the holy Quran—is a vestige of Arab conquest of parts of Africa in the early centuries. In all, the legal systems of Africa are characterized by legal pluralism, often marked by co-existing and mutually competing legal traditions, practices and norms that have the tendency to reinforce patriarchal norms inherent in the parent traditions from which they were established. Notwithstanding the end of colonization, postindependence African countries maintained the inherited legal systems, some with very few modifications. These inherited judicial systems still remain the bedrock upon which many African judicial systems operate (Joireman, 2001).

With the end of colonization in Africa, the continent witnessed momentous political shifts with enduring implications for the development (or lack thereof) of judiciaries. Independence brought liberal democratic political systems to the continent; these political systems were largely short-lived, however, and were often quickly replaced by single party rule, or a usurpation of power by military juntas through coup d'états. The rise of single party governments and military dictatorships meant a couple of things for the judiciary. First, constitutions were oftentimes suspended or even abolished (Prempeh, 1999). Second, and as a result thereof, judiciaries, which had the primary role of interpreting and upholding the constitution, were often put into abeyance. Third, single party and military regimes typically used decrees as the primary sources of law. Executives issued military decrees, leaving little functionality for the legislative and judicial branches (Kumado, 1993; VonDoepp, 2005; Widner, 2001a). Fourth, across the continent during these years a culture of silence descended, as judges and lawyers who were outspoken against the executive were often detained without trial and, in some cases, even murdered (Prempeh, 2006).

Democracy, Judicial Autonomy and Gender Equality

Fast-forward into the late 20th and early 21st centuries, when Huntington's (1991) third wave democracies in Africa begun to mushroom. Transitions to democratic rule may be attributed to a number of domestic and international factors. Domestically, the development of vibrant civil societies characterized by educated elites and comprised of student organizations, women's movements and trade unions played critical roles in putting pressure on dictatorships to end their rule. Additionally, compounded negative effects of World Bank austerity measures begun to unravel regimes by exposing not only their economic deficits, but also their democratic deficits (Joseph, 1998). Internationally, the end of the Cold War, which led to pressure from donor governments and agencies for liberal political reform, reinforced the push for democracy from below.

Judiciaries across the continent benefited from democratic transitions in a number of ways. First and foremost, new constitutions were adopted across Africa; a clear separation of powers between the executive, legislative and judicial branches of government has characterized these. Among other things, these constitutional arrangements were meant to insulate judiciaries from the control of the other branches of government. Prempeh (1999) observes the virtues of these new constitutional developments, in particular the establishment of Constitutional Courts. Creating positions of chief justice or president of the Constitutional Court is another way of insulating judiciaries from executive control. Other matters of significance to judicial independence are the appointment, promotion and removal of judges; these are powers that in most African countries are shared by presidents, legislatures, chief justices and judicial service commissions or other such bodies. Still, in some countries these processes remain dominated by executive branches. Constitutional Courts can only go so far in being the arbiters of the law if their composition—and by extension the selection methods of judges—demonstrates openness, fairness and less executive control (Prempeh, 1999).

A return to democratic governance in many countries presented new political opportunity structures for enforcing the rights of all citizens through constitutional provisions aimed at ensuring equality before the law. Most new constitutions contained language aimed at enshrining human rights and eliminating gender-based discrimination. Gender advocates and women activists who have called upon governments to use new laws to improve the position of women in society have capitalized upon these provisions. Wording in constitutions aimed at increasing the number of women in public office, such as in Rwanda and South Africa, provided an impetus for advocating for more women on the bench. In Tunisia, the secularization of the constitution and the law has helped to increase the number of women on the bench. The results have not been uniform, however. The promise of equality in Egypt's constitution has not translated into more women in the judiciary. The constitutional provisions for the creation of Constitutional Courts equipped with the power of judicial review of executive actions in Benin, South Africa and other civil law countries have not been followed by other countries on the continent (Prempeh, 1999).

As noted, constitutions have contributed to creating open and transparent appointment processes and providing for activist lawyers, women's groups and other civil society actors to be engaged in the appointment process by holding the appointing powers accountable. There are still cases, evidence of continued executive overreach, in which some heads of executives have gone against the recommendations of judicial service commissions and have submitted the names of their preferred candidates to the legislature for vetting and appointment. These cases have the effect of reintroducing 'court packing' by the executive, with the tendency to usurp the autonomy of the judiciary. The lack of executive respect for constitutions and the systems of checks and balances is what Prempeh, (2007, p. 1) aptly describes as 'constitutions without constitutionalism.'

In addition to constitutional provisions aimed at providing a legal basis for women's representation in all public offices, including the judiciary, most African countries have signed and ratified international legal instruments aimed at promoting women's rights. For instance the United Nations Convention on the Elimination of All Forms of Discrimination against Women (CEDAW) has been signed and ratified by all African countries except Somalia and Sudan. In addition, at the regional level, the Additional Protocol on the Rights of Women (Maputo Protocol) has been signed and ratified by an overwhelming majority of African states. Clearly, the mere ratification of these legal instruments is not enough to ensure women's increased access to public office across the continent; still, it is often a first step for women's rights advocates to pressure governments for more women in public office, including in the judiciary.

What We Know About Gender and Judging Globally

Important questions remain to be answered concerning women in the judiciary globally. Available data from the United Nations (2012) confirms the uneven distribution of women in judiciaries across the globe. The regional distribution indicates that at 60%, the Eastern Caribbean Supreme Court, whose jurisdiction covers nine countries, has the highest percentage of women judges. This is followed by Central and Eastern Europe and Central Asia with 40% women. Sub-Saharan Africa is represented by about 28% women in judiciaries. The record for the developed world is quite uneven. As Schultz and Shaw (2013a, pp. 12–13) have demonstrated, the share of women in the federal courts in the United States stood at 30%, Great Britain at 23%, France at 64% and Canada at 33% in the 2010s.

Multiple factors explain the variation we see across continents and among countries. First, the type of legal tradition that exists in the country—whether common law, civil law or a mix—determines the appointment processes used in the appointment of judges. Studies suggest that civil law countries tend to have higher numbers of women in the judiciary, though they may be located in the lower rungs of the courts (Malleson & Russell, 2006). In the case of Canada, judicial reforms aimed at increasing opportunities for women to join the bench have been credited with increasing the number of women judges and the appointment of a female chief justice (Russell, 2006). Other contributing factors that help explain the different distribution of women in judiciaries around the world include the access to legal education, level of gender-based employment discrimination, and women as an alternative to men, the use of judicial appointment commissions, the presence of constitutional quotas for gender parity and many other factors (Shultz & Shaw, 2013a, p. 14–21).

The literature on gender and judging, globally, reveals some interesting recent developments. These studies suggest that the entry of women into the legal, and by extension the judicial, profession is a recent development gaining momentum in the 1970s—a process Menkel-Meadow (1986) describes as 'feminization' of the judiciary. The feminization of the judiciary, however, is not happening uniformly across the world, as alluded to above. In some cases it appears that the feminization of the judiciary is taking place, though only at the lower rungs of the courts. Shultz and Shaw (2013a) argue that a continued predominance of men in the legal profession, and a continued perpetuation of masculine norms within a profession long viewed as a man's, work against women's access to judicial appointments.

Williams and Thames (2008), by contrast, argue that the wide variation in the number of women in High Courts in select developed countries can be attributed to factors such as the prestige of the court, the selection methods utilized and the importance attributed to women's role in society. Legal traditions can also be a factor—whereby civil law countries appear to have a better record than common law countries in terms of the gender composition of judiciaries. The selection methods employed—whether through elections, appointments or nominations—can also, though not always, make a big difference in the gender composition of courts (Cowan, 2006; Kamau, 2013; Kenney, 2008; Malleson, 2006).

A number of themes emerge in existing studies on gender and judging. First, studies have sought to answer the question of why women should be well represented on the bench. Invariably, these studies have argued that the presence of women on the bench promotes judicial legitimacy (Kenney, 2008), democratic values of representation and equity (Feenan, 2009), judicial diversity (Rackley, 2013) and principles of merit (Malleson, 2003a). Furthermore, some of these studies have sought to engage with the debate on the difference women judges bring to the courts and the interpretation of laws as necessary for achieving gender-sensitive rulings (Rackley, 2013).

A second recurring theme in existing studies is how to make that happen. In other words, how are more women persuaded to join the bench? This question has necessitated a discussion of appointment processes and the relative openness or lack of transparency of the different appointment models. For instance, in civil law countries, it is often argued that the civil service/bureaucratic model of appointment creates better opportunities for highly qualified women to become judges (Shultz & Shaw, 2013a). In common law countries, the appointment of judges is often made from the rank of barristers who have connections to gatekeepers such as appointment committees and bar associations. Malleson (2003a) argues the case of 'secret soundings' as detrimental to women's access to joining the bench. In particular, Malleson challenges the principle of 'merit' which does not take into account the work and contributions of women lawyers. Notwithstanding these general trends, it should be borne in mind that there are variations within the civil and common law traditions. For instance, the use of elections and executive appointment of judges to the federal courts in the United States is not a practice common in the British system, where the use of judicial appointment committees has been introduced in an attempt to make the appointment process more transparent. In countries that have tried to make appointments to the bench more open and transparent by establishing appointment commissions, the record indicates that persistent sexism and patriarchy in such commissions continue to limit the opportunities for women to ascend to the upper echelons of the bench (Cowan, 2006; Feenan, 2009; Kamau, 2013; Malleson, 2003a).

A third recurring theme is what do women do once they get on the bench. Or, as some would put it, what should women do once they get to the bench? This discussion is often framed around the 'difference' debate, namely, whether women judges decide cases differently from men due to their lived experiences (Abrahamson, 1998; O'Connor, 1991). Some studies argue that women judges do not judge differently from their male counterparts (McCormick & Job, 1993; Walker & Barrow, 1985; Westergren, 2004). The difference debate remains moot. Malleson (2003a) cautions against the preoccupation with the difference women judges make, as it places too high a premium on the expectations of women judges. Women judges should not be viewed as making a difference only in their judgments, but also, due attention needs to be paid to the representative role of women judges and the multiple ways in which they contribute to collegiality on the bench, mentoring other women judges and defending women's rights through associations to which they belong (Martin, 1993). Overall, there is growing evidence that suggests that women judges do make a difference, whether consciously or subconsciously, in the decision of cases and in challenging existing societal patriarchal norms endemic in the law and in the practice of courtroom cultures.

Many other themes remain to be explored as Shultz and Shaw (2013a) have argued; issues of women's work as judges, judicial education and training and the profiles of leading women judges need to be explored in greater detail around the world.

Women Judges Across Africa; Women's Access to Judiciaries

Within Africa, the lack of current and accessible data on the composition of judiciaries in general is further compounded by the lack of a significant scholarly literature on women judges. Most of the data presented in the chapters in this volume focus on the representation of women in the higher courts, while some have data on a combination of higher and lower courts. Table 1.1 describes some of the attributes of the countries included in this volume.

What then have been the factors helping or hindering women's access to judicial appointments in Africa? A number of factors can be identified. First, increasing access to education for girls and women, and eventually to law school, has been critical, as Menkel-Meadow (1986) suggests for other parts of the world. In Africa, women begin to enter law schools in record numbers

Table 1.1 Selected Attributes of Case Studies, 2015

Country	*Type of Legal System*	*Geographic Region*	*Percentage of Women on Highest Court*	*Woman Chief Justice?**
Benin	Civil/Customary Law Mix	West	28.57%	No
Botswana	Common/Civil/ Customary Law Mix	South	0%	No
Egypt	Civil Law	North	0%	No
Ghana	Common/Customary Law Mix	West	35.71%	Yes
Nigeria	Common/Customary/ Muslim Law Mix	West	18.75%	Yes
Rwanda	Civil Law	East	41%	No
S Africa	Common/Civil/ Customary Law Mix	South	18.18%	No
Tanzania	Common/Customary/ Muslim Law Mix	East	25.00%	No
Tunisia	Civil Law	North	22.22%	No

*Not all countries have chief justices; in some countries the highest position may be president of a Constitutional Court.

in the early 1980s, when universities begun to expand their reach (Owor & Musoke, 2012). The early 1980s marked an increase in the number of universities and law schools, the liberalization of education and the advancement of women's equality through social movement pressures and changing norms (Manteaw, 2008). Consequently, more educational opportunities for women to attend school, university and law school led to an expansion in the pool of women applicants for judgeships.

Second, regime type across the continent in the first decades of independence had a negative impact on judiciaries, as described above, and on women's access to judiciaries. With judiciaries in many instances 'silenced,' many women (and men) lawyers sought refuge in private legal practice in order to ensure their safety and that of their family members. This veil of fear persisted until the transitions to democracy turned to democratic consolidation, with the promise of judicial autonomy. As judiciaries became more robust and more independent, they became places where women could work without fear of retribution for simply doing their work.

Third, selection methods for judicial positions are central to understanding the gender composition of African judiciaries. Selection to the lower courts in civil law and common law countries in Africa is through either the appointment model or bureaucratic (civil service) model or a combination. There are no elections to the bench as occurs in the United States. Within civil law countries such as Benin, Egypt and Tunisia, the process of allowing candidates to join the judiciary through competitive examinations promises to be a vital tool for increasing the number of female judges. These findings are in line with earlier studies discussed above, on the effect of civil law traditions in enhancing the chances of women on the bench.

Part and parcel of the appointment process are the potential 'gatekeepers' to the process. In common law countries these include judicial service commissions, bar associations and presidents. In cases where there is a lack of political will by nominating bodies or persons to nominate qualified women, the chances for the upward mobility of women may be limited. Appointments to the bench are based on the level of the court in question, with lower court appointments often based on a combination of years of service and the completion of an examination and interview process. For higher courts, the appointment process usually relies upon nominations from individuals in conjunction with a judicial service council or commission, followed by executive confirmation. And while the establishment of judicial service commissions is often an attempt to make the appointment process transparent and accountable, as recently in Kenya (Kamau, 2013), male-dominated commissions, not particularly interested in diversifying judiciaries, can end up reinforcing the patriarchal norms inherent in the legal and judicial systems of some countries.

Fourth, the pluralistic nature of African legal and judicial systems can play a role in explaining the appointment, or not, of women judges. For example, in Egypt and northern Nigeria, where Islam and Sharia Courts exert significant influences, we see negative outcomes for women's access to judicial posts. Religion and customary law continue to have important implications for women's access to the judiciary in Africa, in contrast to some other parts of the world. For instance, the earlier prohibition on women serving as judges in Egypt still lingers on in this era, and so is the case with the challenges of women serving as judges in northern parts of Nigeria.

Finally, it may be the case that women judges on the bench will lead to the recruitment of still more women judges as has happened in both Ghana and Rwanda, where women chief justices have advocated for and recruited more women to the bench. Some suggest that the active recruitment of women judges by women judges defeats the 'merit' principle of the appointments process and that such recruitment of possible women judges should rather be left to women's civil society organizations. In Canada, it took targeted recruitment efforts in order to increase the number of women judges and the eventual appointment of Beverley McLachlin as the first female chief justice in 2000. Increasing the number of women qualified to be judges is, however, not the only antidote for increasing the number of women on the bench. Indeed, as Hunter (2008) points out, it requires women judges who have a commitment to women's issues and women's advancement (what she problematizes as feminist judges) to make a difference across a wide spectrum of judicial matters, including the recruitment of other women.

Some of the same factors help to explain why women are gaining greater access to judiciaries in some cases but not in others. Africa has not been left out of a global feminization of the judiciary, though there is tremendous variation across countries and across courts. In some countries like Tanzania and Ghana, the percentage of women judges in the higher courts is higher than in the former colonial power, Britain. At the same time, in a country like Ghana, there are greater percentages of women in the higher courts than in the lower courts, raising a concern about who will replace the senior women judges when they retire.

Impact and Contributions of Women Judges

To those who might ask why we should focus on women in the judiciary, Kenney (2012) has offered a simple response: 'why not women?' Increasingly, women are playing important roles in judiciaries around the world, as chief justices and judges on higher courts such as Supreme Courts, Courts of Appeal and High Courts in common law countries; and on Constitutional Courts, Courts of Cassation and Appeal Courts in civil law countries. Within these higher courts, women judges have the ability to make precedent-setting decisions with the potential for promoting women's rights and gender equality; this is especially so in common law countries where judges make law. At the lower courts, such as Magistrates' Courts, Circuit Courts, and sometimes in Customary Courts and Sharia Courts, though female judges cannot contribute to setting precedent through case law, they may still play critical roles in that most of the cases that come to these courts concern matters pertaining to family—marriage and divorce, inheritance, maintenance and so on—and that affect large numbers of women. This volume provides some insights into the ways in which women judges are having an impact across Africa.

Increasing Judicial Diversity

The presence of women in African judiciaries is also critical to promoting judicial diversity and addressing male bias. As Rackley (2013) points out, judicial diversity is important if the judiciary is to be viewed as an unbiased institution capable of advocating for the rights of all citizens. Such diversity should, however, not be measured in terms only of gender, but should also be viewed through the lenses of religion, sexual orientation, disability, race and ethnicity. Africa represents a continent where diversity can be measured across many spectrums. The limited number, or absence, of women judges, results in a perpetuation of justice being seen as the right of men. A limited number of women judges in courts contributes to limited access to courts for women (Cowan, 2013).

For promoters of women's rights, the presence of women judges can provide not only gender diversity, but can also lead to diversity in terms of legal reasoning and decisions that come out of the courts. It should, however, be pointed out that a gender-diverse judiciary does not necessarily guarantee women's rights in Africa—or any other part of the world, for that matter. As earlier studies have demonstrated, it is not enough to have a large number of women on the bench. Critical mass will not necessarily lead to changing the norms within the judiciary and within society at large. In advocating for women judges, some scholars argue that there must be active recruitment of women on the bench, but more specifically, such recruitment should focus on gender-rights-focused women, those Hunter (2008) refers to as feminist judges. Judicial diversity spans beyond gender diversity. As the chapter on South Africa demonstrates, questions of judicial diversity in terms of sexual orientation, disability and religion are beginning to become important points of discussion. Much research needs to be done in these areas.

Challenging Patriarchal Norms and Institutional Cultures

Women judges in Africa matter as they are placed at a juncture of authority and patriarchy and wield a great deal of power in challenging and changing patriarchal norms and cultures. Female judges, sitting *en banc* with male judges are well positioned to challenge the patriarchal laws on the books. In Benin, women judges have made decisions that have in some cases set the path for expanding women's rights.

The role of women judges in changing judicial culture should not be viewed as limited only to the decisions they make. The presence of women judges has had the impact of gradually socializing fellow men judges on the gendered nature of the law and the need to put on a gendered lens when interpreting and applying these laws. In other instances, the proliferation of country chapters of the International Association of Women Judges (IAWJ) has contributed to creating a forum for women judges to discuss their peculiar challenges and mentor new judges, as in Botswana, Ghana and Tanzania.

Developing Legal and Constitutional Jurisprudence

Women judges are also contributing to the development of legal and constitutional jurisprudence and case law. In common law countries, in particular, the important position occupied by case law and decisions of higher courts has various implications for promoting women's rights. The contribution of women judges in establishing gender-sensitive case law is not without its critics, who argue that a focus on gender-sensitive interpretation of the law has the tendency to diminish the judicial impartiality of judges. In reality, what women judges do is to balance the scale of justice by making it gender neutral. Of course, women judges are not a monolithic group who think and act the same. As some of the chapters in this volume demonstrate, women judges have been at the forefront in making decisions that have the potential to advance women's rights in family, inheritance and employment matters.

Challenging Societal Perceptions of Judicial Corruption

Perceptions of judicial corruption remain endemic in most judicial institutions across the continent. Perceptions of judicial corruption play into the legitimacy, public confidence and trust of judicial institutions. The 2010–2012 Afrobarometer surveys posed the question: 'how many of the following people do you think are involved in corruption, or haven't you heard enough about them to say: Judges and Magistrates?' The results indicate that 45% of respondents felt that 'some' judges were corrupt, 25% felt that 'most' judges were corrupt and 8% felt that 'all' judges were corrupt. While the data are not disaggregated according to the gender of the judges, there is some evidence to suggest that the increase in the number of women judges is having an impact on societal perceptions of the judiciary as a corrupt institution. Cardinal (2013) has suggested the idea that women judges come with 'clean hands.'

Shultz and Shaw (2013a) suggest that

> in many African and Asian countries the participation of women has helped to restore public trust in the judiciary . . . women are less prone to bribery which raises the question whether they are more virtuous than men. In any case it is easier for them than men to resist corruption as they do not need to earn money for the family; they are not the breadwinners.
>
> (p. 16)

This assertion by Shultz and Shaw is a very far-reaching one; it presupposes that the domestic arrangements in families across Africa and Asia are still largely in the hands of male heads of families. This is fast changing and women are equally contributing to the upkeep of their families and hence are important breadwinners. In fact, the role of women as caregivers outside their nuclear families places a higher burden on them. More research is needed in this area to assess the relative perception of judicial corruption between male and female judges in Africa. Until then, one can argue that the idea that citizens feel that women are less likely to be corrupted through bribery may have an impact on access to justice for indigent women litigants and for overcoming democratic deficits in many African countries.

Constitutional and Legal Provisions for More Women in Political Office

With women constituting just over 50% of populations in most African countries, the equal representation of women in all branches of government remains an important condition for signaling and enacting the democratic values of equity and equality of opportunity. In many countries women's movements have successfully pushed the adoption of gender quotas through constitutions or laws for the executive and legislative branches of government, for example in Rwanda and Tanzania. Other countries like Botswana and Ghana have no such provisions in their constitutions or laws. Using quotas for judicial appointments is much more difficult, if not impossible, given the demands of judicial impartiality. Recruiting more women into the judiciary remains a priority in many countries, however, and is the goal of women's associations and local chapters of the International Association of Women Judges.

Why Gender and the Judiciary in Africa Matters

This volume sets the pace for unearthing a rich body of knowledge on women judges in Africa. The formidable roles women have played in judiciaries have remained relatively understudied. The educational experiences, professional contributions and continuing challenges of women judges in Africa are largely representative of extant studies in other jurisdictions around the world. This volume is not another scholarly attempt to simply situate Africa and African women's experiences and contributions within Western experiences and to draw lessons from Western experiences for African women. Rather, this volume makes a case for scholars and researchers to focus on the paramount roles women judges play in the judicial systems of countries across the continent.

The findings in this volume hint at the prospect that, notwithstanding lingering colonial, cultural, and institutional and constitutional explanations for women's access to legal education and recruitment to the bench, African women are standing their ground. Gender and the judiciary in Africa matter—because African judiciaries are setting important lessons that jurisdictions outside of Africa can learn from. With a rising number of African countries having appointed women as chief justices or presidents of Constitutional Courts within the last decade, the role of women judges challenging patriarchal norms and cultures is something from which developed countries can take a cue. The traditional precolonial roles of African women as leaders and guardians of justice are being revived. Gender and the judiciary in Africa matter and greater attention needs to be paid to these important developments on the continent, developments which have the potential to positively affect democratic development.

Organization of the Book

This book includes nine country case studies—with cases chosen from different regions of Africa, a variety of legal traditions, and some with more and some with fewer women judges, and at different places in the judicial hierarchy. The cases are drawn from northern Africa—Egypt and Tunisia, western Africa—Benin, Ghana and Nigeria, southern Africa—Botswana and South Africa, and eastern Africa—Rwanda and Tanzania. We have countries with common law legal systems such as Ghana, Nigeria and Tanzania and civil law legal systems such as Benin, Egypt, Tunisia and Rwanda and those that are a mix such as South Africa and Botswana. In some countries there are still customary law systems in place and in some, sharia influences. In one country, Egypt, women are still 'battling' to make any entry into the judiciary and in another country, Rwanda, women are 41% of Supreme Court judges. The book does not seek to answer all the questions surrounding gender and judging in Africa. Each chapter is an exploratory attempt at combining historical institutionalism and other theoretical approaches to set the context for gaining a deeper understanding of the presence, purpose and product of women judges in Africa.

2 Egypt

The Lingering Battle for Female Judgeship

Mahmoud Hamad

Out of 20 Arab countries, 17 (85%) permit women to be judges, while in the other three (15%) countries, it is either an illegal or a traditionally inaccessible position. Countries that permit women to be judges in the Arab world are Algeria, Bahrain, Djibouti, Egypt, Iraq, Jordan, Kuwait, Lebanon, Libya, Morocco, Qatar, Palestine, Sudan, Syria, Tunisia, and Yemen and the United Arab Emirates.[1] Countries where women are denied access to sit on the bench are Mauritania, Oman and Saudi Arabia. However, even within the majority of Arab states that permit women the ability to serve on the courts, there is a wide variation in the level and depth of female participation in the administration of justice. In some countries, such as Tunisia, Morocco, Algeria and Lebanon, women serve in the majority of judicial posts in adequate percentage of the overall number of judges. In others, like Egypt, Yemen and the Gulf states the representation of women is rather symbolic in number and magnitude.[2] In this second group, females are permitted to assume judgeship in rather insignificant numbers and in some posts and are excluded from most judicial functions.

Egyptian women have been represented in the executive and the legislature since the 1960s, albeit in inappropriate percentages. In the 2011 parliament women held only 1.6% of the seats in the People's Assembly. The 2014 constitution establishes a quota that guarantees at least 70 out of 567 seats (approximately 12%) to women in the House of Representatives. Currently (early 2015) Egyptian women occupy five of 36 cabinet posts. Egyptian females, however, have never assumed the critical portfolios of defense, interior, finance, justice or foreign affairs. Furthermore, Egyptian women were never permitted to occupy the positions of president of the republic, vice president, speaker of the house, prime minister or governor.

Female integration in Egypt's courts started comparatively late, even by the modest standards of the Arab world. This integration was met with increasing difficulty and is still lacking. This is rather surprising if we take into consideration two facts: Egypt's judiciary is the oldest in the Arab world and Egypt has a reasonable record (by Middle Eastern standards) of advancing gender equality. This calls for answers to a number of interesting questions. What kind of obstacles lay in the road of gender equality in the administration of justice?

Why did Egypt lag behind other Arab countries that further advanced the integration of women in the judiciary? What reforms could be implemented to increase the numbers of women judges? What are the prospects of women judgeship in 21st century Egypt?

Women and the judiciary is the subject of this chapter, which is divided into five sections and a conclusion. The first section outlines briefly Egypt's legal history and gender representation. The second section explains the organizational structure of Egypt's judiciary. The third section is devoted to analyzing the representation of women on the bench. The fourth section investigates the effect of women judges on the courts' rulings and the development of law and politics. The fifth section underlines the societal, political and historical obstacles that complicate women's full access to the judiciary. The conclusion explores the future of female judges after the passing of the 2014 constitution, which included for the first time in Egypt's constitutional history a provision mandating the appointment of female judges.

First, Egypt's Legal History and Gender Representation

Since their establishment over a century ago, the modern Egyptian courts have not only become important parts of the social and political landscape but have been imitated and replicated throughout the Arab world (Brown, 1997, p. 1). The modern Egyptian legal system could be traced back to 1875, when the Mixed Courts were established.[3] In the 19th century, Egypt as an Ottoman province suffered from the principle of extraterritoriality. This meant that European laws, not Egypt's, applied to Europeans residing in Egypt. Extraterritoriality was an upshot of the capitulations system. Under this system, foreigners and others who enjoyed expatriate status were immune from prosecution in Egyptian courts. All litigation between foreigners and Egyptians had to be brought before one or more of the Consular Courts of the 17 capitulatory states recognized by the Ottoman Sultan. Egyptians and their government were in an extremely vulnerable or helpless position. The Mixed Courts were a remedy for the legal problems of the capitulations system.

The Mixed Courts structure was modeled on the French legal system and has left an enduring mark on the administration of justice in Egypt. The 1875 Charter of the Mixed Courts established their locations and jurisdiction. There was one Court of Appeal in Alexandria and three Courts of First Instance: Alexandria, Cairo and Mansura. The Mixed Courts radically changed the Egyptian judicial process (Brinton, 1968).

The establishment of the Mixed Courts, hearing disputes between Egyptians and foreigners and between foreigners of different nationalities, was so successful that it was imitated in the National Courts. The National Courts were set up in 1883, one year after the British Occupation of 1882. The National Courts have had all-encompassing jurisdiction over all legal disputes among Egyptian citizens. The 1883 National Courts' codes were based on the Mixed Courts' codes of 1875. National Courts' judges were mostly Egyptian but there was some foreign representation, and they tended to follow the Mixed Courts' interpretation of the law.

As Enid Hill has noted, the 'French' institutions in Egypt have sometimes developed in a slightly different way than they did in France. Furthermore, the Egyptian legal system has since developed some institutions that are not found in France, but are found in other civil law legal systems (Hill, 1979, p. 1). The most important of these is the Supreme Constitutional Court (SCC). The Egyptian legal system is thus *sui generis*.

Nevertheless, all of Egypt's judicial institutions are a byproduct of its institutional history: traditional and Western. The traditional influence came from the residual weight of a millennium of religious or Sharia Courts that dominated Egypt's litigation processes up until the 19th century. While Islam has provided women with a plethora of civil and political rights, traditional Islamic practices forbade women from serving as judges. The courts remained an exclusive domain for men in most Arab and Muslim countries even after the establishment of the modern states in the 19th or the 20th century.

Besides, when Egypt's courts were first constituted, women in Europe did not enjoy political rights nor were they admitted to the bar. The male-dominated nature of the European judiciary molded the Egyptian courts. No European female judge was ever appointed to either the Mixed Courts or the National Courts. In France, women did not earn the right to become judges until 1946, two years after they were enfranchised. Even when women were admitted to the courts, they were never treated on equal footing with their male counterparts (Kimble, 2014, p. 49).

Second, Court Structure and Organization

Egypt has a number of judicial institutions: some with adjudication functions, one performs only prosecution and one represents state interests before the courts. The three judicial institutions with adjudication functions are: the courts of general jurisdiction—hereafter the ordinary courts (established in 1883),[4] the administrative judiciary—Council of State (established in 1946) and the Supreme Constitutional Court (established in 1979). The Administrative Prosecution Authority (established in 1954) prosecutes legal offenses by civil servants, while the State Cases Authority (established 1875) acts as the government attorney. Egypt also has a separate military judiciary as part of the armed forces structure. Figure 2.1 illustrates the structure of the Egyptian judiciary.

First, the ordinary court system is composed of a Court of Cassation, Courts of Appeal and Courts of First Instance. The Courts of First Instance have general jurisdiction over small claims and minor offenses. In civil cases, they are composed of one judge, while in criminal cases they may be composed of either one judge or three judges, depending on the seriousness of the possible penalty. Above those courts are the Courts of Appeal. Currently, there are seven Courts of Appeal in Egypt that are composed of three judges. At the pinnacle of the regular courts of Egypt stands the Court of Cassation. The Court

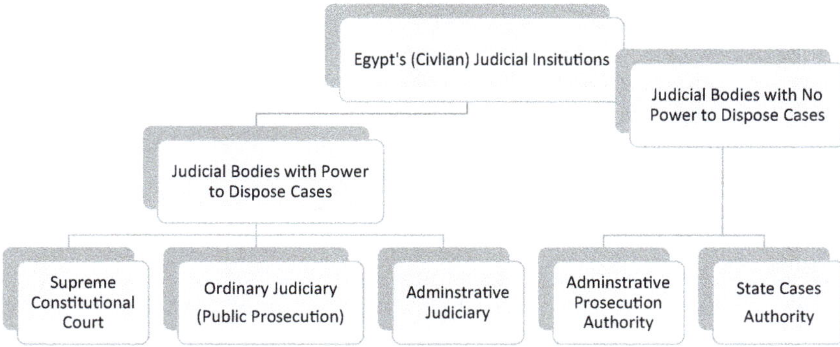

Figure 2.1 The Structure of the Egyptian Judiciary

of Cassation, which sits in Cairo, accepts petitions on judgments rendered by the Courts of Appeal only on two grounds: mistakes of law and violations of due process. There is no appeal from the Court of Cassation.

Second, there is a parallel 'administrative' court system with jurisdiction over challenges to executive actions. If a citizen or a resident wants to argue that an executive action or administrative decree is inconsistent with the law passed by the legislature, he/she must bring a legal action in the administrative court system. 'The Egyptian Council of State has many similarities with the French *Conseil d'État* and is composed of three sections which are the judiciary section, the advisory section (of the Government), and the legislative section' (Kosheri & Riad, 1995, p. 127). Like the general court system, there are administrative Courts of First Instance and appeals courts. The final authority within the administrative court system is the High Administrative Court. There is no appeal from a decision of this court.

Third, the Supreme Constitutional Court (SCC) is an independent judicial body. The SCC was established in 1979, and according to its legal framework it has three main duties: (1) to serve as the final authority in the case of a jurisdiction dispute between two Egyptian courts; (2) at the request of some high-ranking government officials, to issue authoritative interpretations of legislative texts; and, (3) finally, and most important, it has the sole right to perform bona fide judicial review.

The Administrative Prosecution Authority (APA) was established through a legislative act in 1954. It is tasked with the investigation of significant financial and administrative violations (even if they do not involve criminal offenses) committed by government employees and by others subject to the competence of the administrative prosecution. APA members enjoy many of the guarantees of other members of the judiciary and the structure resembles its counterpart in the Public Prosecution Department (PPD). A special council composed of the seven most senior members manages the APA.

The State Cases Authority (SCA), established in 1874, is the oldest of Egypt's judicial institutions. Despite being legally stigmatized as an independent judicial institution, the SCA does not perform a truly judicial function. Its role is confined to representing the Egyptian state before national and international courts and arbitral tribunals. The law states that the SCA has the power to plead on behalf of the state. When it comes to the organizational structure of the SCA, it is divided into seven parts, each capable of representing the state in the areas of its jurisdiction.

Female access to the employment at these judicial institutions varies greatly. As shown in Figure 2.2, there is no single female currently serving or having ever served at the administrative courts. As for the Supreme Constitutional Court, currently no females sit on Egypt's highest court, but a single female justice, Tahani el-Gebali, served on the court between 2003 and 2012.[5] Two female members were appointed to the SCC Commissioners Department. Sherin Farhoud currently serves at the rank of president of the SCC Commissioners Department and Faten Shaarawy served in the same capacity for a year 2008–2009.

As for the courts of general jurisdiction (civil, criminal, family, etc.), there are currently 42 female judges out of approximately 12,000 judges and prosecutors. No females have ever served in the Public Prosecution Department, the traditional gateway to the courts. Egyptian women are comparatively more represented at the SCA and APA. Among 1,134 members in the 2013 SCA promotion list there was a total of 101 female members, or just shy of 9% of the members (Youm 7, June 20th, 2013). The APA has the highest female representation, with 1,832 female prosecutors out of 4,442 members. Female administrative prosecutors have reached the pinnacle of the legal career at the institution, with two female prosecutors assuming the presidency of the APA: Consular Hind Tantwai (1998–2000) and Consular Lila Gafaar (2000–2001). What is noticeable is the increasing number of female members in the lower

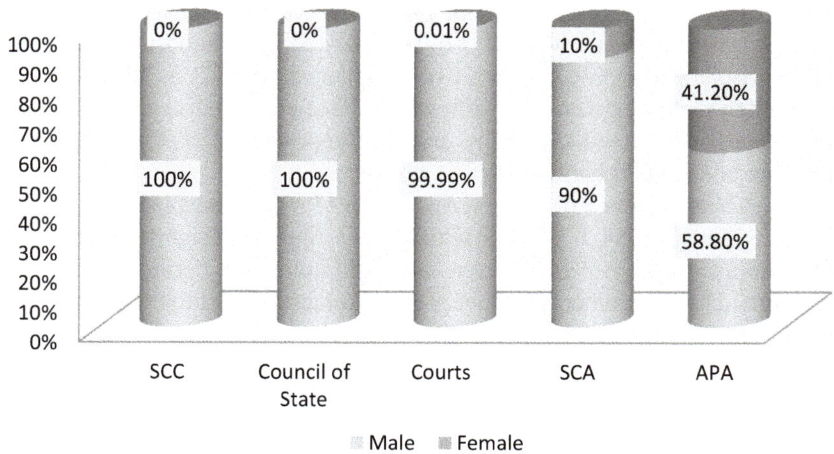

Figure 2.2 Percentage of Females Serving in Egyptian Judicial Institutions, 2015

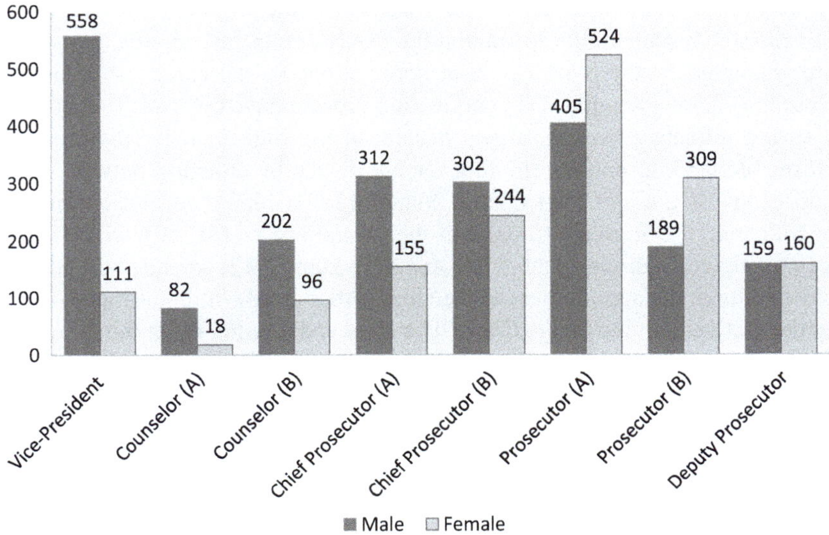

Figure 2.3 Number of Women Members in the Different Ranks of the APA in Egypt

ranks of the APA. While females represent 16.6% of the APA highest rank, vice president, women are half or more in the lowest three grades, as shown in Figure 2.3.

Third, Gender and Representation in the Different Judicial Institutions

Upon graduation from law schools, graduates have the liberty to choose between seeking judicial appointment, working as lawyers or embarking on other legal or nonlegal functions. Judicial appointment is highly prestigious and extremely competitive. 'Judges, especially those in senior positions, and their counterparts in the *niyaba* (public prosecution office) are definitely of high status in Egyptian society, and are accorded considerable respect. They are paid, even at the lower levels, relatively well as government salaries go,' according to Hill (1979, p. 41).

The appointment processes for all these judicial institutions with the exception of the SCC follow the career path of civil law bureaucratic institutions. Young law graduates apply for judicial posts shortly after graduation.[6] Each institution has a near-monopoly over the appointment of new recruits.[7] The screening process includes a background security check, detailed review of family history, a medical checkup and finally, an interview by the most senior judges in each organization. Nominated individuals are subsequently appointed by a presidential decree.[8] This procedure has led to accusations of favoritism with regard to sons and daughters of judges and high-ranking government officials in the appointment process.

As for the SCC, per Article 5 of the Courts Law, the president of the republic had the sole responsibility to appoint the Court's chief justice. SCC's justices are appointed by the president from nominations by the chief justice or the Court's general assembly. This nomination process gave the executive branch a strong influence over who gets placed on the high bench. This allowed Hosni Mubarak to appoint the first female justice by enlisting only the support of the SCC Chief Justice Fathi Naguib (2001–2003).[9] After the removal of Mubarak, the Supreme Council of the Armed Forces (SCAF), which ruled Egypt between February 12th, 2011 and June 30th, 2012, amended the SCC's law to require the appointment of the chief justice from within the ranks of the senior justices serving on the Court. The 2014 constitution made this a constitutional guarantee. Article 193 stipulates, 'The General Assembly of the Court [SCC] shall elect its President [the title used in Egypt for the chief justice] from among the most senior three vice-presidents [justices] of the Court. It shall further choose the vice-presidents and the members of its Commissioners, and the appointment thereof shall be made by virtue of a decree by the President of the Republic.'

Therefore, any female appointment would have to receive the support of the Court's general assembly and does not depend on the intention of the executive branch. Because the SCC's general assembly has a tradition of appointing justices who served on the Court's commissioners department, the probability of female justices seems remote in the short run. There is a single female that currently serves at the rank of president of the SCC Commissioners Department alongside 13 males who serve in the same rank. Seven of the male commissioners outrank the only female commissioner and theoretically should be appointed before she has the chance to serve as SCC justice. In 2003, Mubarak appointed the first female justice to the SCC. Women's rights organizations called for female admittance to the courts and the Council of State. In September 2006, the minister of justice requested High Judicial Council (HJC) approval in principle to appoint female judges in accordance with the Law of Judicial Authority and Article 40 of the 1971 constitution. The HJC approved the request and conducted interviews with 124 female members of the APA and SCA who had applied. In April 2007, Mubarak issued a presidential decree to appoint 31 female judges in mid-level positions. Figure 2.4 shows the points of entry for female judges. Those female judges, however, never served in the PPD and were mostly placed in family courts or the then newly established economics courts. Calls by women's rights groups to allow females to join the courts on equal footing with men were largely ignored.

This partial success left only the Council of State with no female representation. The executive convinced then Council of State President Mohamed el-Housiny to allow females to compete in the entry exam. The unilateral decision alarmed administrative judges, who believed that the president was doing the executive's bidding for personal reasons. The general assembly of the Council of State, which convened in an extraordinarily rare meeting, voted overwhelmingly to ban the appointment of female judges. The Council's

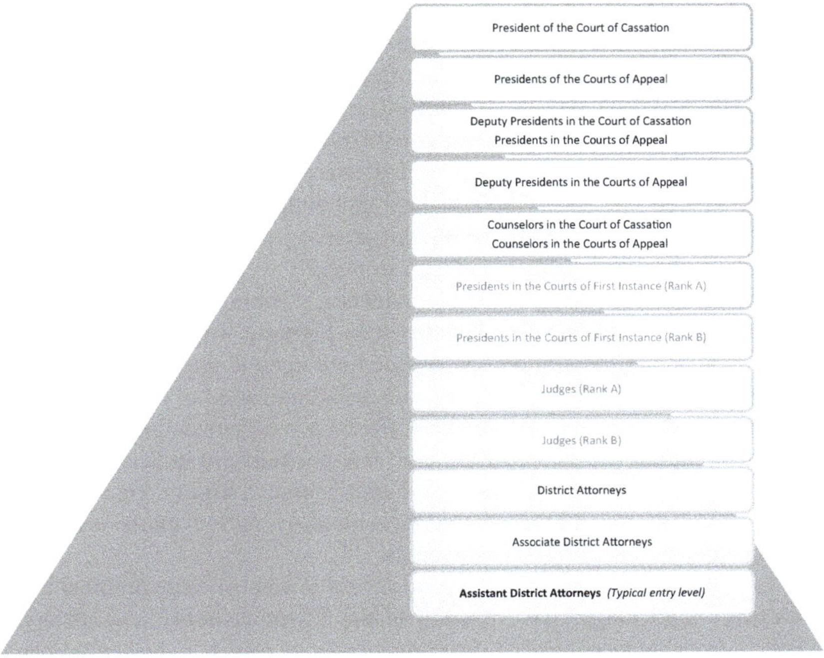

Figure 2.4 Hierarchies of the Ordinary Courts in Egypt (ranks in bold delineate the entry points and current ranks of female judges), 2007–2015

Taken substantially from The Law of the Judicial Authority of 1972 and 1984.

highest authority, the Special Council of Administrative Affaires (SCAA), later overruled that ban, but the general assembly was steadfast. The general assembly reconvened and reaffirmed its position. The executive enlisted the support of the reliable SCC, which ruled that the general assembly did not have the authority to determine who may serve on the court, that only the supervisory committee may approve new judges and that female judges may serve on the Council. The general assembly considered this to be an affront to judicial independence and opposition grew more intense, forcing the Council's leadership to table the issue. Many judges interviewed regarded the effort to appoint judges as bowing to pressure from the first lady, at that time Susan Mubarak.[10] As with many other initiatives under Mubarak, this was a public relations gesture, rather than a genuine effort to further gender equality. The regime wanted to put on a liberal face to mask its illiberal policies.

Fourth, Women and the Judiciary

Egyptian women's experience on the bench has been rather short in length and limited in magnitude: one SCC justice for less than a decade and roughly

40 judges on the ordinary courts (or about 0.006%) of sitting judges for fewer than nine years. Some female judges are using their new status to advocate for women's rights and particularly access to the judiciary. Three female judges, Judge Sana Sayed Ahmed Khalil, Judge Dina Hussein Mahmoud Hassan and Judge Amal Mahmoud Atta Ammar, are members of the National Council for Women (NCW) thirty-member governing board.[11] The NCW has worked to advance women's access to the judiciary, including receiving judicial delegations from other countries, publishing the success stories of female judges and lobbying for women's rights in the legal domain.[12]

There is, however, scarce credible evidence of women's judicial behavior and particularly how female judges seek to promote women's rights. Most female judges and prosecutors interviewed are keen to state that there is no difference between their adjudication and the adjudication of their male counterparts. The downplaying of gender difference is understandable if we take into consideration the nature of the civil law bureaucratic judiciary of Egypt and the novelty of female judgeship in Egypt's judicial history. Female judges could be more assertive in presenting their ideological predispositions as time goes on and when their number increases.

Taking into consideration the expanded profile and the large political influence courts and judges have exerted in the Egyptian polity and society it seems reasonable to argue that the appointment of female judges would be a double-edged sword in relation to legitimacy of judicial institutions, at least in the short term. Women's rights groups and liberals would welcome a more representative court system and would perceive the judiciary more favorably if women would sit on the bench on equal footing. At the same time, the appointment of female judges could further damage the legitimacy of the courts in the eyes of the millions of conservative Egyptians who already see the judiciary as a vestige of Western non-Islamic influence in a largely Muslim society.

Women judges, however, could break the gender stereotypes that still hinder the socioeconomic development of 21st century Egypt. Furthermore, women's equal access to the courts could increase the faith and confidence of the appointment process, where merit has not particularly been the deciding factor. Female appointments could conceivably enhance the qualifications of judges as many females seize the best grades in many law school graduating classes.

Fifth, Challenges and Obstacles

Egyptian women have strived to secure a number of legal, political and social rights since Huda Sha'rāwī founded the Egyptian Feminist Union in 1923.[13] Furthermore, working as a lawyer is not new to women in Egypt. The first Egyptian female lawyer opened her private practice in 1939. Egypt was the first Arab country to grant women their political rights in 1956. Egypt has also signed and ratified many international treaties that affirm equality between males and females.[14]

The contemporary debate on female judicial appointment in Egypt dates back to the 1950s. When Aisha Ratab, later first female law professor and first female minister, applied for a judicial post at the Council of State and was turned down, Ms. Ratab sued the Egyptian government for not permitting her to become a judge despite her academic qualifications. The lawsuit was dismissed with the response that limiting the judiciary to men does not demean or discriminate against women. The Court reasoned that 'social circumstances' prevent women from assuming judicial posts. Females were never admitted to the courts—administrative or ordinary—and this is where things rested until the beginning of the 21st century, when a handful of females were appointed as judges on the ordinary courts and the Supreme Constitutional Courts.

There are a number of social, institutional and cultural hurdles facing the full incorporation of women in the Egyptian judiciary. The main challenge is a conservative understanding of Islam.[15] The appointment of women as judges in some Muslim countries remains a controversial issue, due to a general perception that such appointments might not be in conformity with the sharia. Some scholars cite historical precedence as a justification for being male as a condition for judgeship. They note that there has never been a woman judge in the 14 centuries of Islamic history. As one scholar put it the 'resistance to women judges in Egypt is largely the result of a theological vision of the female gender role' (Ammar, 2003, p. 69).

It is nevertheless significant to mention that 'Notably, the Quran and Hadith literature do not provide explicit provisions setting forth necessary qualifications or credentials concerning service in the judiciary—although Islamic scholars will later draw upon both of these textual sources to support opinions on the subject' (Abdelkader, 2014, p. 318).

The four grand schools of Sunni jurisprudence (the dominant sect of Egyptian Islam) are: Hanafi, Shafi, Maliki, and Hanbali.[16] The teachings and principles advocated by these four 'founding fathers' continue to command a great deal of authority in the modern Islamic discourse, with each holding sway in a specific region of the Muslim world (Hallaq, 2009).

These schools stipulate that a judge should possess seven qualities. Out of these seven, all agree on five, including: adulthood, sanity, sense of justice, ability to hear and see, and knowledge of the rules of arbitration. They, however, disagree on two conditions, namely, whether being male and freedom (from slavery) are conditions for being a judge. The Maliki, the Shafi and the Hanbali schools view being a male as a necessary condition for a judicial post. The Hanafi school is the only school that does not consider gender to be a condition for judgeship. In the Hanafi school women may become arbitrators in all cases except *hudud* and *qasas* crimes (equivalent of major felonies). There is a minority of jurists within the Hanafi school who argue further that women may be arbitrators of all crimes.

Individuals against the appointment of female judges have developed a multitude of arguments in order to anchor their opposition on religious foundations.[17] The 'Islamic School of Law Argument' finds its roots in the gendered division of social roles advocated by many premodern Islamic scholars. These scholars understood men and women as fulfilling distinct and complementary social roles. They cited Quranic verses and the Prophet's statements to support a gender hierarchy. Further, since one verse presumably assigns men guardianship over women, some reasoned that women cannot undertake judicial authority because they could then exercise guardianship over men.

Another group bases their opposition on the 'Testimony Argument.' They cite a singular Quranic verse, which pertains to financial transactions making male testimony superior to female testimony in financial matters to assert more broadly that female testimony is deficient. By extension, women cannot preside over a court in which her testimony is not accepted.

The 'No Positions of Authority Argument' characterizes judgeships as a form of public authority for which women are unqualified. Here again a singular Hadith is commonly cited as evidentiary support. The principle thus derived is a perceived general prohibition against women assuming positions of sovereign power, and the judiciary is viewed as an extension of such power.

The 'Nature Argument' holds that women's judicial exclusion is justified on account of an emotional nature that renders them incapable of judicial administration in an objective and decisive manner. Relatedly, the 'Physiological Differences Argument' renders women unqualified for judicial posts due to various aspects of their physiology. First, women are unfit to hold judicial office because menstruation symptoms leave them 'nervous, unstable, and prone to sudden changes.' Second, maternity leave will cause undue delays to the court's administration. Third, judicial work requires long hours and overnight activities not suitable for women.

Accordingly, many Egyptians do not see the appointment of female judges as compatible with sharia. The state enlisted the support of the 'official' religious authorities to change popular perception in this regard, but this had less than the desired effect. The Sheikh of Al-Azhar issued a *fatwa* on September 25th, 2013 on the official website of Dar Al-Iftaa stating women may assume judicial posts and senior state positions without prejudice to sharia law. This, however, was less than convincing because these institutions lost a great deal of credibility due to their closeness to the regime. In addition to conservative understandings of religion, biased and stereotypical representations of Arab women have a long and complex history in both nationalist and colonial discourses. An awareness of this history and its contemporary reproductions in modern discourse is crucial in any attempt to map the sociopolitical status of Arab women in the 21st century. A patriarchal view of society remains strong in Egypt. The political and intellectual elites do not see women. Women's rights groups have failed to frame the issue in a way that is advantageous to their cause and accessible to the general public. Women's participation in the judiciary has become a religious argument first and foremost and not an issue of inclusion or of human rights.

Discriminatory attitudes against women are a reflection of the public dispositions toward women. Egypt lacks effective educational or media efforts to enhance the standing of women in society. One public opinion survey conducted by the Ahram Center for Political and Strategic Study in 2007 revealed that more than 70% of the populace were against the appointment of women judges. What was noticeable was the strong opposition among Egyptian women to such appointment. Table 2.1 shows that seven out of ten women disapproved of the appointment of females as judges. This is comparable to the percentage among males (eight out of each 10 males disapproved of such appointment). It was also interesting that more women were against the appointment of female judges than other significant positions such as ministers or even prime minister. The only explanation for such attitudes is that Egyptian women have assumed the position of cabinet members for decades and society (particularly the female portion) became accustomed to and comfortable with women assuming such responsibilities.

The archaic nature of the Egyptian judicial system is another explanation for the opposition to female judgeship. The male-dominated tradition of the courts' structure is arguably the most significant institutional problem facing the advancement of female judges in 21st century Egypt's judicial associations. The resistance of judges concerning the advancement of female judges is particularly pronounced in the Council of State. Judges in general and Egyptian judges in particular, are traditional and conservative. This is problematic because a traditional view of women does not support calls for gender equality. Being traditional and conservative is not a generational problem that time will solve. Young administrative judges are as opposed to the appointment of female judges as their senior colleagues. Some senior judges are supportive of female appointment because they could personally benefit from opening the doors to appoint their daughters on the bench.[18] Those judges are worried that the feminization of law faculties may result in the feminization of the profession of judges. This is critical from the perspective of administrative judges because of the nature of work in the administrative courts. Unlike judges in the criminal, civil or family courts who interpret legislation, the administrative judiciary actually make[s] the law. Many judges interviewed seemed to

Table 2.1 Percentage of Women and Men Who Disapprove of Female Appointment to Specific Professions in Egypt

Female	*Profession*	*Male*
32.9	Lawyer	48.9
67.8	Police Officer	83.6
72.5	Judge	81.2
73.4	Governor	81.8
48.8	Minister	59.6
68.7	Prime Minister	82.2
84.3	President of the Republic	91.4

Source: Al-taweel, 2012, p. 38.

hint at their belief that women are not qualified to undertake such immense responsibility.

This seems to be a byproduct of a conservative view of the role of women in the legal sphere as well as a negative assessment of the experience of female judges. The experience of former SCC Justice Tahani el-Gebali was not conducive to the prospects of female membership in High Courts. Justice el-Gebali was considered by most to be highly political. Many inside and outside the judicial corps criticized her frequent appearances on TV programs and her undisciplined discourse (Kirkpatrick, 2012). Some even claimed in off-the-record conversations that in almost a decade on the court (2003–2012), she never wrote a single court opinion. It is highly unfortunate that political connections (el-Gebali was believed to be close to the former first lady Susan Mubarak) rather than merit were behind such a cardinal appointment. 'Many notable female law professors could have done a much better job on the bench,' a mid-level administrative judge stated in a personal interview. Most judges, interviewed during the research for this work, believed that she has done more harm than good to the reputation of the Supreme Constitutional Court and the stature of female judges.

Besides, some female prosecutors have done their gender a disservice by demanding 'special' consideration for their 'family circumstances' and refusing to serve in remote places or to work extra hours to finish cases. Taking advantage of the fact that most of their parents are high-level judges, some of these prosecutors frequently enlist their parents to secure easy assignments in Cairo and other major cities, as the President of APA, Anani AbdelAziz, stated in a newspaper interview (Al-wafd, September 24th, 2012, p. 8).

The anti-female position is not only prevalent among administrative judges but it is also common among judges in the ordinary courts who comprise the largest majority of judges in Egypt. Many judges have condemned the HJC decision in 2006 to appoint a small number of female judges. This could well be the reason why such appointment was repeated only once in 2008, when 12 female judges were appointed. This vocal opposition also explains why the plans to allow women to compete on equal footing for the judiciary entry examination was put on hold indefinitely.[19]

Conclusion

Egyptian constitutions since 1952 have explicitly guaranteed gender equality. The 1956 constitution, promulgated under Nasser, stipulated in Article 31 that, 'Egyptians are equal before the law and equal in rights and public duties. There is no discrimination between them on the basis of sex, origin, language, religion or conviction.' In the same vein, the 1971 constitution, written after Sadat's ascendancy to power, maintained in Article 40 that 'citizens are equal before that law and in rights and duties; there is no discrimination between them on the basis of sex, origin, language, religion or conviction.' These constitutions, however, did not lead to the realization of gender equality in the public sphere. Furthermore, successive constitutions did not mandate gender equality in the court system. The 2014 constitution is different.

The 2014 constitution issued after the military takeover of July 3rd, 2013 was met with a great deal of appreciation from women's rights groups. Article 11 stipulates that 'The state shall ensure the right of women to hold public and senior management posts of the state and *ensure the appointment of women in the judicial bodies and authorities with no discrimination against them*.'(emphasis added)[20] This idea was a novel change in Egypt's constitutional history. For the first time, the state committed itself to female representation in the courts. In addition, for the first time in the Egyptian history, this constitution introduced a provision that explicitly commits the state to enforce international human rights treaties upon ratification.[21] This should have an enabling effect, as many of the treaties that Egypt ratifies affirm gender equality and women's rights.

Some expected the new provisions to usher in a new era in female access to the courts. The notion of a complete transformation, however, is premature optimism.[22] The High Judicial Council agreed in February 2015 to appoint a new group of female judges.[23] The HJC, nevertheless, did not agree to allow women equal access to the courts. The HJC is only going to interview only female members from the ranks of the APA and the SCA. No females will compete for the entry exam (Shrouk, February 23rd, 2015). The same discriminatory policies persisted despite the constitutional texts.

Even more troubling news came from the administrative courts. After the constitution did go into effect a number of recent female law school graduates attempted to apply for the entry posts within the Council of State but were denied access to the application materials. The Director of the National Council for Women, Mervat al-Talawy, sent a communiqué to the Council stating, 'I have learned that a meeting of the State Council's Special Board will be held to decide on the acceptance or rejection of female applicants in your esteemed council. . . . If this is true, please note that the 2014 Constitution should be taken into account; violating the constitution would prompt legal action against the Council of State' (El-Omda. M. & R. Abdallah, January 20th, 2014). The letter was met with an uproar within the Council.

The Council responded on the same day, stating that Talawy's letter 'lacked courtesy,' and that it would refer the matter to the president of the republic. The Council Judges Club sent a letter to the president of the Council, calling on him to file a lawsuit against Talawy for interfering in the affairs of the Council. The Council judges are steadfast in their opposition to female entrance into the administrative courts. They maintained that these constitutional articles do not 'oblige' the Council to appoint women, adding that 'current circumstances' prevent them from being judges. They added that the idea of female judges is unacceptable in sharia law.

Religion, however, is not the main obstacle for female judgeship; the interpretations of Islam have evolved over the past 1400 years (Keddie, 1991, p. 15). The conservative nature of the courts is the obstacle. A genuine integration of females in the administration of justice in Egypt would not only require change in the attitudes of the citizenry but also a transformation of how judges themselves perceive gender roles in the society and the legal community. Massive changes in a bureaucratic judiciary that prides itself on following tradition is no easy task. The realization of full and equal female integration in the judiciary would require time, effort and political will. The goal of gender-blind admission to judicial posts will not materialize any time soon. These will not be the last words on this important topic.

Notes

1 Two of the members of the League of Arab States were excluded from the analysis. Somalia was omitted for the absence of a centralized state and Comoros was omitted for lack of credible information.

2 In Yemen, women have theoretically been permitted to enroll in the High Judicial Institute since 2007. The Institute is the gateway to assume a judicial post. However, no females were actually admitted. Currently there are 32 female judges, compared to 1200 male judges. Nonetheless, these women all became judges in South Yemen before the unification in 1990.

3 Islamic courts dominated Egypt's adjudication for more than a millennium. The administrative deterioration of the Ottoman Empire left its mark on Egypt. The judicial administration of Egypt in the 17th and 18th centuries largely resembled other Ottoman provinces. The judicial system was corrupt, outdated and dominated by officials who were neither versed in law nor Arabic (El-Nahal, 1979).

4 In Egypt, the Public Prosecution Department (PPD), responsible for prosecuting all offenses on behalf of the state, is an integral part of the courts. Junior judges serve for about 10 years in the PPD and may return later in their careers. The Public Prosecutor heads the PPD and is also a member of the High Judicial Council, the highest authority within the ordinary court system.

5 Justice el-Gebali was removed from the court when the 2012 constitution went into effect. Article 176 of the constitution stipulated that: 'The Supreme Constitutional Court is made up of a president and ten members.' El-Gebali was number 12 in the rank of seniority and, hence, was retired from the bench. What is noticeable is the fact that some of the judges that were removed returned to the SCC after the removal of President Morsi and the suspension of the 2012 constitution.

6 Law school in Egypt is an undergraduate degree and generally attracts high school graduates with below average grades. Law education in Egypt is conducted through national universities, Al-Azhar, and the Police Academy. The curriculum includes all of the normal courses in any modern law college such as Roman law, the history of legal systems, civil law (as divided into several courses relating to obligations, torts, contracts, ownership, theory of rights, etc.), criminal law, procedure, commercial law, constitutional law and administrative law. Certain other groups of courses are related to Islamic legal system, which includes family law, inheritance, principles of jurisprudence and modes of interpretation. Moreover, students study several additional courses such as legal philosophy, criminology, agriculture, public and private international law, evidence and maritime law. Thus the construction of the syllabus for LL.B in Egypt is a reflection of the history of the legal development in the country. See Serag, 2001–2002, p. 616.

7 The official conditions for access to the office of magistrate are: (1) to be an Egyptian citizen who enjoys his civil rights, all the required guarantees of morality and good reputation, (2) to have an LL.B. from an accredited university or an equivalent degree from Al-Azhar, (3) to be at least of 21 years for the office of public prosecutor, and 30 years for the Court of First Instance.

8 The applicants' files are tightly screened to confirm their appropriateness for the bench. The applicant ought to have two important characteristics. First, he should come from a suitable family background. In practice this usually meant that he should be from the upper-middle or the upper stratum of society. Second, no one of his immediate relatives has been accused of anti-regime sentiments or activities.

9 Chief Justice Naguib's support for women's rights was well known. Tahani El-Gebali, Egypt's first female judge, said she 'would never be mistaken if I said that he is Qassem Amin of this era,' referring to an Egyptian proponent of female emancipation active at the turn of the 20th century (Nafie, 2003).

10 As part of research for this chapter, the author conducted 32 interviews with judges and prosecutors from the APA, the Council of State and the courts and PPD. These interviews were carried in Cairo between January 2014 and March 2015. Most interviews were conducted in person, while a handful were telephone interviews. All judges spoke on the condition of anonymity.

11 The National Council for Women, www.ncwegypt.com/index.php/en/about-ncw/members-of-the-council

12 The National Council for Women, www.ncwegypt.com/index.php/en/component/content/archive?year=2012&month=11

13 The birth of the modern feminist movement coincided with the anti-imperialism movement in the post-World War I era. The first women's organization developed was the Egyptian Feminist Union in 1923. The Egyptian Feminist Union described its institutional mission as raising women's awareness of their rights and contributions in the society in order to realize political and social equality with men. This organization was particularly significant because of its close association with the 1919 revolution, where women participated in anti-British activities alongside their male counterparts for the first time in Egypt's history. This organization, however, suffered from its socioeconomic composition as most of its members came from the ranks of middle and upper class educated women, who considered women's rights an intrinsic part of the modernization process in Egypt. In 1948, another pioneer in the feminist movement, Doria Shafiq, established the Bint al-Nil organization with the goal of attaining gender equality in the social and political spheres (Sika & Khodary, 2012).

14 Egypt signed and ratified the Convention on the Elimination of All Forms of Discrimination against Women in 1981. On 4 January 2008, the government of Egypt withdrew the reservation to article 9 (2) made upon ratification, concerning the granting to women of equal rights with men with respect to the nationality of their children.

15 The greatest majority of Egyptians are Muslim Sunni, and Islam continues to play an integral part in shaping public attitudes towards female roles in politics and society. According to a worldwide survey by the Pew Research Center, published in 2013, 74% of Muslims in Egypt favored making sharia the official law in Egypt. 'Sharia, or Islamic law, offers moral and legal guidance for nearly all aspects of life—from marriage and divorce, to inheritance and contracts, to criminal punishments. Sharia, in its broadest definition, refers to the ethical principles set down in Islam's holy book (the Quran) and examples of actions by the Prophet Muhammad (sunna). The Islamic jurisprudence that comes out of the human exercise of codifying and interpreting these principles is known as fiqh. Muslim scholars and jurists continue to debate the boundary between sharia and fiqh as well as other aspects of Islamic law.' *The World's Muslims: Religion, Politics and Society*, www.pewforum.org/2013/04/30/the-worlds-muslims-religion-politics-society-overview/

16 In Egypt, although the population follows the Maliki School, the codification of laws mostly follows the Hanafi School. This distinction is particularly interesting in light of the issue of women judges.

17 This discussion was taking substantially from Abdelkader, 2014.

18 Author interview with a mid-level administrative court judge.

19 A public opinion study revealed that 53% of the judges asked utterly refused the appointment of female judges, while 22% approve of such appointment if females would work in advisory functions without assuming the bench. Only 12% of judges expressed support for the appointment of women judges in all ranks of the court system (Al-taweel, 2012, p. 40).

20 This issue was not the only one that the supposedly liberal 50-member committee 'watered down.' 'The text of article 11 was proposed to be 'the state shall endeavor to take measures to ensure a fair representation of women in representative assemblies,' but some male members of the predominantly liberal 50-member committee, pressured to change "fair"' to "adequate" because fair might mean 50 percent.'

21 Article 93 of the 2014 Egyptian constitution states that: 'The state is committed to the agreements, covenants, and international conventions of human rights that were ratified by Egypt. They have the force of law after publication in accordance with the specified circumstances.'

22 The first wave of governors appointed by the president of the republic in February 2015 did not include a single female governor. The executive branch actions do not match its discourse on empowering women. The president of the NCW, a generally reliable regime supporter condemned the government decision. www.ncwegypt.com/index.php/ar/media-centre/ncw-news/142–2013–02–25–07–14–24/1608–2015–02–09–08–55–25

23 The High Judicial Council, chaired by the president of the Court of Cassation and including in its membership the top five judges in the Court of Cassation and the Courts of Appeal in addition to the public prosecutor, is the highest authority within the ordinary court system. The HJC has competence in all matters pertaining to appointment, promotion and discipline for the entire judicial corps in the PPD, the Courts of First Instance, the Courts of Appeal and the Court of Cassation. The composition of the Council changes every year due to the mandatory retirement of senior judges. The current composition is opportune for the appointment of female judges. None of the current HJC members has openly declared his opposition to the matter (as was the case with the 2011–2012 composition for example). The cause of women judges is further served by the fact that the current public prosecutor, Hisham Barakat, is supposed to desire to transfer his daughter, Marwa, an administrative prosecutor, to the court.

3 Botswana

Delayed Indigenization and Feminization of the Judiciary

Gretchen Bauer and Rachel Ellett

Since independence in 1966 Botswana has experienced a very different political and economic trajectory from the majority of sub-Saharan African countries. Botswana has held free and fair elections every five years, with successful leadership transitions from one elected president to another, albeit with no alternation of political power from the ruling Botswana Democratic Party (BDP), and it has experienced steady economic growth such that by the early 1990s Botswana was classified as a middle-income country with one of the highest per capita incomes in Africa. And yet despite this status as an 'African miracle' (Samatar, 1999), Botswana has struggled to bring women into leadership positions in all three branches of government. Since the 2014 election Botswana has one of the lowest representations of women members of parliament (MPs) in Africa and in the world—9.5%—and this has been the case for decades.[1] In 2012, only 12.5% of cabinet ministers in Botswana were women, the lowest in the Southern African Development Community (SADC) after the Democratic Republic of Congo and Mauritius—compared to 39% in South Africa and 29% in Mozambique (SADC, 2013, p. 40). In 2010, Botswana ranked lowest of all SADC countries in women judges on the High Court—only 6% compared to 65% in Lesotho or 54% in Zambia, although Botswana had the second highest percentage of women magistrates in the region—56%—and the only woman attorney general in the region (SADC, 2013, p. 45).[2]

In this chapter we focus on why there have been so few women judges in the higher courts in Botswana, compared to many other African countries, and why their numbers have increased so slowly. Since the appointment of the first woman judge in Botswana—Unity Dow in 1998—there has been an intensification of the debate around judicial appointments broadly, and the appointment of women judges more specifically, and gradually the number of women being appointed to the higher courts is increasing. We explore a number of possible explanatory factors including: a slow and fairly recent indigenization of the higher courts, and a limited supply of potential candidates overall with men dominating the legal professions and serving as the 'gatekeepers' to higher court appointments. Further, we consider wider contextual factors such as lack of transparency and executive overreach in the judicial appointments process, and a lack of political will to appoint more women.

We then consider the impact of women in the judiciary by reflecting on the work and careers of Botswana's most prominent early female judges. Finally, we raise the relationship between the women's movement and the appointment of women into political posts. We observe that at the height of women's activism we begin to see women appointees to the judiciary, the first women chiefs and the highest—to date—percentage of women MPs. Today we see an increase in women judges but a decrease in women MPs. This raises interesting questions for future research. Public office positions—whether appointed or elected—are not filled in a vacuum, but instead reflect a broader range of intersecting social, political and economic dynamics.

Historical Overview

Like many African countries, and as a legacy of colonialism, Botswana has a mixed legal system in which civil and common law exist side by side with customary law. Known then as Bechuanaland, Botswana was made a British protectorate in 1885. Uniquely in Africa, Bechuanaland was administered by high commissioners sitting outside the territory—in Cape Town and Pretoria in neighboring South Africa. Through a series of proclamations, South African common law was extended to Bechuanaland during the protectorate years.

Aguda (1973, pp. 55–56), who served as a justice on the Court of Appeal in Botswana from 1972 to 2001, describes the establishment, also by proclamation, of courts in Botswana during the protectorate period: the High Court, with effect from January 1939 (with unlimited jurisdiction in criminal and civil cases); a Court of Appeal in 1954, to take appeals from the three High Commission Territories (Bechuanaland, Basutoland and Swaziland), with a separate Court of Appeal for Botswana created by the country's constitution at independence; a Judicial Committee of the Privy Council in 1955 (abolished at independence); subordinate courts (with limits on claims amounts and certain offenses) also created in 1939; Customary Courts, touched upon in 1919 and 1934 proclamations but more fully regulated by the Native Courts Proclamation in 1943, superseded by the African Courts Proclamation of 1961. The High Court as created in 1939 was primarily for Europeans, as were the subordinate courts, while the customary or African courts were open only to Africans and had no jurisdiction over non-Africans. As Aguda points out (1973, p. 60), 'the whole scheme of legislative programme for this country from 1885 to 1959 was to create two different administrations: one for Africans and the other for the others.' In sum, colonial rule in Botswana 'left its mark' on the legal system in the country, as in other African countries, although certain aspects of the legal system such as those of a 'racially discriminatory nature' were able to be removed by the mid-1960s when Botswana attained its independence (Aguda 1973, pp. 53, 61).[3]

In addition to ruling Bechuanaland from neighboring South Africa, the British sought, as in other colonies, to administer Bechuanaland as cheaply as possible which meant a heavy reliance on traditional systems of rule—in the case of Bechuanaland, the kgosi/dikgosi (chief[s]) and the kgotla/dikgotla (place[s] of assembly where the chiefs hold court). Dikgotla 'operate at all levels of Tswana society, from the family cluster to larger lineage and ward groupings, to the central kgotla of the morafe (tribe or polity)' presided over by the paramount chief (Morton, Ramsay, & Mgadla, 2008, p. 171). Justice, as administered by the dikgosi or chiefs within the dikgotla, was based on unwritten law, the source of which 'lay in custom and tradition, with no distinction made between civil and criminal law' (Morton et al., 2008, p. 156). Since independence a series of proclamations have reduced the powers of chiefs, weakened the autonomy of Customary Courts and eroded customary law (Bauer, 2014; Sharma, 2009). And yet, according to Sharma (2009, p. 5), most Batswana today access the judicial system through the Customary Courts; Customary Courts handle approximately 80% of criminal cases and 90% of civil cases in the country.

Court Structure and Organization

The superior courts of Botswana consist of the Court of Appeal, the High Court, and an Industrial Court.[4] The most important inferior courts are the Magistrates Courts and the Customary Courts. The organization of the courts reflects the dual legal system in the country, in that the first three courts are concerned primarily with common law and the Customary Courts deal with customary law (Fombad, 2011). The Court of Appeal is 'the highest and final court in the land [. . .] the final arbiter of all legal matters in Botswana.' The High Court was created with unlimited original jurisdiction to hear and determine any criminal and civil cases under any law. There are three High Court divisions in Botswana—in Lobatse, Francistown and Gaborone. Magistrates Courts are not created by the constitution, rather by statute. The judges' roles in the administration of justice are stated in Part VI of the constitution of Botswana, with the constitution and other laws regulating their appointment and dismissal, tenure, status and independence from the other two branches of government (Fombad, 2011). Magistrates Courts have gone through a complete transformation since independence, from courts that were presided over by administration officers to courts wholly manned by professional magistrates with legal qualifications (Republic of Botswana, Republic of Botswana, n.d., Administration of justice: About Magistrate Courts). There are 24 Magistrates Court centers in Botswana today. Until 1998 no woman had ever served on the Court of Appeal or High Court. The first women were appointed to the Magistrates Courts in the late 1980s.

The Customary Courts derive their authority from the Customary Courts Act (1969). The Customary Law Act (1969) also guides the courts in determining whether customary or common law applies. The Customary Courts have jurisdiction to deal with a wide variety of matters of civil and criminal law such as financial disputes, petty theft, marital disputes, divorce (where the couple is married under customary law), livestock theft, insults and defamation, among others. The jurisdiction of the Customary Court is limited by the potential penalties or fines to be imposed, or the particular types of crimes or disputes to be adjudicated (Fombad, 2011). The Customary Courts are presided over by chiefs, of whom historically very few have been women. From the late 1990s onwards a small number of women in Botswana have asserted a right to be chief—whether sub-chief, senior chief, headman of record, headman of arbitration or even paramount chief—perhaps a symbolic representation effect of having more women holding formal political office in the country. In 2011, of the reported 2430 chiefs in Botswana—at all of the different levels—a 'very insignificant number' were women—perhaps a few dozen—and those primarily at the lowest or ward level, as headmen of arbitration. The first woman chief joined the House of Chiefs in Botswana in 1999 (Bauer, 2014).

Gender and Representation

Botswana remains a laggard in the SADC region in regards to appointment of women at the Court of Appeal and High Court ranks. No women have ever been appointed to the Court of Appeal in Botswana. Six women have been appointed to the High Court bench, of whom the first two—Unity Dow (1998–2009) and Athaliah Molokomme (2003–2005)—are no longer serving. Of the current 24 High Court judges, four[5] are women: Leatile Dambe, appointed in 2010, Mercy Garekwe and Phadi Solomon, appointed in 2011, and Tebogo Tau, appointed in 2012. Thus in 2015, women comprise 17% of the judges at the High Court level. As noted earlier, women comprise a majority of appointments—56%—at the magistrates level (SADC, 2013, p. 45). While it is clear that the trend in Botswana is now moving in the direction of increasing women's representation on the bench—jumping from 5.6% in 2010 to 17% in 2015—it is also the case that Botswana historically has lagged far behind its neighbors. As the late University of Botswana Law Lecturer Keneilwe Lekoba lamented: 'the appointments of Phadi Solomon and Mercy Garekwe to the High Court bench is not worth celebrating because Botswana's judiciary is marred by a lot of gender imbalance [and] "vertical segregation by gender" is still an issue of concern, especially within the judiciary' (Modise, 2011).

In this section we explore four potential explanations for this disparity: first, a judicial appointments process marked by a lack of transparency and executive overreach; second and third, historical institutional factors, namely, a limited supply of potential candidates and a male-dominated legal profession that has entrenched male hegemonies within the judiciary; and fourth, a lack of political will—with the indigenization of Botswana's higher courts near completion and the expansion of the bench, seats are available and yet still not being filled with significant numbers of women.

The judicial appointments process in Botswana has been mired in controversy in the last few years. The Law Society of Botswana (LSB) (2011) and others are concerned about appointment processes insofar as the significant role of the executive branch in appointments to the courts undermines the independence of the judiciary by allowing too much influence from the executive.[6] The president of Botswana alone appoints the chief justice and the judge president of the Court of Appeal; as such the process has 'tended to be shrouded in some secrecy,' according to the Law Society (2011, p. 4). The judges of the High Court and Court of Appeal, meanwhile, are appointed by the president, on the advice of the Judicial Service Commission (JSC). As such, the composition of the JSC becomes important: the chief justice (who chairs the JSC), the president of the Court of Appeal (not being the chief justice or the most Senior Justice of the Court of Appeal), the Attorney-General, the Chairman of the Public Service Commission, a member of the Law Society nominated by the Law Society, and a person of integrity and experience not being a legal practitioner appointed by the president—thus five of six members are appointed by the president—and the body is neither inclusive nor representative (Law Society, 2011, p. 5).[7] In addition, according to the Law Society, the procedures of the JSC are not well regulated and not accessible to the public.

In 2009 the Law Society shifted from quiet disapproval to a very public campaign against executive overreach in the appointments process. At that time, members of the Law Society publicly expressed their chagrin over President Khama's rejection of the candidates recommended by the JSC. In 2010, according to Mooketsi (2010), President Khama overlooked one woman who submitted her application for a High Court appointment, prompting a call for more women judges in Botswana. This generated critical coverage in the local media. A Gaborone lawyer reflected on this development:

> [t]he woman has demonstrated outstanding ability not only in private practice. 'I feel she was qualified even more than some people who have been appointed. If you look at her experience, she could not have been a better candidate,' she said. She added that some of the recently appointed judges were people from the corporate world, while others were academics without the hands on experience. 'You should wonder why the appointing authorities did not go out of their way to appoint this woman,' she questioned [. . .] She said the issue of gender balance does not seem to have been taken into consideration in the judiciary. 'Women with abilities should have made it to the bench.' The attorney said it was a high point for women when Dow was appointed as the first woman judge in the country. However, she said, since then women have been overlooked when it comes to the appointment of judges.
>
> (Mooketsi, 2010)

Part of the challenge in understanding the obstacles to appointment of women judges is the opacity of the process and the heavy—and sometimes arbitrary—hand of the president. In 2011 the LSB publicly distributed a paper focusing on the language contained in Section 96(2) of the Botswana constitution. Section 96(2) provides that the president must appoint 'in accordance with the advice of the JSC.' The Law Society interprets this language to mean that the president does not have the discretion to reject nominations put forth by the JSC. In early 2015 President Khama rejected the recommendation of the JSC for the appointment of Mr. Omphemetse Motumise to the High Court. The JSC defends the right of the president to do so, claiming its role is only 'advisory.' The Law Society is now threatening to commence litigation against the president and the JSC to determine the constitutionality of the president's action and seek clarity on the constitutional language moving forward (Mosikare, 2015). Reports in the media suggest that Motumise's appointment was blocked to make way for a BDP sympathizer: 'Although the President allegedly did not give any reasons for rejecting Motumise, the JSC went on to appoint Kebonang, who is believed to be pro ruling Botswana Democratic Party and allegedly has not been actively practicing law for some time now' (Baaitse, 2015).

While there is no direct link between the opacity of the appointment process and women candidates, the general concerns point to a politicization of judicial appointments. Politicization and opacity may not directly block potential female appointees, but they are not conducive to the appointment of women either. A more transparent process, such as in Kenya or South Africa, would allow for broader societal input into the vetting of candidates. The recent global shift towards merit-based appointments is, in part, an effort to diversify the bench in societies with a stubborn persistence of appointees drawn only from narrow elite strata of society. It is believed that the judiciary will be more legitimate and gain greater compliance if it comprises a bench of judges more reflective of society. One way to achieve this is broadening representation on the JSC. For example, in Kenya the new JSC comprises the chief justice as chairperson, three judges, the attorney general, two lawyers, a member of the public service commission and two members of the public (Sec.171(1) Kenya Constitution). Furthermore, attention is drawn to the question of gender equality by specifying the appointment of 'one woman and one man.' The debate in Botswana over judicial appointments does not appear to be moving in the direction of constitutional change, but rather strengthening and clarifying the role of the JSC in the process, rather than reforming the JSC itself.

Historically Botswana has generated a very small indigenous legal community, leading to a heavy reliance for many years (far longer than most other African countries) on expatriate judges. Following British colonial rule, Botswana was characterized by an almost nonexistent indigenous bureaucratic class, a low number of citizen-based political organizations, a heavily skewed class structure, and a parallel authoritarian traditional political structure (Holm & Molutsi, 1990). Between 1971 and 1989 there were only 83 law graduates in total from a joint University of Botswana Lesotho and Swaziland program.[8] The impact of more than a quarter century of extraterritorial legal education is not simply felt in terms of supply. The small number of lawyers graduating during this period further served to preserve the realm of law for the elite (Ellett, 2010).

The Botswana civil service was notoriously slow to indigenize and the upper echelons of the judiciary remained entirely expatriate well into the 21st century. For more than two decades after independence, judges of the High Court were expatriate judges who were appointed on contract for two to three years. The localization of the High Court began in 1992, when two citizen judges were appointed. Historically, appointments to the Botswana Court of Appeal have included (only male) judges from Ghana, Guyana, Lesotho, Nigeria, Scotland, and (heavily) South Africa (Ellett & Mafukidze, 2013, pp. 30–31). Rather rapidly in the last two years the Court of Appeal has localized. According to the government of Botswana's website on the judiciary the Court of Appeal is 'currently going through a process of localization' with four local judges and four expatriate judges sitting on the bench (Republic of Botswana, About the Court of Appeal).[9] This has occurred in just three short years; it was not until 2012 that the first Motswana was appointed to the Court of Appeal, Justice Elijah Legwaila.

For years now the Law Society has called for an acceleration of the process of indigenization with regard to the appointment of judges to the Court of Appeal and High Court, suggesting, among other things, that Botswana could not 'afford to import foreign judges when there were qualified citizen judges at home' (Ellett & Mafukidze, 2013, p. 21). As Lekgowe and Motswagole (2011) argued in a news article, in certain cases the Court of Appeal has avoided rendering judgments on certain issues because 'the foreign judges in the case lacked the knowledge and understanding of the public policy considerations in Botswana.'

In that same article, Lekgowe and Motswagole (2011) make reference to indigenous knowledge and culture; they posit:

> That knowledge and understanding of indigenous circumstances and systems is significant for a judge [. . .] While qualifications are indispensable, it is equally important that a judge must possess knowledge of the culture and language of the people upon whom he renders justice [. . .] Therefore, it is a well-placed grievance that has been raised before that the people of Botswana, to whom the machinery of justice is meant to serve and protect, do not know who these foreign men are, and that, on the other hand, these foreign men do not know the people of Botswana, so, exactly how are these men, unknown to us and us unknown to them, supposed to define, craft and enrich our future aspirations and hopes when they are not from or amongst us.

Two aspects of this eloquent argument are noteworthy. First, they continually make reference to the fact that all expatriate judges have been men. These expatriate men have therefore literally and symbolically blocked the pathways for local women judges. Second, we should reflect on the fact that their arguments about possessing knowledge of local culture and people must surely also apply to 50% of the population: women. The intensification of public debate around indigenization of the Botswana judiciary has clearly reaped rewards and we see the rapid departure of expatriate judges. However, because public discourse around judicial appointments has been dominated by this single issue, it has crowded out the space for activism and debate around women appointees.

To end our discussion of the historical legacies of expatriate-dominated institutions it is instructive to turn to comparative examples once more. First, if we compare Botswana to other SADC countries with expatriate-staffed apex courts, as in Table 3.1, we see Botswana ranks poorly among this subset of cases.

In other SADC countries the process of indigenization began earlier (Zimbabwe) or the demand for indigenization was not as high or intense (Lesotho). Or it was accepted that the Court of Appeal was different because it did not sit year round and it made sense to staff it externally. Or alternatively, equilibrium may be reached where the court is staffed with a combination of expatriate and local judges as we see in Namibia. We must conclude, therefore that the slow indigenization of the superior courts in Botswana was a necessary, but not sufficient, condition for explaining low representation of women in the judiciary. Other important factors are also at work.

Turning to the supply of potential candidates for appointment to the judiciary—the current membership of the Law Society of Botswana stands at over 500 lawyers.[10] A significant proportion of these members are working as lawyers in government, many of whom are women. Michelson's (2013, p. 1118) data from 2010 indicates that there were 453 lawyers total, of whom 139 were women, thus placing women lawyers at 39% of the total population of lawyers. Within the region Botswana is performing well, indeed there are a greater percentage of women lawyers in Botswana than Malawi (27%), Lesotho (25%) and Zambia (29%). It is only South Africa (46%) that ranks higher in southern Africa (Michelson, 2013, pp. 1115–1119). Women are now entering the legal profession in greater numbers than ever before; this much cannot be disputed. But this increase has been in place for some time now, so should we not be expecting to see a greater percentage of senior women lawyers and, consequently, appointment of women to the bench? Do the arguments about the supply of women judge candidates still hold today?

Table 3.1 SADC Countries With Expatriate-Dominated Apex Courts According to Percentage of Women Judges at High Court Level, 2010

Country	*Percentage of Women Judges at High Court Level*
Botswana	5.6%
Namibia	17%
Seychelles	20%
Swaziland	25%
Zimbabwe	29%
Lesotho	65.2%

Source: Adapted from Table 8 'Women in the judiciary in SADC member states,' in SADC (2013, p. 45).

Barmes and Malleson (2011, p. 254) find that in the United Kingdom

> between the point at which newly qualified lawyers enter the profession and the point at which judicial selection decisions are made, intervening factors work systematically, on the one hand, to channel members of some practitioner groups into, and on the other hand, to exclude others from, the different recruitment pools from which the judiciary is drawn.

They conclude that reaching gender parity (in the absence of explicit affirmative action provisions) will remain elusive as long as there are skewed internal hierarchies and ascriptions of value in the legal profession writ large. While we do not have data on University of Botswana law graduates and their career pathways, many of these forces are clearly at work. As one University of Botswana Law Lecturer[11] argues: 'There are not many senior women lawyers who can be judges. Currently, we have only about five senior women lawyers who have been at the bar more than twenty-plus years. It is only in recent years that women are making partner in law firms or running their own practices.' The rapid expansion of the bar in Botswana does appear to go hand in hand with a feminization of the bar. But as Michelson (2013, p. 1103) reminds us, 'Lawyer feminization on a massive scale does not preclude the possibility of truncated female careers and enduring female ghettoization in lower- status segments of the bar.' More research needs to be undertaken in Botswana and across sub-Saharan Africa to better determine the career paths of the burgeoning numbers of women law graduates.

It is noteworthy that the Law Society of Botswana has had a significant number of women in important leadership roles. Most prominently, Justice Sanji Monageng was executive secretary of the Law Society after its establishment as a statutory body in 1996. She was also the first chief executive officer, a role she performed for over eight years.[12] 'Today the Law Society is synonymous with my name,' Justice Monageng has publicly stated.[13] Justice Monageng has gone on to a very prominent career as an international judge. She is currently vice-president of the International Criminal Court (ICC). She previously sat on the African Commission on Human and People's Rights and at the High Court in Swaziland and Gambia. Monageng was first appointed a magistrate in Botswana in the late 1980s; she describes the relationship between her reception as one of the first women magistrates and the beginning of the women's movement:

> [T]here were maybe three of us only, female magistrates, initially I think it was a little strange for women to be in a very important seat then, but we were not made particularly uncomfortable, in a lot of ways there was a lot of excitement. That at long last we have female magistrates instead of women being made District Commissioners all the time. Botswana by then had progressed [. . .] the women's movement had started agitating [. . .] for gender equality. So people were a little bit careful, except for the fact

> that we were still grappling with some laws that were gender insensitive. But then these were not particularly against us they were against a society. Botswana is not doing too badly at all; there are a lot of women in some powerful positions, even at the High Court. For a long time we only had one female judge [. . .] but the government has started recruiting more and more women [. . .] but we could do much better.[14]

It is noteworthy that Monageng did not sit at the High Court in Botswana. There is no record of Monageng herself suggesting she was deliberately overlooked for the High Court bench, but others have suggested that this is the case (Mooketsi, 2010). It is possible that she simply did not put her name forward for consideration. According to the University of Botswana Law Lecturer, 'there are many amazing senior women lawyers [who] have never submitted their names for consideration for judgeship to the JSC.'[15] Research conducted in Botswana and elsewhere in the region, suggests that it is rare that a potential candidate for a High Court judgeship simply opens the newspaper, sees the advertised position and independently applies for the job. According to Ellett (2013; 2014) it is commonplace for individuals to receive quiet phone calls from chief justices, members of the JSC or sometimes even individuals outside of the JSC, through which they are asked to submit an application.

Botswana stands apart in regards to the prominence of the Law Society in the appointments procedure. Law Society recommendations help generate the shortlist of candidates, and in the last round of appointments two women were shortlisted (one an acting judge and another a judge of the industrial court).[16] There are ways in which this could be helpful, or could simply be another gate for women to push through. Another former chief executive officer of the LSB, Tebogo Sebogo, has publicly urged the government to continue to prioritize gender balancing in the judiciary: 'Sebego said there has to be some kind of affirmative action to bring a balance. He said there should be a deliberate effort by the government to ensure this. The law society official said they are going to encourage their women members to apply for the posts of judges' (Mooketsi, 2010). If women lawyers make up over one-third the total number of lawyers, and over 50% of the magistrates, it seems to suggest that the supply of potential candidates should be sufficient.

Finally, we need to turn our attention to the politics of appointments and to examine the political will for feminizing the judiciary. We suggest that a lack of political will has contributed to the small number of women appointed as judges to the higher courts in Botswana. The weak political commitment to appointment of women judges is located first and foremost in the presidency. The executive holds tremendous actual and symbolic power in the appointment of judges in Botswana. A similar lack of political will from President Khama, has been identified in relation to women members of parliament and women cabinet members. According to Bauer (2011, pp. 32–33), women activists interviewed in Botswana in 2009 suggested 'a highly centralized and powerful executive seems increasingly indifferent to a women's rights agenda.' They noted that upon becoming president in 2008, one of Khama's first actions was to remove one woman minister and one woman deputy minister, without adding women in any other ministerial positions. In addition, in strong contrast to Presidents Masire and Mogae, President Khama has not used the opportunity of specially elected (appointed) seats in parliament to bring more women into parliament, the 2014 appointment of Unity Dow notwithstanding. Women political leaders in Botswana such as Margaret Nasha are on record criticizing President Khama's record of failing to nominate more women MPs and failing to support women's political leadership more broadly (Bauer, 2011, p. 33).

Women and the Judiciary

In Botswana, with so few women in the higher ranks of the judiciary, it is difficult to draw any conclusions about whether and how women judges have sought to promote women's rights. The four women judges currently sitting on the High Court have only been appointed in the last five years. In this section, then, we examine briefly the tenure of the first two High Court women judges, Unity Dow and Athaliah Molokomme, also taking into account two cases that have had particular significance for women's rights in Botswana, the Citizenship Case[17] of the early 1990s and the much more recent Mmusi Case,[18] two cases in which the two women were, respectively, involved (though in neither case while they were serving on the High Court).

Unity Dow and Athaliah Molokomme are highly accomplished and highly regarded women lawyers and longstanding women's rights activists in Botswana. Dow (also the author of four novels, as well as other books) served in the attorney general's chambers as state counsel after finishing law school in the early 1980s and then joined Botswana's first all-women law firm. She was one of the founding members of the women's organization Emang Basadi in the mid-1980s and of Women in Law in Southern Africa in the late 1980s, for which she served as coordinator between 1992 and 1994. She started the Metlhaetsile Women's Information Centre in Mochudi in 1990, serving as its director from 1994 to 1998, when she was appointed to the High Court. She gained world renown for her role as plaintiff in the seminal Citizenship Case, in which she successfully challenged an amendment to the Citizenship Act of 1984 that sought to establish citizenship through a father only (Dow, 1995).

The High Court ruling on the Citizenship Case agreed with Dow that the Citizenship Act 'violated women's rights to liberty, the right not to be subjected to degrading treatment, and the right not to be discriminated against on the basis of sex.' The Botswana Court of Appeal upheld the High Court decision (Segwai, 1998). In her own compilation of the documents surrounding the Citizenship Case, Dow (1995) extended her 'sincere thanks to Judge [Martin] Horwitz for significantly advancing the cause of women. His decision demands more than the formal "as the court pleases."' Mobilization around Dow's Citizenship Case and Emang Basadi's legal reform efforts in the 1980s and 1990s led the government of Botswana to undertake a comprehensive review of its laws to identify instances of gender discrimination, resulting eventually in the abolition or amendment of many laws in the early 2000s and the adoption of other laws such as the 2008 Domestic Violence Act and the 2009 Children's Act, both of which 'cater to women's interests' according to one woman member of parliament in 2009 (Bauer, 2011, p. 30; Ellis, 2012).

Dow was appointed by President Quett Masire as Botswana's first female judge of the High Court in 1998. Of her appointment to the High Court, Dow has said: 'What better evidence of the independence of the judiciary is there than in a citizen who can sue the state in a high profile case, and then join the judiciary in that particular country? In another country that could never happen' (Segwai, 2008). In his autobiography, Masire (2006, p. 142) says: 'I later appointed her to the High Court as a judge, which clearly showed I held nothing against her for pressing her case.' Two important cases that Dow handled while High Court judge include the Child Maintenance Case of 1996–97 and the Battered Women Syndrome Case of 1997, both of which had important legal ramifications for women. The most high profile case Dow presided over concerned the right of the Basarwa or Khoisan people of the Central Kalahari to retain their ancestral lands and hunt game in what was proclaimed the Central Kalahari Game Reserve in the early 1960s.[19] Dow upheld the rights of the Basarwa to their ancestral land in a trial that was the longest and most expensive in the country's history. This was seen by many as a human rights victory and as a reflection of Dow's background and experience (Segwai, 2008).

Dow also played an important role within the judiciary as founder of the Botswana Women Judges and Magistrates Association in 1999. She had become active in the International Association of Women Judges (IAWJ) and decided to start a chapter in Botswana. The organization remains small, in part due to the weak participation by women magistrates, who view the organization with some suspicion because it is not an official government body.[20] This body is an important networking opportunity for female judges both domestically and internationally.

In 2014 Unity Dow stood for parliament as a BDP candidate from Mochudi West. She had hinted at this possibility already in a 2012 interview when she said: 'I'm a lawyer and I've been a judge, but there's one thing that I have not done so far and that is to make laws. I would love a plan to join politics and to run for a political office as a member of parliament and therefore join the legislature' (Ellis, 2012). She narrowly lost the election and then was the only woman to be brought into parliament as a Specially Elected Member by President Khama. She was subsequently appointed Minister of Education and Skill Development by President Khama. On her place as a lawyer and a judge, Dow was firm in her position that women should be just as well represented in the legal professions as men. In an interview in 2012 she observed: 'When you start to practice you realize how just the language of the law is so male, the culture of the law is so male,' she says. 'You're beginning to think, "I don't think it should be like this, I have a right to be here, I've earned the right to be here and therefore this whole environment should be about me as well"' (Ellis, 2012).

Athaliah Molokomme, Botswana's attorney general since 2005, served a much shorter term on the High Court, for only two years before being appointed attorney general. Like Dow, Molokomme finished law school in the early 1980s but then went on to obtain a PhD in the early 1990s and pursue an academic career as a member of the Faculty of Law at the University of Botswana. Also a founding member of Emang Basadi in the mid-1980s, as a law lecturer Molokomme was invited by government and women activists to put her research and advocacy skills to work examining laws that discriminated against women in Botswana (see Molokomme, 1993), leading to many publications. In 1998 she started and then directed the Gender Unit at the Southern African Development Community Secretariat and in 2003 she was appointed to the High Court where she served for only two years before becoming attorney general.

In her position as attorney general—and representative of the government—Molokomme recently found herself confronting—and emerging as one of the primary defenders of—customary law in Botswana.[21] This was in stark contrast to a long career advocating for legal reforms to end gender discrimination and enhance women's rights in areas of maintenance, marriage and representation in political office, among others. In the case of Ramantele v. Mmusi and Others, four sisters sought to inherit their family homestead rather than have their nephew do so, simply because he was the sole surviving male relative. The High Court and Court of Appeal rejected the argument that under customary law only sons were allowed to inherit the property. High Court Justice Key Dingake wrote that: 'It seems to me that the time has now arisen for the justices of this court to assume the role of the judicial midwife and assist in the birth of a new world struggling to be born. Discrimination against gender has no place in our modern day society' (Laing, 2012).[22] Judge President Ian Kirby of the Court of Appeal wrote that 'any customary law or rule which discriminates in any case against a woman unfairly solely on the basis of her gender would not be in accordance with humanity, morality or natural justice. Nor would it be in accordance with the principles of justice, equity and good conscience' (Lee, 2013). In her defense of the government position/customary law, Attorney General Molokomme had argued 'that it was not in the public interest to find the practice of favoring males in inheritance to be unconstitutional, because a majority of the population followed such practices, and it was too soon to abandon such culturally ingrained rules' (Roht-Arriaza, 2012).

The citizenship and inheritance cases demonstrate that progressive, pro-equality male judges have rendered decisions that positively impact women in Botswana. But this should not be interpreted as a signal that women judges are not necessary; in fact the message it should send is the opposite—imagine what could be achieved with a bench of individuals who substantively represent all of Botswana society, not just a narrow segment of it.

Conclusion: Challenges and Obstacles

Botswana has generated a steady supply of prominent women public figures in government, in civil society, academia and industry, and yet the number of women sitting in the upper levels of the judiciary has remained stubbornly low. This chapter has examined a number of possible explanations for the slow feminization of Botswana's High Court and Court of Appeal. While it is clear that the opaque and politicized appointments procedures and the slow indigenization of the courts have hindered the expansion of women judges, these do not fully explain the phenomenon. Nor can it be true that there is a dearth of qualified women candidates given that women make up over 30% of the lawyers and over 50% of the magistracy. The answers, we suggest, lie somewhere at the intersection of gatekeeping in the legal profession and career paths for women lawyers on one hand, and weak political commitment to feminization of the judiciary on the other. Further research needs to carefully examine the politics of the legal profession to shed further light on this problem.

Another interesting avenue of research is to further trace the connections between civil society, the media and political appointments. The women's movement in Botswana was highly active and focused in the 1990s. Emang Basadi successfully increased awareness of women's issues, which in turn became a regular feature of public discourse. At this time we saw the first appointment of a woman to the High Court, the first women chiefs and the highest number of women MPs. The number of women MPs has now dropped off, but we are beginning to see an increase in the number of women High Court judges. This raises intriguing questions about the relationship between women's activism and the feminization of government—in both elected and appointed positions. The symbolic value of women in prominent leadership positions may have a laggard effect, rather than an immediate effect.

While nobody can predict the future with any certainty, it seems safe to suggest that the number of women judges in Botswana will continue to increase over the next few years. The question instead is at what rate will women be appointed? And from where will these women judges come? Will they be lawyers from private practice, lawyers from the government or sitting magistrates? Will any patterns emerge in terms of the independence and or activism of women judges being appointed from different sectors? Several of the recent women appointees have come from government lawyer positions—will this impact their independence given the dominance of a single political party in Botswana?

Notes

1 Retrieved from www.ipu.org/wmn-e/classif.htm. The highest representation of women in Botswana's National Assembly was achieved in 1999–17%—following a significant mobilization of women's organizations led by Emang Basadi. Since then the percentage fell to 11% in 2004 and 8% in 2009. See Bauer, 2010.

2 In 2015 the percentage is slightly higher as will be discussed later in the chapter. The cited SADC table is somewhat ambiguous on years, offering 2010–2012. In 2010, 5.6% of judges on the High Court in Botswana were women.
3 See also Redgment, 1988 and Kakuli, 1997.
4 Sec. 127, Constitution of Botswana.
5 It should be further noted that a review of the current High Court Rolls for Botswana (www.justice.gov.bw/Court_Rolls/high-court-Gaborone) indicate other women currently sitting at the High Court level, for example, Anna Mphetlhe, a Registrar at the Administration of Justice.
6 Botswana's appointments process and in particular the early heavy reliance on expatriate judges has also been used to explain the limited judicial activism in the country: 'On the whole, the judges in Botswana in spite of certain landmark cases like Attorney-General v Dow have not been as "activist" as one would expect from Africa's oldest democracy.' An early study on judicial activism in the country (Quansah and Fombad, n.d.) has provided evidence to suggest that the country's contract system of judicial appointments has not helped because the contracts of some of the judges who displayed strong traits of judicial and constitutional activism were not renewed.
7 As Morima (2013) observes: 'It is submitted that, considering its majority in the JSC, the executive can ensure that only candidates sympathetic to government are appointed as judges though they do not meet the fit and proper criteria, thereby compromising judicial independence from the very beginning.'
8 Rachel Ellett data collected from University of Botswana Academic Calendars/Graduation Books and Chancellor College Law Department website.
9 An out-of-date version of the same website noted that there were 'currently,' eight expatriate judges of the Court of Appeal, drawn from different parts of the Commonwealth. The website continues: 'This has enriched the court and brought diversity and dynamism in the court. To date, no Motswana has ever been appointed to the Court of Appeal, although arrangements have been made for Judges of the High Court to sit in that court during its session, to expose them to its operations. This is also intended to prepare judges of the High Court for the eventual localization of the court.' Republic of Botswana, Hierarchy of the Courts.
10 Rachel Ellett interview with Law Society Executive Secretary, Gaborone, February 2013.
11 Email correspondence between Rachel Ellett and University of Botswana Law Lecturer, April 2015.
12 Retrieved from www.icc-cpi.int/NR/rdonlyres/E42E92F1-A149–45E2-B7DB-39CB1F450F34/278351/ICCASPEJ2009NVBENG.pdf
13 Interview with Sanji Monageng for the IAWJ 'Pioneering women judges on international courts.' Retrieved from http://iawj-womenjudges.org/hon-sanji-mmasenono-monageng/
14 Transcription of portion of interview with Sanji Monageng for the IAWJ 'Pioneering women judges on international courts.' Retrieved from http://iawj-womenjudges.org/hon-sanji-mmasenono-monageng/
15 Email correspondence between Rachel Ellett and University of Botswana Law Lecturer, April 2015.
16 Email correspondence between Rachel Ellett and University of Botswana Law Lecturer, April 2015.
17 Unity Dow v. Attorney-General BWHC [June 1991].
18 Mmusi & Others v. Ramantele & Another, BWHC (2012).
19 Sesana and Another v. Attorney General (Misc. No. 52 of 2002) [2006] BWHC 129 (13 December 2006).

20 Rachel Ellett interview with Botswana Women Judges and Magistrates Association member, Gaborone, June 2009.

21 As in several other African countries, the constitution of Botswana not only lacks a provision requiring that customary law be brought into line with individual constitutional rights but also includes a provision that exempts customary law from equality and nondiscrimination provisions of the constitution (Scribner and Lambert, 2010, p. 53). According to Gender Links (2013, p. 62), constitutional and statutory reform is necessary in order to seal the loophole that allows customary law to discriminate against women. Unity Dow has been quoted as saying: ‘It is not unfair to say that if gender discrimination were outlawed in customary law, very little of customary law would be left at all’ (Gender Links, 2013, p. 60).

22 Another publication quotes Dingake differently—referring to the new world to be born as ‘a world of equality between men and women as envisioned by the Botswana Constitution’ (Miller, 2012).

4 South Africa

A Transformative Constitution and a Representative Judiciary

Cathi Albertyn and Elsje Bonthuys

For nearly three and half centuries of colonial and apartheid rule in South Africa, the incumbents of judicial positions were exclusively white and male. At the cusp of democracy in 1994, only two judges were female and one was black. Twenty-five years into democracy, in 2014, 63% of all High Court judges are black and 32% are women (Law Society of South Africa, 2014, p. 46). Such a profound demographic change is the direct result of the transition to democracy in the early 1990s, and the concomitant aspiration of transforming the judiciary from one that 'collaborated, largely by omission, silence and inaction, in the legislative and executive pursuit of injustice' under apartheid (Truth and Reconciliation Commission, 1998, para. 158), to one that is a legitimate and independent guardian of the democratic constitution. Indeed, the appointment of black and female judges, as well as the justifications for greater judicial representativity and diversity must be understood as part of wider debates on the nature, scope and meaning of political, economic and legal transformation in post-apartheid South African society.

This chapter explores the constitutional, political and legal context for the appointment of women judges in South Africa, and considers the extent to which it is possible to identify and evaluate their impact. It starts with a brief history, illustrating that gender is only part of the picture in South Africa. Because of the historical exclusion of black people from tertiary education and from the apartheid legal profession, race has generally been a more prominent and persistent theme than gender. It then considers the constitutional provisions that require a more representative or diverse judiciary in South Africa and the debates on the meaning of judicial transformation mandated by these provisions, as well as the manner in which the appointing bodies have carried out this mandate. The barriers that women face in the legal profession are discussed before looking at the impact of women on the judiciary. Here we traverse some local and global theoretical debates and concepts before examining the situation in South Africa. In concluding, we note the wider contextual factors—constitutional, legal and political—that have been important in securing progressive and women-friendly judgments and provide some lessons from the South African experience.

Historical Overview: History, Race, Apartheid and Transformation

The origins of the modern South African judiciary lie in the 1827 Charter of Justice of the Cape Colony, which introduced a legal system, based on the English common law model, with a divided legal profession, Supreme or High Courts and Lower Magistrate's Courts, and an independent judiciary comprised mostly of judges trained in England (Sachs, 1973, ch. 1). The establishment of the Union of South Africa in 1910 saw he extension of this model throughout the country. Magistrates' presided over magistrates' and Regional Courts, and judges staffed the various provincial divisions of the Supreme Court from which appeals lay to the Appellate Division as court of highest appeal.

It is important to note that alongside this civil court system, the early South African state maintained a clear divide between civil law (for whites) and customary law (for blacks). Despite recognizing customary law, colonial and state authorities nevertheless regarded it as an inferior system of law, as evidenced by the informal status of the bodies which have administered these rules (Hoexter, 2014). Customary law was administered by Magistrates' Courts sitting as commissioners' courts, as well as by a different and inferior system of customary or traditional courts, presided over by male elders and traditional leaders, which left virtually no space for women to preside or indeed act as litigants or witnesses (Koyana & Bekker, 1998, p. 256). These latter courts still exist, and although their roles and functions have been the subject of a lengthy law reform process, this has stalled largely because of significant popular opposition to the proposal to retain their conservative and patriarchal character (Claassens & Weeks, 2009). This chapter, however, deals with the civil courts, focusing in particular on the judges who staff the higher court levels.

South Africa's adoption of a Westminster model of government and parliamentary sovereignty in 1910 meant that the judiciary, while independent, had limited ability to challenge unjust laws. While the South African judiciary achieved a reputation of being 'formally independent from political influence, manifestly incorrupt and consciously impartial' (Corder, 1984, p. 240), it did not escape criticism for its failure to use the legal means at its disposal to stem the tide of racial segregation and apartheid. In particular, the majority of judges adhered to a legal culture of "formalism," namely a tendency to ignore the role of values and attitudes in the interpretation of law, and thus to deny the possibility of judicial choice and creativity in the face of racially oppressive laws (Dugard, 1971). As a result, Corder notes, the judiciary failed to 'display a positive commitment to justice on those occasions when the legislative will was advancing injustice in the social formation' (Corder, 1984, p. 240).

Academic criticism of apartheid judges thus focused less on the white, male character of the judiciary than on the narrow legal culture and limited methods of adjudication that constrained its capacity to contest racial oppression. In contrast to this, criticism from within the national liberation struggle challenged both the racial composition of the judiciary and its acquiescence in apartheid laws and policies (Albertyn, 2014, pp. 248–254). As political change became more likely in the 1980s, the African National Congress (ANC) called for 'an independent and non-racial judiciary' (ANC, 1989a; 1989b, paras. 16.6–16.7).

Gender was almost entirely absent from all these conversations. As Chanock (2001, p. 26) writes of the period up to 1932:

> It is significant that there are no women's voices in any of the sites in which law was talked about: no women lawyers, no women politicians, no women 'experts.' An alliance of patriarchies relegated African women to the bottom of the social structure, and simultaneously elevated white women.

With few exceptions, this remained true until 1990. Indeed, it was only in the conditions of the democratic transition that gender equality emerged as a core principle of the new democracy (Albertyn, 1994; Hassim, 2002). As a result of sustained gender activism around the new constitution, the ANC in 1992 expressed a commitment to a racially *and* gender-diverse judiciary that would inspire greater legitimacy through inclusive decision-making (ANC, 1992; Albertyn 2014, pp. 256–257).

Court Structure and Organization

The Democratic Constitution and the Transformation of the Judiciary

South Africa's 1993 constitution established a constitutional democracy. Often described as a legal revolution, the old system of racialized parliamentary supremacy was replaced by a justiciable constitution, in which all law and conduct were subject to the human rights and democratic principles enshrined in the constitution and enforced by the courts. The judiciary was thus given extensive powers of judicial review in the new democracy. Unlike the apartheid judiciary, it would be able to test and strike down discriminatory law and conduct for violating the constitution, providing an important constitutional basis for advancing women's rights.

In the cut and thrust of *realpolitik* that characterized the negotiations for this constitution in the early 1990s, parties agreed on the retention of the apartheid judiciary (Constitution, 1993, section 241). Anxieties about the character of this judiciary and its capacity for protecting and enforcing fundamental rights were partly deflected by the creation of a new Constitutional Court, which was to be the apex court in all constitutional matters (Constitution, 1993, s 99(2)) and would therefore drive the jurisprudence on the Bill of Rights, including women's rights. The crucial role of this court meant that the appointment of its judges was critically important, resulting in a requirement that these judges be 'representative in respect of race and gender' (Albertyn, 2014, pp. 255–259). The two-tier hierarchy of lower Magistrates' and Regional Courts on the one hand, and provincial High Courts (which replaced the various provincial divisions of the Supreme Court) on the other hand, was retained, as was the Appellate Division, now named the Supreme Court of Appeal (Hoexter, 2014). The requirement that judicial officers be representative in terms of both race *and* gender applies to both levels of courts and is discussed in more detail in the paragraph below.

Although all parties agreed that a stable transition required continuity in the legal system, the ANC (as the government-in-waiting) saw 'transformation' of the judiciary as a longer term objective. The achievement, over time, of greater racial and gender representativity in this judiciary would be central to this transformation (ANC, 2012, para 1). Thus democracy provided the context and the impetus for profound changes to the character, composition and work of the South African judiciary, placing racial and gender representation at the center of its transformation. (Albertyn, 2014, p. 257).

Constitutional Provisions and the Meaning of Judicial Transformation

The task of judicial selection is governed by section 174(1) and (2) of the Constitution. Section 174(1) requires judges to be 'fit and proper' and 'appropriately qualified,' the so-called merit requirement. This is supplemented by section 174(2) which requires that '[t]he need for the judiciary to reflect broadly the race and gender composition of South Africa must be considered when judicial officers are appointed.' This second provision is central to the appointment of both women and black judges and thus to the transformation of the judiciary.

Of course, this idea of transformation was always contested, and has become even more so. We can identify two key themes which are often interwoven in the strongly disputed and sometimes emotive political, popular and legal debates on judicial appointment. First, there is disagreement about the appropriate relationship between the requirements of merit and transformation as set out in the two subsections of the constitution. Second, and nested within the first theme, is the question of what exactly judicial transformation entails.

At the heart of the second question is whether the requirement of a representative and transformed judiciary in section 174(2) would be satisfied by demographic representation only, or whether it connotes something deeper, namely, a greater diversity not only of race and gender but also of judicial values, experiences and modes of adjudication. On the one hand are those who emphasize demographic representation as important in and of itself, responding to the pre-democracy academic and political criticisms of the exclusively white male occupancy of the bench. They suggest that transformation is achieved through representation, the mere presence of black and female judges. This enhances the legitimacy of the institution, which failed to inspire respect and confidence in the majority of people in apartheid South Africa. In the light of South Africa's history, few would argue with this. Nevertheless, some who make this argument assume that the relationship between representation and the quality of justice operates in a rather essentialist manner: being black or female inevitably affects one's judgments and leads to better outcomes for oppressed groups. More commonly, it is argued that race and gender connote different life experiences and attitudes that impact the interaction, reasoning and decisions of such judges. However, this relationship is indirect and not inevitable.

On the other side are those who argue for a deeper and more nuanced understanding of diversity and transformation. They suggest that the stark legacy of apartheid and patriarchy means that not only have the benefits, opportunities, norms and qualifications for advancement in the legal system largely been the preserve of white men, but the character, outlook and culture of the apartheid judiciary has been shaped by a small elite, schooled in legal formalism under a system of racialized parliamentary sovereignty. The achievement of diversity is thus bound up with at least two broad challenges. The first is to achieve a diverse judiciary in which multiple intersecting differences of class, culture, sexual orientation, religion, ethnicity, and so forth enrich the institution. The second is to transform the values, norms and culture of the judiciary (and judicial decision-making) to fit the new constitutional democracy. Such a judiciary would be likely to understand the values of the constitution, including gender equality, in a progressive way and to proactively dismantle systems of racial and gender oppression inherited from our apartheid history.

One can thus identify a spectrum of different understandings of the relationship between professional 'merit' and demographic representation in section 174. One approach tends to regard gender and racial representation as mandatory and either overriding or at least being equally valuable as other elements of professional expertise and experience. In this view, demographic representativity functions as a screening or filtering criterion that trumps the merit of other candidates. Transformation is a thin concept associated with mere racial and (to a lesser extent) gender representativity, while other issues such as a judicial commitment to constitutional values and progressive judicial philosophy are of lesser significance. A second, contrasting approach prioritizes a narrow, unchanged notion of technical merit and experience within the traditional branches of the legal profession over representativity, insisting that competence always limits positive action to diversify the judiciary (Albertyn, 2014, pp. 276–277).

The third and more substantive approach views race and gender representativity as mandatory, but locates this within a wider understanding of multiple axes of difference, including class, background, ethnicity, culture, sexual orientation and religion. In this approach, sections 174(1) and (2) are read cumulatively, balancing both merit and transformation, while simultaneously interrogating and expanding the traditional concept of judicial merit. Important here is a commitment to constitutional values, empathy and progressive judicial philosophies as elements of judicial merit. In this view transformation is a broader concept linked not only to the judiciary's demography, but also to a wider concept of multiple axes of difference and diversity and to its norms, values and modes of operation, and its capacity to advance the values of the constitution (Albertyn, 2014, pp. 276–283).

As discussed below, the appointing bodies, the Judicial Service Commission (JSC) and Magistrates' Commission, have tended to follow a narrower approach, in which they have often prioritized race over gender. The narrow approach can be good for women insofar as demographics are concerned (although the record has been uneven), but it pays little attention to the values of judicial candidates, thus running the risk of appointing judges, including women judges, who might be insensitive to the gendered principles and values of the constitution, and less likely to advance women's rights. We argue, therefore, that deeper judicial and legal transformation does not only require the appointment of large numbers of women, but that all judicial appointees should be committed to protecting and advancing a progressive notion of gender equality.

Gender and Representation: Appointing Women Judges

Women Judges and Magistrates in the South African Courts: How Far Have We Come?

Accurate and up-to-date figures are hard to come by, but it is generally agreed that women, particularly black women, are best represented in the lower tiers of the judiciary. The statistics for the magistracy indicate that, in November 2013, 39% of all magistrates were female and that almost half of regional court magistrates (who are senior magistrates) were women. Moreover, four of the nine Regional Court presidents were women (Olivier, 2014a, pp. 329–330).

The picture is slightly less optimistic in the High Courts, the seniority of women judges. There has been significant improvement from a situation where virtually all judicial posts were held by white men in predemocratic South Africa (Olivier, 2014b, p. 119) to the position in April 2014 when 63% of all permanent judges were black, and 32% were female (Law Society of South Africa, 2014, p. 46).

To appreciate the extent to which these figures reflect the national demographics, it is necessary to know that black people currently constitute just over 91% of the population and whites just 8.7%, while women make up more than half of the population (51.2%) (Statistics South Africa, 2013, p.10). The proportion of black judges represents almost 69% of the demographic target and it has been more rapidly achieved than the proportion of women judges, which currently represents 63% of the target. The difference is most acute in the Constitutional Court where only two of the eleven judges are female and in the positions of judge presidents of the various courts, only one of whom is female while one woman is an acting judge president. Likewise, there is only one woman deputy judge president (Department of Justice and Constitutional Development, 2015). In the High Courts, therefore, the lack of women is most severe in the most senior positions.

Table 4.1 Women Judges in South Africa by Racial Category, 2015

Race	*African women*	*White women*	*Colored women*	*Indian women*
Percentage of superior court judges	14.5%	9.5%	3.3%	4.9%
Percentage of the total South African population	41%	4.5%	4.6%	1.3%
Women as percentage of all judges of their race	32%	26.4%	34%	50%

In South Africa, however, the category 'women' can never be taken at face value and we need to disaggregate these figures according to the apartheid-based racial categories to judge the contemporary impact of the history of racialized privilege amongst women. Thus, we find that African and colored women are most underrepresented, while the percentages of white and Indian women judges are disproportionately large. The most pressing issue is the lack of African women judges. Whereas 44% of all judges are of African origin, only 32% of all African judges are female (Law Society of South Africa, 2014, p. 46). The overrepresentation of therefore comes at the expense of an underrepresentation of African and colored women, as can be seen in Table 4.1.

Different factors influence the numbers of women in the most senior judicial positions, and the uneven distribution of women across the judiciary. These include the constitutional provisions that require that the judiciary reflect the race and gender composition of the population; the extent to which the appointment process and criteria encourage or discourage the appointment of women and black people; and the historic and current barriers faced by different groups of women in entering the legal profession as a precursor to being appointed as judges. Important too, are the open processes of judicial nomination and appointment, and the ability of civil society participation and advocacy to influence these. We turn to these issues next.

The Judicial Service Commission and Civil Society Participation in the Appointment Process

Magistrates are appointed by the minister of justice, in consultation with the Magistrates' Commission. Interviews for these positions are not open to the public or media and, perhaps because of their less prestigious nature and the less significant political impact of judgments by the lower courts, the appointments of magistrates excite less public interest and debate than those of High Court judges. Nevertheless, the relative weight of different appointment criteria such as experience, professional qualifications, gender and disability have resulted in two court challenges and subsequent changes and clarifications to the appointment processes and criteria for magistrates (Olivier, 2014a, pp. 330–332). These cases grapple with essentially similar policy and definitional issues as those applying to the appointment of judges, as we discussed in the section above. This is understandable, given that the constitutional provisions on judicial appointments apply to both the magistracy and the judiciary alike.

Prior to democracy, South Africa followed the British convention of a 'tap on the shoulder' in appointing judges, who were drawn exclusively from the ranks of senior advocates and appointed by the executive. In practice, the Judge Presidents and the minister of justice would identify suitable candidates and secure their appointment (Olivier, 2014b, pp. 117–119). Under democracy, South Africa has introduced an open and transparent system of judicial appointment in which the procedure for the appointment of judges is highly visible, often contested and connected to current political debates about race and gender. Although the final power of appointment ultimately lies with the President, this is constrained by the powers and functions of the Judicial Service Commission (JSC), which receives nominations, conducts interviews and recommends judges for appointment to the President (Constitution, 1996, sections 174, 178; Judicial Service Commission Act 9 of 1994).

By comparison with other judicial appointment bodies, the JSC is considered unusually transparent in the sense that it accepts nominations from a wide range of legal actors; members of the JSC are appointed from the broad array of constituencies; and its interviews (but not its deliberations) are open to public and media attendance (Du Bois, 2006). This openness has created opportunities for lively political debates and contestation by political parties and public commentators and for civil society, in the form of NGOs and academic bodies, to mobilize around appointment processes (Bonthuys, 2015). In the past five years, gender activists have been particularly active and effective in drawing attention to the relative paucity of women judges by critiquing the President's failure to appoint more women to the Constitutional Court, when there was ample opportunity to do so (Underhill, 2012). They have also argued that both the president and the JSC lack the political will to address gender disparities to the same extent as racial imbalances and fail to nominate and appoint suitable women candidates (Du Plessis, 2013a; Khan, 2013). Recent interventions have drawn attention to the overwhelmingly male membership of the JSC itself and to the failure of certain of the government-appointed women on the JSC to actively promote the nomination of more female judicial candidates (Masengu & Tilley, 2013).

Recent evidence suggests that criticism and advocacy by civil society organizations may have contributed towards increasing the number of women judicial nominees. Indeed, responses by the JSC, and the chief justice in particular, reflect an acute awareness of these criticisms, and in recent interview panels, several women were recommended for appointment at once. During the period from March 2012 to April 2014, the proportion of women in the judiciary increased from 28% to 32% (Law Society of South Africa, 2014, p. 46; Manyathi, 2012, p. 4). Moreover, instances of blatantly sexist questions or remarks directed at women judicial nominees that were reported in the past (Rickard, 2007) were not repeated in the past five years. In fact, the JSC has regularly and publicly invited women candidates to put themselves forward for consideration (Rabkin, 2011; Schroeder, 2013).

Despite these encouraging responses to concerns expressed by gender activists, the JSC's positions on certain crucial aspects of the transformation debates which we described above have been unclear and often contradictory. First, the JSC's nomination patterns and public statements on what would constitute sufficient professional expertise and merit and the relationship between transformation, representation and merit sometimes create the impression that demographic representation would trump professional expertise as a criterion. For instance, the chief justice, in response to criticisms that the JSC failed to nominate a suitable female candidate was reported as saying at a press conference that 'it is not a constitutional imperative to appoint the best of the best' (Tolsi, 2013). Indeed, the JSC has failed, on occasion, to nominate a suitably qualified female candidate for office, or nominated a man where the female candidate was more suitable. In 2013, for instance, three candidates applied for the position of deputy judge president of the North Gauteng Court. Although the male candidate, who was recommended, was the most senior of the three, this was only by one year and one of the female candidates gave a very good interview. Nevertheless, the JSC did not take this opportunity to improve gender equality in leading judicial positions (Rabkin, 2013). Such failures to recommend suitably qualified women for appointment call into question the JSC's frequent statements that there are too few qualified female candidates.

On the other hand, in response to being criticized for failing to nominate sufficient numbers of women, the JSC has more than once stated that too few women apply for appointment and that some female applicants lack the requisite professional experience (Schroeder, 2013). Another frequent theme is that the traditional 'pool' from which female candidates can be selected has been exhausted and that there are simply not enough competent women to appoint to judicial office. During public interviews the JSC has frequently asked female candidates to describe their experiences in practice and appointment from the ranks of attorneys, magistrates and academics has helped to substantially increase the appointment of women and black judges.

Perhaps most damaging for women candidates are the ways in which the uneasy relationship between gender and race as criteria for transformation is sometimes exploited to score political points. Bonthuys (2013) has argued that, in the public fracas which surrounded the appointment of Justice Mogoeng as chief justice in 2011, certain conservative political and legal professional stakeholders used arguments related to gender to further agendas which had little to do with gender equality. In turn, the chief justice, in his position as chairperson of the JSC, has reacted defensively to recent criticisms of the JSC by insinuating that all criticism proceeds from racial or other inappropriate motives. Although the point that some people call for gender equality to deflect concern from the primary need to transform the racial composition of the profession may be understandable, and sometimes be legitimate, it also dismisses real concerns about gender equality and prioritizes racial transformation (Bonthuys 2015). Setting up a dichotomy between gender and race in transformation is misleading because, as the table in the paragraph above shows, the most dramatic demographic gap is that of African women, who constitute 41% of the population, but only 14% of judges. Although white women are overrepresented as judges, they constitute only 26% of all white judges, with white male judges continuing to predominate. The problem is therefore one of *both* gender and race and its roots lie in the demographic, social and normative structures of the legal profession, to which we turn next.

The Legal Profession

The JSC's point about women's underrepresentation in the legal profession has some merit. The South African legal profession is organized in accordance with the divided British model and consists of attorneys or solicitors in the side bar and advocates or barristers who practice at the bar. Traditionally judges were appointed from the ranks of senior advocates. In apartheid South Africa both sectors of the legal profession were virtually the exclusive domains of white men. Given that currently equal numbers of women and men graduate with legal qualifications, the profession could be expected to normalize in the future. However, this has not happened in South Africa and, as in other countries, rapid change is unlikely without active and effective intervention.

Statistics indicate that the numbers of women admitted as attorneys approached parity with men in 2004 and has exceeded the numbers of men since 2006. Nevertheless, in March 2014 the numbers of men practicing as attorneys far surpassed the numbers of female practitioners (Law Society of South Africa, 2014, pp. 26, 35). Clearly therefore, large numbers of women become attorneys, but they are discouraged by factors within the profession. In their interviews with women candidates, members of the JSC have frequently asked questions about candidates' experience in the profession and the answers usually reveal the litany of sexism and marginalization familiar in legal professions throughout the world (Rabkin, 2014). These range from a failure to accommodate family responsibilities, to sexist and stereotypical professional norms, attitudes that limit their access to particular areas of legal work, exclusionary social networks, and lack of access to position of leadership and authority (Cowen, 2005).

The situation at the bar is no better and comes as no surprise, given that advocates are briefed by senior attorneys, who remain for the most part white men. Twenty years after the advent of democracy this most lucrative and high-status sector of the legal profession continues to be dominated by white men and has failed to include significant numbers of black men and women. In every White men account for 56% of all advocates in the country. In all racial groups men outnumber women considerably. In 2014 the figures showed that white women accounted for only 22% of white advocates, African women 23% of all African advocates, colored women 45% and Indian women 11.6% of all Indian advocates (Law Society of South Africa 2014, p. 45).

The 'pool' from which judges have traditionally been appointed is therefore neither demographically representative, nor likely to become more representative in the near future. Even where judicial candidates are recruited from those parts of the profession in which women predominate, such as academia, the magistracy, the side bar and the corporate legal sector (Masengu & Tilley, 2013), nominees from these nontraditional backgrounds can be unfavorably compared with senior white male advocates whose experience is regarded by the profession as more suitable to judicial office.

Hard work is required to remove the traditional barriers of exclusion in the legal profession. Women will not automatically 'trickle up' unless there is a concerted attempt to recognize their parenting role, address attitudes and culture, unpack and adapt gendered norms and actively mentor promising young women, especially young black women (Cowen, 2005). But it is perhaps worth pointing to two mechanisms that have assisted women in overcoming some of the traditional barriers of exclusion. The first was a series of programs for fast-tracking aspirant women judges, funded by the state and conducted under the auspices of the chief justice (Wesson & Du Plessis, 2008, p. 10). The second aimed to increase the opportunities for women to be appointed as acting judges, which is considered particularly important for judicial candidates from nontraditional legal backgrounds. Recently, activists focused on the failure of judge presidents to appoint women as acting judges, thus depriving them of crucial experience in what has been seen by many as an informal requirement for appointment (Masengu & Tilley, 2013). This has been effective in leading some Judge Presidents to actively solicit women lawyers for acting judicial appointments, thus enhancing their chances of appointment.

Women and the Judiciary: Women's Impact in the Judiciary

Although there are still too few women in the South African judiciary, it is important to question whether those women who are already on the bench have made any impact on the institution of the judiciary or on the quality of its judgments. This includes questions of institutional authority, legitimacy and culture, as well as judicial decision-making and the question of whether women are more active in upholding the rights of female litigants and reforming patriarchal legal rules and concepts.

The assumption or the hope that women judges will confront and change patriarchal law and legal systems cannot be the only or even the most important reason why they should be appointed as judges. Firstly, this ignores the important legitimacy rationale of a representative judiciary, namely that a greater judicial representation of the major social groups in society can help to establish a judiciary's credibility and increase public confidence in it, particularly amongst previously excluded and disadvantaged groups. Although perhaps more important in respect of race in South Africa, the presence of women in the judiciary has significant symbolic value.

Another hitherto neglected but nevertheless vital rationale to appoint more women judges is simply that failure to do so would mean that certain positions of power and influence in society and in the public service remain less attainable for women than for men (Albertyn, 2014, pp. 271–275). In other words, women have a simple constitutional claim to access state institutions and positions on an equal basis with men. The removal of sex discrimination and the achievement of substantive equality in the legal profession is a worthwhile aim in and of itself and would justify increasing the numbers of women judges, even if there were no proof that women judges are more active in fighting patriarchy than male judges or that they dispense a different and better quality of justice. The need for equal participation in the South African legal profession and in the South African judiciary is amply justified by the way in which these institutions have historically been dominated by white men. Both women and black men therefore have a legitimate claim to be appointed as judges, and to have the continued domination of the legal profession by white men addressed.

The question of women's impact on the quality of justice is far more difficult to answer and, as Malleson (2003a) has demonstrated, implies several assumptions which need to be interrogated more closely. Expecting women judges to shoulder the burden of achieving gender equality as precondition or justification for judicial appointment is both unfair and unrealistic. It is unfair because patriarchy is not primarily a problem for women to solve—as a pervasive social challenge it should be addressed by all judges, whether male or female. It is also unrealistic because it can be extremely difficult for women judges to swim against the tide in conservative and male-dominated institutions like the judiciary and legal profession.

Canadian and Australian research has provided clear, though anecdotal, evidence of the backlash faced by women judges who openly challenge patriarchal norms and privilege. Backhouse's description of the treatment of Judge L'Heureux-Dube after her judgment in the Ewanchuk case on sexual violence (2003) and Graycar's account (2012) of the imprisonment of an Australian female chief magistrate who was seen as 'threatening' a male junior magistrate illustrate the dangers facing women judges who are openly feminist in sexist societies. Moreover, feminist judges are likely to be in short supply. The socially conservative nature of the legal profession and the need for advocates to conform to common professional values and modes of behavior in order to obtain briefs, mean that it is unlikely that the most fervent feminists would rise to the top of the profession and gain the necessary experience for judicial appointment. Selection processes and criteria add to the impetus to appoint the least radical, most conformist and compliant women as judges (Thornton, 1996, p. 221). Expecting this group of women to overturn long established legal principles, especially when they are still junior and work in environments which have been described as sexist and hostile by female judges (L'Heureux-Dube, 2001, p. 15), is probably overly optimistic.

The pressures preventing women judges from making a difference are therefore formidable. Recent writings have suggested that these pressures might be overcome by establishing a 'critical mass' of female judges (Collins, Manning, Kenneth & Carp, 2010; Johnson, Songer & Jilani, 2011; King & Greening, 2007; Moyer, 2013). Critical mass theory posits that once the numbers of women within the judiciary reach sufficiently high proportions (30% or more), the need to conform to masculine norms and modes of thinking will abate, allowing women judges to show their true feminist colors and to influence their male colleagues to adopt similarly progressive views. Such sanguine expectations have not been conclusively borne out by studies in other fields (Childs & Krook, 2006, p. 528). Indeed, much of the research has shown that the changes women make to institutions depend on a number of interrelating factors (Dahlerup, 2006, p. 520; Grey, 2006). These include the importance of 'critical acts' (Dahlerup, 2006, pp. 512–513) and 'critical actors' (Childs & Krook, 2006, p. 528) rather than critical numbers. In respect of the judiciary, we suggest this means that we should focus on identifying what women judges do when they appear to make a difference, and what are the characteristics of those judges who do influence the law in a positively gendered manner.

Evidence of Women's Impact in the South Africa Judiciary?

Since the advent of democracy in 1994, South Africa has made significant strides in the legal entrenchment of women's rights. Although many of these emanate from law reform, important gains have been made in the courts, especially in customary law, gender-based violence and family law. For example, women have secured rights to inheritance and property in monogamous and polygynous, customary and religious marriages; the right to consent to a second wife in some customary marriages; and the right to be recognized as a traditional leader by their communities. These cases have provided important practical relief for women and have shifted family norms towards ideas of gender equality and women's agency. (Albertyn, 2011; Bonthuys, 2014). In the area of gender-based violence, the courts have defended progressive legislative gains and expanded the duties of the state, especially the police services, to protect women against violence and sexual assault (Albertyn, 2011). In addition, there is evidence of a progressive and gendered jurisprudence in some courts, in which evidence of the reality of women's lives underpins a legal approach to equality which is both substantive and potentially transformative (Albertyn, 2011). However, the extent to which this can be directly attributed to individual or groups of women judges is less clear.

South Africa provides no clear proof for the claims of critical mass theory in the judiciary. Although women make up almost 40% of the magistracy, there is as yet no solid evidence that the justice dispensed in that part of the legal system has become more understanding of women's problems and perspectives, nor that female magistrates have been particularly active in challenging patriarchal legal rules or interpretations. Although women are more likely to be involved in cases in the Magistrates' Courts than the higher courts, in sexual offenses, family and maintenance matters, and although female magistrates are often assigned to these courts, we do not yet know whether that makes a difference in the treatment of women and outcomes in those courts. This may be a topic worthy of future research.

The subordinate position of the Magistrates' Courts within the court hierarchy limits their ability to make significant impacts on jurisprudence as compared to higher level courts like the Constitutional Court and the Supreme Court of Appeal. For instance, despite the Constitutional Court having the lowest ratio of women judges, certain women and men judges on the Constitutional Court have authored key judgments that have had a widespread effect in changing legal thinking and judgments in the lower courts on issues such as maintenance orders, domestic violence and sexual assault (Bonthuys 2008b). For example, in Bannatyne v. Bannatyne the Constitutional Court drew attention to the way in which inefficient legal enforcement of children's maintenance entitlements increases the burdens upon primary caretakers, who are usually women, and exhorted courts to improve the enforcement of maintenance orders. Lower courts responded by limiting the legal and procedural loopholes which allowed fathers to escape their maintenance duties and by crafting a range of innovative mechanisms to obtain maintenance from reluctant fathers, thus amplifying the effect of the Bannatyne judgment.

The level of seniority of women judges and the power of precedent in common law systems are therefore factors which could have a greater impact in advancing women's rights than the numbers of women judges. This supports the suggestion that critical acts and critical actors, rather than critical mass, are important for the achievement of gender equality in common law systems.

Central to the claims of critical mass theory is that *women* would judge differently from men. Although this is a claim sometimes made in the political arena (Albertyn, 2014, pp. 262–269), academic literature problematizes this position in two ways. First, as we have shown in the paragraphs above, race is and has historically, politically and socially been more central in the South African context. Moreover, both race and gender are further complicated by multiple cross-cutting axes of differences such as class, sexual orientation, rural origins, religious affiliation or cultural heritage—all of which have concrete and complicated effects on the life experiences of different women. This means that the question must be asked: *which* women judges and *whose* interests? We cannot assume that the judicial appointment of irreligious urban, middle-class white women will bring about positive changes for rural impoverished African women who are subject to customary law simply because they are all women. The multiple aspects of social identities are generally acknowledged to be far more complex. Thus when a lesbian South African judge, Kathy Satchwell, was asked about the impact of her sexual identity on the bench, she pointed to variety of intersecting influences—ethnicity and race, social class, education and political beliefs—that affected her position and, she believed, distinguished her from other lesbian judges (Moran, 2006, pp. 572–575).

Another issue which needs to be carefully unpacked is the relationship between judicial diversity on the one hand, and judging on the other hand, and the ways in which this relationship is mediated by various competing conceptualizations of impartiality or objectivity—a concept which stands central to the identity and activities of judges.

Apartheid-era judges were criticized for failing to recognize the extent to which their personal experience and bias (including but not limited to race) might have affected their exercise of the judicial function (Dugard, 1971). For this reason, former Constitutional Court judge Kate O'Regan argues that judicial officers in postapartheid South Africa need to make 'a self-conscious appreciation of the impact of their background on their way of thinking and a conscientious attempt at all times to be *impartial*' (O'Regan, 2012, p. 1176). This process of impartial decision-making is greatly enhanced by a diverse bench:

> So requiring diversity on a collegial court enables judges to interrogate their own prejudices or blind-spots. The more alike judges are, the more likely that they will mistake prejudices for simple truths; the more different they are, the more likely that they will interrogate the correctness of their assumptions. If our backgrounds are the same, it is very comfortable and easy to reinforce the prejudices that such backgrounds foster. When we are different, prejudices masquerading as 'common sense' or 'the ways things are' are much more likely to be uncovered.
>
> (O'Regan, 2012, p. 1176)

These arguments make particular sense when judges sit 'en banc,' as in the United States or Canadian Supreme Courts or the South African Constitutional Court and Supreme Court of Appeal. However, a diverse bench also benefits individual judges, whose interaction with colleagues outside the courtroom can develop their ability to appreciate diversity and understand that others—including those who appear before them—can hold different values, assumptions, expectations and motivations. As former chief justice Langa noted in a public address, diversity 'improves the quality of decisions by increasing judicial debate' (2007, p. 371).

Nevertheless, the outcome of any particular litigation can never simply be determined by the race or gender of the parties or the judicial officer: 'Judges must decide cases impartially and not on the basis of their identity or the identity of those who appear before them' (O'Regan, 2012, p. 1176). Rather than directly impacting the outcome of a particular case, the effect of diverse judicial perspectives should be on the process of judicial deliberation and the quality of reasoning.

In the final analysis, the arguments in support of diversity dispel the classical liberal 'myth' of judicial neutrality or objectivity—as adjudication that is or can be divorced from the values, prejudices and assumptions held by a judge. Rather, adjudication is a process of making visible one's 'inarticulate premise' and through reasoned engagement to achieve a result that has taken all aspects of a case into account, including the previously unknown perspectives that may flow from being a woman or being black, and associated differences of class, culture, politics and so forth. The aim is not to replace one (unacknowledged) partiality with another, but to open up the process of justice to a wider range of perspectives.

The multi-layered and sophisticated relationships between numerous axes of difference and the process of judicial reasoning are difficult to capture empirically. For this reason, empirical research on whether women judge differently from men often flounders on the difficulties of multiple identities, or is based on essentialist and erroneous gender stereotypes, for instance that women judges will vote more 'liberally' than male judges by deciding in favor of plaintiffs in civil rights cases and in favor of defendants in criminal law cases (Johnson et al, 2011, pp. 246–247). The better kinds of empirical research, and the ones in which differences between female and male judges are more likely to manifest, are therefore narrowly focused on cases which actually have gender dimensions like rape (King & Greening, 2007). Nevertheless, it is difficult to measure the texture and weight of persuasive legal argument in a precedent-based legal system by way of large scale empirical research.

How then do we establish whether women judges make a difference? One way would be to do a textual analysis of actual judgments on topics where gender is salient to see whether women judges use different arguments, legal authority or modes of reasoning from their male colleagues. This would work best in high-level courts where judges can question existing precedents and therefore have more scope to question and develop existing legal principles. Another, which works well in courts where judges sit together, is to analyze the extent to which women judges agree with one another in cases involving gender, as compared to cases which do not have explicit gender dimensions. O'Connor and Yanus's (2010) small-scale study of judges O'Connor and Ginsberg of the US Supreme Court showed that, although on average the two women agreed with one another only 52% of the time, in gender discrimination and abortion cases they agreed with one another 90% of the time. Although the numbers are small, the evidence appears to be significant. A similar small-scale exercise was undertaken on the South African Constitutional Court from 1996 to 2007 (Bonthuys, 2008a). It found that the two women judges and the male judge identified as a feminist tended to agree with one another more frequently in cases involving gender than was the case in all cases. Conversely, they agreed less with the other judges in gender cases than was usually the norm. Moreover, in cases which involved gender, these three judges were far more likely either to author the main judgment of the court, or to author a dissenting or separate concurring judgment than was usually the case. This study does not provide compelling evidence; the sample is very limited and it has not been updated to include recent cases. It nevertheless suggests that women judges tend to agree with one another and with feminist men more often in cases involving gender, which may be an indication that women judges think differently than men judges.

When asked about their judicial role, South African women judges have argued that they bring particular experiences, perspectives and knowledge to law and legal reasoning (Democratic Governance and Rights Unit, 2009, p. 23; Mokgoro, 2010). Similar claims have been made about black judges who have experienced racism and apartheid. Budlender alludes to the 'connectedness' that black judges currently have with 'the life experiences and concerns of the people who constitute the majority in the country' (2005, p. 716).

There are, however, strong arguments to suggest that the sex or race of a judge is less determinative of their reasoning than their judicial approach. It may be that thoughtful and skilled judges who have a strong sense of constitutional values and context in relation to gender (and other) inequalities can make a difference, regardless of their sex. These can be women, but not inevitably, and not all women are included in this group.

Indeed, the more important divides between different judgments in the Constitutional Court, for example, relate to broader world-views and judicial philosophies of which gender is only a part. An analysis of the reasoning of the Constitutional Court judges on the rights of women in customary law shows that all the groundbreaking judgments which substantially extended the rights of women were penned by African male judges, with significant support from other male and female judges. The court was more divided in cases on the extent to which customary law should be developed in line with the dictates of the constitution, and the degree of deference which should be shown to existing cultural norms. In these cases a minority of judges, including a woman judge, resisted the more progressive outcomes by asserting cultural difference. It appears that in these cases more conservative and traditionalist judges—both male and female—are more likely to defend culture.

Concluding Thoughts: Lessons from the South African Experience

The South African experience teaches the value of constitutional reform, as does that in many other African countries. Not only did the democratic constitution provide a new and more open mechanism for judicial appointments and a provision which explicitly requires the presence of women in the judiciary, but it also signaled a break from a past in which the legal system was deeply implicated in various forms of racial and gender oppression. As such, the democratic constitution provides and sustains the impetus towards gender equality, not only in relation to the appointment of judges and magistrates, but more broadly in law and society. Where judges—both female and male—issue judgments which enhance the rights of women, they act in terms of the constitutional imperative to do so. The Constitution thus provides the larger framework within which aspirations toward gender equality can be realized.

A second point is the value of an open and transparent appointment process which provides the necessary space for a wide array of civil society actors vigorously to interrogate and engage the bodies which appoint judges and to advocate not only for the appointment of women judges, but for judges who will understand and uphold progressive constitutional values.

That women should be appointed as judges brooks no opposition, but the South African context also shows that other factors like race, religion, cultural background and so forth may be equally important for achieving a broad and valuable diversity of opinions, views and values that will enrich the reasoning and jurisprudence of our courts. Most important is to appoint judges who are committed to transformative processes and outcomes. Although women judges and feminist judges may be particularly committed to dismantling structures of gender oppression, this should not be a task that falls to women only. Nor are women and feminists the only judges who produce positive outcomes for women in a constitutional democracy. Generally, progressive judges who adjudicate with due regard for constitutional values (including gender equality) and context should do so. However, the fact that progressive male judges may also advance gender equality in no way detracts from the constitutional need for the appointment of more women. Appointing women as judges is politically and constitutionally required for a range of other reasons, including the attainment of substantive gender equality in government positions, for reasons of legitimacy and enhancing the diverse range of experiences on our courts.

The need to appoint a more diverse range of judges alerts us to the way in which, 20 years after the advent of democracy in South Africa, both levels of the legal profession continue to be dominated by a small and historically privileged part of the population. Structural and cultural issues within the profession that exclude women and black men and other minorities should be addressed, by way of legislation, if necessary. Finally, the trend by the JSC to expand the pool from which judges are appointed is to be welcomed, not only because it increases the chances of appointing previously marginalized groups, but more fundamentally because it questions and transforms the hitherto limited concept of what constitutes judicial merit and competence.

5 Nigeria

Women Judges Enhancing the Judiciary

Hauwa Ibrahim

> On July 16, 2012, Honorable Justice Mariam Aloma Mukhtar, Grand Commander of the Order of Nigeria, was sworn in as the very first female head (chief justice) of the Nigerian judiciary. A pioneer and pace setter for Nigerian women on the bench, Justice Mukhtar was one of the first female lawyers in northern Nigeria, the first female High Court Judge from the north, the first female second in command in the Kano State judiciary, and the first Nigerian female judge to be elevated to the Court of Appeal, where she served for over 17 years. She also became the 13th indigenous chief justice of Nigeria. Justice Mukhtar has been the recipient of numerous awards, having been honored by the International Association of Women Lawyers (2003), receiving the Fellowship of the Nigerian Law School (2004), and becoming the Grand Commander of the Order of Nigeria in 2012. Currently she is the first and only female permanent member of the country's highest advisory council to the president of Nigeria.[1]

The heterogeneity of Africa's cultures—55 countries, one billion people, 3,000 ethnic groups and over 2,000 languages—is evident as well in the diverse legal systems of these countries. Increasingly, African women are taking active roles in their national judiciaries, in countries like Nigeria, Ghana, Botswana and Kenya.[2] Justice Mukhtar's record and achievements preface this chapter because she has become emblematic of the small but significant gains towards pluralism and gender equality in Nigeria's judiciary and, in some small measure, of the gains made in Africa at large.

In addition to extensive legal research, this chapter on women's participation in the Nigerian judiciary is informed by numerous interviews with female judges across Nigeria, including Justice Mairo Nasir (High Court of Abuja), Justice Rabi Umar (High Court of Bauchi), Justice Yellim Suleiman Bogoro (High Court of Bauchi), Justice Aisha Ndume (High Court of Abuja), Justice Adedotun Onibokun (High Court of Lagos), and Honorable Justice Donli, former president of the Economic Community of West Africa Court of Justice [ECOWAS]. It is worth noting that Nigeria has contributed female judges internationally as well—from Honorable Justice Donli to Justice Nkemdilim

Izuako, with the latter currently serving as one of the three judges on the United Nations Dispute Tribunal (United Nations, 2008).

Gender and Representation: Nigerian Progress in the Context of Judicial Culture

One of the first countries to appoint a female Justice of the Supreme Court and several judges in the higher court of record and Customary Courts, Nigeria prides itself on having achieved one of the highest rates of female judgeship on the African continent. These successes are especially meaningful given the lack of written laws or formal policies prescribing preferential treatment towards women. But as enormous as these triumphs are, they are not realized across all legal institutions. The appointment of judges in Nigeria is constitutionally provided and the criteria and process are the same for men and women. However, the appointment of judges depends on other factors as well. In appointments to federal courts, for example, consideration is given to the region (north/south) of Nigeria. Where you are from, and at times, whom 'you know' can be the most important criteria. And because these are informal criteria, they are not transparent—which in a patriarchal society often works against female justices.

Judicial powers in Nigeria are vested in the federal and state courts. These courts are required to accord primacy to the 1999 Constitution of the Federal Republic of Nigeria (CFRN) and its amendments. While the constitution of Nigeria is the most important source of law, there are other sources of law as well, including English law, local legislation (state and federal), Nigerian case law, and customary law. Different sources of law mean different opportunities for women judges. Nigerian Sharia Courts, for example, have still not appointed any female judges or registrars. It is in jurisdictions where common law is entrenched that female lawyers are, by and large, not discriminated against and appointed to serve on the bench. We would, in this way, be doing a disservice not to acknowledge the pockets of conservative strongholds that discriminate against women on and off the bench and, further, set hurdles for existing female judges to adjudicate effectively.

Disparities, thus, manifest geographically as well as across legal institutions. The greatest feats of gender diversity in the legal structures have been attained in southern Nigeria. Northern Nigeria is still vastly nonpluralistic. So saying, the north has produced female Chief Judges in state High Courts such as in Zamfara, Sokoto and Kano. One of the key milestones was the appointment of the late Justice Nana Aisha Abdullahi, the first female member of the High Court in 2010 in the conservative state of Jigawa. Indeed, the aforementioned first chief justice of Nigeria, Justice Aloma Mariam Mukhtar, is from the northern Nigerian Kano State.

In southern Nigeria, we must note, the inclusion of women in the judiciary has been structural rather than ad hoc, as we see in the north. Local media have reported that women currently dominate the Lagos judiciary.[3] The reasons for this are predictably sociocultural too. The south has a better education system that is more inclusive of women. More women in the south read law;[4] they also come from many generations of educated family members. In the rural north, it is unfortunately not the norm to encourage girls to attend school beyond the elementary level. This lack of educational opportunities has resulted in fewer women holding judicial office in northern Nigeria. There is a sense in which female judges from southern Nigeria feel that they have a fair shot, whereas judges from northern Nigeria feel that women are not fully represented on the bench. But this seems to be more because the north does not have the education system and cultural support to provide the qualified women for the job. During our recent interview, for instance, Justice Mario Nasir noted that the first female judicial officer in the northern Katsina State was appointed in 1988, while in the southern Lagos State the first female judge, the late Justice Modupe Omo-Eboh, had been appointed almost two decades earlier, in 1969.[5]

The 1999 CFRN provides for a federal system of governance, consisting of 36 independent states and a federal capital territory (FCT). Appointments for chief judge of a state are made by the state governor on the recommendation of the National Judicial Council, and are subject to confirmation by the House of Assembly of the state. The chief judge of a state is usually the most senior judge and the judicial and administrative head of the state judicial system. Though the patriarchal culture in Nigeria may not be friendly to female judges, scores of women have actually served as chief judges of the state judiciaries and some are still occupying these offices. In the 36 states of the federation, 10 women serve as chief judges of the state judiciary.

Female chief justices serve in Lagos State (Hon. Justice Ayotunde Phillips [June 2012]), Osun State (Hon. Justice Oyebola Adepele Ojo, President of the Customary Court of Appeal [July 2010] and Chief Judge [June 2013]), Niger State (former First Lady of the Federal Republic of Nigeria Hon. Justice Abubakar Justice Fati Abubakar named chief [June 2013]), Akwa Ibom State (Hon. Justice Idongesit Isua appointed chief justice [September 2008]), Oyo State (Hon. Justice Bolajoko Olateju Adeniji), Abia State (Hon. Justice Nnenna Chioma Otti [April 2014]), and Kano State (Justice Patricia Mahmoud [Jan. 2015]).

Historical Overview: Nigerian Legal History

The progress and setbacks in gender pluralism in the judiciary in Nigeria are rooted in both the opportunities and the obscure convolutions that have been historically produced in the legal system's adoption of laws from diverse external sources. Nigerian legal scholar and former Judge Akintunde Olusegun Obilade (1979, p. 54) has noted that 'English law has had a tremendous influence on the Nigerian legal system and forms a substantial part of Nigerian law.' Even apart from the influence of foreign laws, countries' legal systems are generally very complex due to legal pluralism, namely, the existence of more than one legal system within a society. Indeed, Nigerian law consists of many sources: the 1999 constitution, legislation, English law, Islamic (sharia) laws, customary law, and judicial precedents (Tobi, 1996, p. 66).

Northern Nigeria incorporated a great deal of Islamic law (civil provisions) into its codes in the aftermath of the 19th century Fulani Jihad (Smith, 1960, p. 84). And while the Nigerian laws today are mostly codified, there are also unwritten laws that emanate from custom that still hold great sway. It is the intricate interplay between and attendant interpretations of these sources that have propelled women to the top of the judiciaries in some areas of Nigeria and are holding them back in others.

The 1999 Nigerian constitution regulates the legislative arm of government, the National Assembly, which has been vested with the power to make laws for the peace, order, and good governance of the federation. It also requires that all criminal laws must be written (Section 36(12)). While there are no written laws that guarantee women equal access to service in the judiciary, there are no such laws that forbid or hinder access either. In southern Nigeria this has led to staggering rates of participation on the part of female judges. Failure, however, to review the dynamic between the multiple sources of legal thought, including unwritten, aforesaid laws that emanate from customary and Islamic traditions, has obstructed our ability to determine if they are in conformity with current societal norms, especially in the field of criminal law.

For Nigerian women, as well as for Nigerians in general (on and off the bench) this has sustained the existence of impracticable laws or legal provisions that are disregarded more often than they are observed. But when they are disregarded, conservative groups in our society protest and blame female judges for what they see as social transformations that pose a danger to the patriarchal structures that keep these groups in power.

The context of legal tradition in Nigeria is shifting, from the postmodern to premodern—from rational legal authority to self-expression. Political and social theories are turning to traditions for the maintenance of social coherence and identity. Ongoing discussion by lawyers and scholars, about the efficacy of laws and their application, suggests that beyond the structures of the legal system and legal traditions, it is imperative that we appropriately relate the formal methods of law with indigenous traditional and cultural systems, which may prove to be less expensive and time-consuming than politicians would like us to believe.

The common law system in Nigeria, for example, regulates the criminal, administrative, commercial, civil and family justice arenas. It is in areas that are regulated by common law that we see the most progress for women in the judiciary. Common law is codified into civil and criminal laws, classified as the penal law in northern Nigeria and the criminal code in southern Nigeria. The civil law is classified accordingly as well. Common law is based on statutes, legislative decisions and judicial decisions. It is distinct from the sharia legal system, which grounds ideas and rules about justice in religious ideologies of human dignity.

While the Islamic law of sharia has always been part of Nigeria's legal system, on October 1999, the sharia laws ceased to operate as we knew them.

In 1999, with the advent of the new governor in Zamfara State and the introduction of the 'New Shariah,' crime was added under the purview of sharia jurisdiction, which had up to that point only regulated matters of a purely civil nature. The newly added criminal statute swung the pendulum too fast, necessitating new interpretations to help women navigate their place within this system as judges, but, more importantly, as individuals subject to this legal system.

The 'New Shariah' legal laws adopted by the 12 northern Nigerian states in 1999 contain provisions that raise serious concerns in terms of human rights. Examples of punishments promulgated in these laws include the amputation or stoning of Muslims, a treatment contrary to universally recognized norms of human dignity. These laws sometimes even contradict binding international treaties. Treaties that prohibit torture and other degrading and inhumane treatments are, for example, included in some of the international conventions that Nigeria has ratified.[6] Nonetheless, the Supreme Court in Nigeria held inter alia that 'Islamic law is not the same as customary law as it does not belong to any particular tribe. It is a complete system of universal law, more certain and permanent and more universal than the English common law' (Palacio, Sage & Woolcock, 2006, p. 153).

Thus, in order to understand how women participate in the Nigerian judiciary, it is best to situate that participation within a larger discourse of the distinctness of Nigeria's legal system. Indeed, nowhere is the diversity of the legal system more palpable and far-reaching than in Nigeria.[7] The Nigerian legal context derives from Nigeria's many ethnic groups, tribes, cultures, religious sects, languages, dialects and history. At the federal level, the legal system is applicable throughout the country. At the lower levels, each state (including Abuja) has its own legal system. Female judges fare a lot better at these first two levels. At the local level, however, both sharia and customary laws are applicable in some states.[8] While this diversity implies a world of creative possibilities for judicial pluralism—racial, gender-based, ethnic, religious and so on—it also poses the practical problem of how to apply multiple legal systems. It fundamentally begs for coherent ideologies of coexistence, or interexistence, between and within the different legal traditions. The hierarchies of courts within the judicial system play a fundamental part in attempts to formulate coherent and consistent practices of Nigerian law.

Court Structure and Overview

Figure 5.1 represents the court structure in Nigeria. The Supreme Court is at the apex of the judicial hierarchy. It is established by the constitution (Section 232(1)) and has, as such, both original[9] and appellate jurisdiction (Section 234), including overseeing and supervising the conduct of Superior Courts of Record.[10] It is important to note the doctrine of stare decisis, according to which the decisions of the Supreme Court are final, not subject to an appeal, and entrenched in all courts, which are required to use such decisions as precedent. The Court of Appeal is next in the judicial hierarchy, and its decisions are binding on all lower courts. Established under the constitution (Sections 237 and 239), the Court of Appeal has appellate jurisdiction.[11]

The Nigerian constitution also establishes the Federal High Court,[12] and its original jurisdiction[13] extends throughout the entire country. The court has, however, limited, but exclusive, jurisdiction in civil and criminal cases or matters as set out in Section 251 of the constitution. There is, accordingly, a High Court in each state of the federation and the Federal Capital Territory. The High Courts' general jurisdiction[14] includes the determination of any criminal proceedings involving or relating to any penalty, forfeiture, punishment or other liability with respect to an offence committed by any person.[15]

The National Industrial Court of Nigeria (NICN), established by Section 264B of the constitution, boasts the widest definitive jurisdiction.[16] It provides that notwithstanding the provisions of Sections 251, 257, and 272, anything contained in the constitution, and in addition to such other jurisdiction as may be conferred upon it by an Act of the National Assembly, the National Industrial Court shall have and exercise jurisdiction to the exclusion of any other court in civil causes and matters.

The Shariah Court of Appeal exists for the Federal Capital Territory and any state in the federation that requires it (Section 275). The Shariah Court of Appeal has appellate and supervisory jurisdiction in civil proceedings

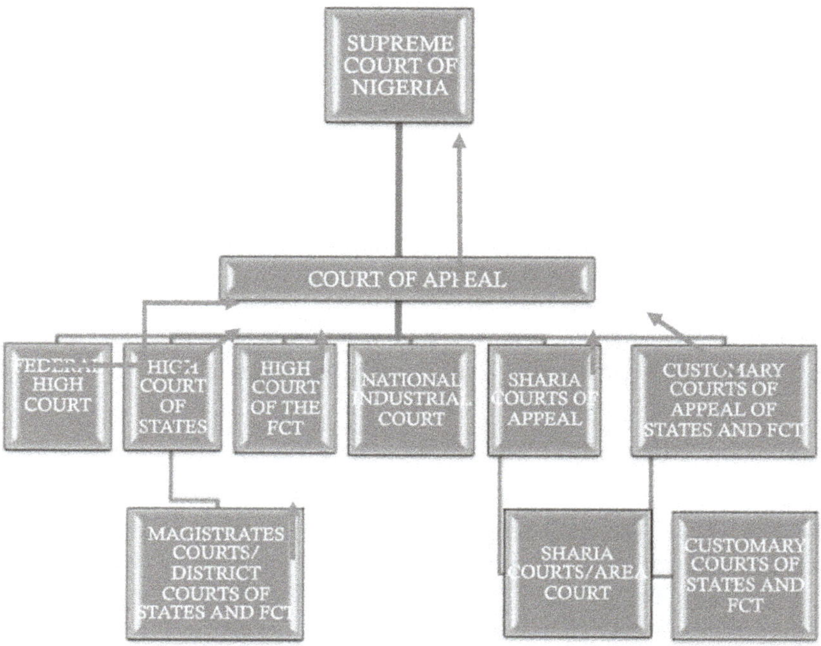

Figure 5.1 Court Structure in Nigeria

involving questions of Islamic personal law, which the court is competent to decide in accordance with the constitution. To be eligible for appointment as a Grand Khadi of the Shariah Court of Appeal of the Federal Capital Territory, Abuja, by the president or of a Shariah Court of Appeal of a State by the State Governor, the judge must be male, a legal practitioner in Nigeria for a period of not less than 10 years, have obtained a recognized qualification in Islamic law, and have considerable experience in the practice of Islamic law or be a distinguished scholar of Islamic law. All appointments are made on the recommendation of the National Judicial Council and are subject to confirmation by the Senate or the House of Assembly of the State (Section 261).

The Customary Court of Appeal exists for the Federal Capital Territory and any State that requires it (Section 275). This court has appellate and supervisory jurisdiction in civil proceedings involving questions of customary law. The Customary Court of Appeal has no original jurisdiction, but has both appellate and supervisory jurisdiction in civil proceedings involving customary law as may be prescribed by laws of the House of Assembly, in the case of a state, or act of the National Assembly, in the case of the Federal Capital Territory.

There are in addition Inferior Courts of Record, courts established by states and the Federal Capital Territory, Abuja, and include Magistrate Courts of States and the FCT,[17] District Courts,[18] Area Courts,[19] Sharia Courts,[20] and Customary Courts.[21]

Women and the Judiciary: Experiences of Female Judges in Nigeria

Historically both the federal and state judiciaries have functioned largely under male dominance. The country did benefit from deliberate governmental policies in the 1990s in states like Lagos—policies that sought to increase the number of women inside the judicial system. And women today are taking more active roles and positions in the judiciary by virtue of their education, but also by virtue of the opportunities for gradual change that the multiple legal sources, hierarchies, and structures, mapped above, have made possible in states where people want women to advance. The judgments, reputations, and increasing popular acceptance of female judges in Nigeria show that these female judges are tenacious, efficient, fearless, well-educated, honest, transparent, and competent (Okechukwu, 2005).

That is not to say that female judges in Nigeria do not encounter profound challenges. Hon. Justice Hansine Napwaniyo Donli, in her written exchange,[22] stated that the challenges on the bench are numerous, but learning to turn them into opportunities has kept her going and so she never felt discriminated against because of her gender. But for most female judges some challenges are not so easy to bear. During recent interviews, female judges expressed deep concerns about balancing work and family as well as the perception, sometimes, of women in the judiciary in northern Nigeria, as inferior.

Some of the judges admitted that the workload could be too much, especially because they do not have access to well-equipped libraries for research. They agreed that litigation has increased at an alarming rate in the past 10 years with the decline of alternative dispute resolution, which has compounded pressures on common law courts in which these judges serve. Most of the judges interviewed believe that the demands of the job have caused intense pressures for their families and children, with some female judges turning to separation and/or divorce. Judges from northern Nigeria reported particular distress in their quest for perfection because they felt that as pioneers they must dispel the notion of female inferiority. Some reported burning out.

There are, of course, still too many states where the number of women in the judiciary is merely nonexistent or the positions are given to them 'as a token.' The very ambiguity of jurisdiction that benefits women in southern or federal judiciaries also opens up opportunities for patrimonial and patriarchal interests to exclude women from judiciaries in the north and at local levels, often exploiting customary and sharia laws. Some resulting challenges are directly discriminatory. A judge described how she was molested at a social gathering. When she was seated on a 'high table' to the chagrin of a traditional chief, he pulled away the seat under her. He was appalled at the prospect of a woman being accorded such honor. Another judge described how a male lawyer repeatedly addresses her without decorum. They are frustrated that many members of their society expect them to be housewives and mothers instead of judges.

That is why many are quick to note that it was not until the emergence of Hon. Justice Mariam Aloma Mukhtar in 2012, with whose story this chapter commenced, that we started to see some progress. For 52 years, since 1960, exclusively male justices had always occupied the position of the chief justice of Nigeria. The judges I interviewed alluded to an 'approval syndrome;' they felt that Hon. Justice Mukhtar had to sacrifice too much to prove herself as a pioneer. While none of my respondents doubts that Hon. Justice Mukhtar has the best interest of the Nigerian judiciary at heart, she has a reputation for being too hard and at times too harsh. One of the judges quoted a colleague who had complained that 'our best was not good enough for Justice Mukhtar, and it seems she was trying to find fault with everything and everyone.'

Justice Mukhtar herself has embraced this reputation, stating that she intends to change the perception of the Nigerian judiciary by 'flushing out the bad eggs' and eventually filing Petition 337 with the Nigerian Judicial Council (NJC) against many judges.[23] The Nigerian Judicial Council, led by Justice Mukhtar, asked President Goodluck Jonathan on February 28, 2013 to compulsorily retire Justice Charles Archibong of the Federal High Court on grounds of corruption. The Council also set up a 'Fact Finding' Committee to investigate allegations leveled against Justice Abubakar Talba of the FCT High Court, who was suspended for 12 months for failing to exercise his discretion judicially and judiciously. Justice Dalhatu Adamu, the Presiding Justice of the Court of Appeal in the Kaduna Division, received a warning letter for deliberately absenting himself from duty. The Council also warned Justices A.A. Adeleye of the High Court of Justice in Ekiti State and D.O. Amaechina of the High Court of Justice in Anambra State for low performance. The Hon. Chief Justice believes that 'elevation to higher courts should be based on performance rather than seniority—no judicial officer should climb to totem heights in the judiciary by merely marking time in the bench.'[24]

While some dismissed claims of corruption and see Justice Mukhtar as being on a witch hunt, others suggest that the terrible conditions of service in the judiciary drive some judges to accept bribes. Funding of the judicial branch is inadequate. And judges report having to improvise for basic tools needed in their courts. Security is another commonly reported concern. Judges have had to arrange extra security from their own funds while on the bench. Many of the judges' residences are not secure in a country that is experiencing violent upheaval in its northern region. Many justices fear litigants' reprisal after cases have concluded. One justice stated: 'I want to stay late in the office to study and to write my judgments because at home, with the children, I am unable to do much. But I cannot stay because of the security situation in the country. So I will look out my office window to check if people are still around; if not, I pack my bag and leave immediately.'

Conclusion

The issue of diversity on the bench is 'relative to states, regions, and personnel.'[25] When the question 'is there equity and merit in the appointment of female judges?' is posed, the answer seems to be generally 'yes.'[26] But it is never that simple, and sometimes merit is waived off as 'affirmative action' due to the Nigerian zoning system, which aims to ensure that at both state and federal levels different people and communities are represented, as a way of encouraging diversity. In the Federal Capital Territory High Court in Abuja, for example, 38 judges represent the 36 states of Nigeria. Only eight of them are female.

And where there is progress, it has often been suggested that it is due to declining interest among men to take judgeships because they see them as 'civil-service-like' jobs. Some men in the legal profession who are eligible to be appointed as judges reportedly consider a judgeship not as 'challenging and productive as legal representation of clients in courts.' These kinds of narratives attribute the high number of female judges in the state judiciary to the idea of the judicial systems being 'a soft-landing arena for women.' Of course, some arenas, especially in the north, are harder than others.

Some of these narratives are reactionary because higher participation of women in the Nigerian judiciary has brought news ways of thinking about the law and the courts in many jurisdictions. Women judges' accomplishments can be demonstrated even by simple administrative decisions to ensure that cases are filed electronically. Prior to these creative ways to mainstream case management and improve transparency, most of the judgments were often contested. As a result there have been fewer accusations of corruption made against the judges.

It is also true that women are in a unique position to advance the rights of women and children through the judicial system without compromising justice. This is especially the case in communities where women and children are systematically marginalized. Female judges can act as catalysts for the sustainable rule of law by protecting and empowering the less privileged women and men and creating a court environment that is accessible to these marginalized people (Schultz & Shaw, 2003b).

So to analyze the historical and structural contexts for the successes and the setbacks of women in Nigeria, we must inquire into not only statistics but also the court structures and hierarchy and the appointment of judges in the context of the sociocultural changes that the country is experiencing. Critical legal scholarship has taught us that the legal and social lives of the law are not always congruent, and our analysis will never be complete without the qualitative narratives and oral histories from female judges themselves, who can shed light into their role in enhancing justice, and into their journeys, challenges and hopes. In this way, this chapter outlines the legal context and points to the need for further research into the sociocultural aspects of gender bias within legal diversity in Nigeria and Africa at large.

The role of women in the judiciary must be considered in both its pre- and postcolonial history, which have sometimes problematically comingled and co-opted indigenous legal, political, and cultural institutions with colonial laws. As a result of our colonial past, women figure prominently as symbolic of justice, and not only in Nigeria. In Western and postcolonial traditions, women are thought to personify the grace of dignity, to be phenomenal in their passion for justice, and are literally to embody the Lady Justice, seen frequently in courthouses, libraries, law schools and institutions of legal relevance. The canon even stretches back to ancient mythology: Themis, the Greek goddess of justice, was known for her clear-sightedness. And in Roman mythology, Justicia (Justice) was one of the four virtues, along with Prudence, Fortitude and Temperance (Resnick & Curtis, 2011, p. 234). It is no wonder, then, that it boggles our minds when patriarchal structures seek to exclude women. The colonial experience is ours to own too. The challenge is to acknowledge the ways in which we can productively channel this tradition so as to throw into relief the ways in which our indigenous and religious legal heritage can empower the women on the bench, and, more important, the women who come in front of the bench.

The 2013 swearing-in of three new judges—two females and one male—in Lagos by Governor Babatunde Raji brought the total number of High Court Judges in the state to 57. Statistics from the Lagos Judicial Service Commission show that 40 of these judges are female and the remaining 17 judges are male. At the magistrate level, 73 of 101 magistrates are female. There are many hurdles still, but the numbers portend astounding promise for young southern Nigerian women today. What most of the female judges interviewed during the course of research for this chapter felt gave them an edge on the bench was a sense of purpose—a zealous determination to excel at all times. In addition to passion, hard work and empathy, these successful female judges also rely on what Hon. Justice Adedotun Onibokun describes as 'proper preparation to prevent poor performance.'

Commenting on ways to encourage young Nigerian women to enter the judiciary, Justice Onibokun advised that we 'sensitize parents to the fact that boys and girls have the same potential if exposed to the same circumstances and educational opportunities without discrimination.' She also urged all Nigerians to 'discourage early marriage, prevalent in some areas in Africa, and to provide information on the importance of education and make learning materials more accessible.' Only these broader approaches will expand prospects for women to enter the judiciary in Africa.

Notes

1 From 'The Trailblazer,' the speech of President Goodluck Jonathan at the swearing in ceremony for Chief Justice Mukhtar on 16 July 2012. Other first female Chief Judges of State Court include Hon. Justice Kulu Aliyu, Chief Judge of Zamfara State, Hon. Justice, Aisha Sani Dahiru, Chief Judge of Sokoto, Justice Patricia Mahmoud, Acting Chief Judge Kano State (a Christian female Chief Judge in a predominantly Muslim state), Justice Constance Ayashe Rekhia Momoh, Chief Judge of Edo State, and Hon. Justice Roseline Ukeje, first female Supreme Court Judge.

2 Georgina Theodora Wood made history when she was appointed the first female chief justice of the Supreme Court of Ghana in June 2007; in 1998 Unity Dow became the first female judge on the Botswana's High Court (Steady, 2011, p. 30; Hallward-Driemeier and Hasan, 2013, p. 124).

3 *The Daily Trust*, Nigerian newspaper, March 10, 2014.

4 *The Daily Trust*, Nigerian newspaper, March 10, 2014.

5 Author interview, Justice Mario Nasir, March 5, 2015.

6 Office of the United Nations High Commissioner for Human Rights, Framework for Communications. E/CN.4/2002/73/Add.2, Para. 168 and 228.

7 Layish, 1989, p. 2; this may not be new in Nigerian society, as suggested by Layish, but in Libya the intensive interaction and mutual fertilization of systems culminated in the integration of Islamic and customary laws. In practical application customary laws in tribal areas enjoy autonomy, nonetheless.

8 Sections 275 and 280 of the CFRN (1999) provide that at the state level, 'There shall be for any State that requires it a sharia court/customary court of appeal for that State.'

9 Its original jurisdiction includes resolving disputes arising between (a) the federal government and any state and (b) between states, and (c) such original jurisdiction as may be conferred by the National Assembly. The Supreme Court has, to the exclusion of any other court, original jurisdiction in any dispute between: (a) the National Assembly and the President; (b) the National Assembly and any State House of Assembly; and (c) the National Assembly and a state of the Federation. See also, CFRN, 1999, Section 232(1).

10 Courts of Appeal, High Courts of the States and the High Court of the Federal Capital Territory, and other courts created by the states.

11 Section 240 of the CFRN provides that the Court of Appeal shall have appellate jurisdiction to the exclusion of any other court of law in Nigeria to hear appeals from the Federal High Court, State High Courts including FCT and other lower

courts. And Section 248 of the CFRN empowers the president of the Court of Appeal to make rules for regulating practice and procedure of the Court of Appeal. It has original jurisdiction on the following executive matters: whether a person has been validly elected to the office of the president or vice president; whether the term of the office of the president or vice president has ceased; or whether the office of the president or vice president has become vacant.

12 Established by Section 249(1) of the CFRN, the Federal High Court consists of a Chief Judge and such number of judges as may be prescribed by an act of the National Assembly.

13 It has original jurisdiction in matters such as taxation, custom and excise, but it has no appellate jurisdiction.

14 As established by Sections 257(1) and Section 272 of the CFRN.

15 State High Courts are established for each state of the federation by Section 270(1) of the CFRN; the High Court of the FCT is established by Section 255; see also Section 272(1).

16 According to Section 254C of the CFRN: The National Industrial Court, importantly, exercises jurisdiction and powers in criminal cases and matters of which jurisdiction is conferred on the National Industrial Court by this section or any act of the National Assembly or by any other law.

17 Magistrate courts are established by the Magistrate Court Law of States and have limited jurisdiction. The Chief Judge of the State divides states into magisterial districts, and magistrate courts are established for each district. For example, in Kaduna State there several grades of magistrate courts.

18 Established by the District Court Act, or, in the case of FCT, the Laws for the Federal Capital Territory, Abuja, and the states of northern Nigeria. The various states in the north have their own laws establishing and defining the jurisdiction it covers. In the Federal Capital Territory, Abuja, for example, there are six grades of district judges.

19 These exist in the northern parts of Nigeria, and including the Federal Capital Territory, Abuja. For example, in Katsina State, there are three grades of Area Courts. The jurisdiction of the Area Court includes all questions of Islamic personal law, matrimonial cases and matters between persons married under customary law, suits relating to custody of children under customary law, civil actions involving debt and damages, matters relating to inheritance and the administration of estate under customary law, and matters concerning private property.

20 Since 2000, Sharia Courts have acquired expansive jurisdiction to include issues of criminal law, far beyond the mandate of adjudicating on civil matters. These courts are found mostly in northern Nigeria. By virtue of the Shariah Courts Law, Katsina State has three grades of courts: Upper Shariah Court; Higher Shariah Court and Shariah Court.

21 Established by the Customary Court Laws of some states of southern Nigeria; like the Area Courts in the north, they are founded upon the need to interpret and adjudicate matters brought under the customary laws of the locales in which they are established. The jurisdiction of Customary Courts includes matrimonial cases and other matters between persons married under customary law, suits relating to guardianship and custody of children under customary law, matters relating to inheritance upon intestacy and the administration of intestate estate under customary law, and other cases or matters for debt or damages.

22 Personal email communication, March 6, 2015.

23 *National Mirror*, Nigerian newspaper, March 11, 2013. Justice Mukhtar disclosed this in the speech entitled 'The Rule of Law—The Bedrock for Sustainable Democracy' that she delivered at the opening ceremony of a two-day workshop organized by the Nigerian Bar Association (NBA) Action Group and held at the Lagos City

Hall on May 13–14, 2013. She stated that she inherited 139 petitions, 106 of which were vexatious or baseless. After becoming chief justice, 198 fresh petitions were filed, 150 of which were found to be frivolous.

24 *National Mirror*, Nigerian newspaper, March 11, 2013.

25 Author interview with Hon. Justice Aisha Ndume, February 2015.

26 Author interviews with almost all seven judges of the High Courts, as indicated above.

6 Tunisia

A New Constitution and More Women Judges

Salsabil Klibi

Since 2011, Tunisia has been undergoing a transition to democracy,[1] characterized mainly by the reconstruction of its legal framework. This reconstruction has focused, in the first place, on the state's fundamental law, its constitution. In 2014, Tunisia adopted a new constitution, only the second to be adopted since the country's first constitution, adopted in 1959. Within the framework of this reconstruction, marked by a break with the old regime, has emerged the issue of the status of women in both society and politics. And yet, in spite of avant-garde legal rules regarding women's rights in an Arab country, the number of women in public office remains relatively low today. For example, in the late 2014 elections of the Assembly of the Representatives of the People, 68 out of 217 members elected are women, or 31%. Although there is much emphasis on the presence of women in the executive and legislative branches, little attention is given to women's place in the judicial branch, whether by researchers or activists.

The most important power in Tunisia today certainly resides in the judiciary, not only because it allows the implementation of laws, but also because it is the inherent protector of rights and liberties. For that reason, the weight of women in the courts requires as much attention as their presence in the other branches. It is thus important to examine what role Tunisian law has given to women in the judiciary, under what conditions, and with what results.

Historical Overview

The Tunisian legal tradition, influenced by the French system, which is a civil law legal system, contains very few elements of Islamic law. Indeed, the new constitution, adopted in 2014, as well as the 1959 constitution, is based on a principle of people's sovereignty and does not provide for sharia as a source of legislation. The new constitution has seen major progress with regard to establishing the rule of law, guaranteeing the equality of men and women in terms of rights and liberties, and providing for the independence of the judiciary, which is necessary for protecting those rights and liberties.

But this progress brought by the new constitution is in fact nothing more than the enhancement of existing principles, originating in Tunisia's first constitution in 1959, adopted shortly after at independence in 1956[2]— and the enactment of other determining laws, with a strong impact on the Tunisian society, which preceded the adoption of the 1959 constitution. The most important of these laws are the ones that changed the very nature of the judiciary, breaking the link with the Muslim and Jewish faiths and rendering Tunisia more republican and breaking the link with the former colonial power through the abolition of French courts in the country. The enactment of the Law on the Organization of the Judiciary in 1967 was the culmination of this process and will be examined here for its impact on the presence of women in the judiciary. In addition, this chapter will examine the potential impact of the feminization of the judiciary on case law, in other words, how law is interpreted and applied when it comes to issues related to women, their rights and liberties.

One of the most important decisions made by the Tunisian state just after independence was the abolition of Sharia Courts in 1956 and of rabbinical courts in 1957. Those measures reflected a strong political will to break the link between justice and religion. Indeed, Muslim doctrine suggests that only men may be judges, and Maliki rite is very strict on this issue.[3] If Tunisia had kept its religion-based judicial system, women would have had neither the right nor the opportunity to become judges. The Tunisian constitution, adopted shortly after those two fundamental decisions related to the judiciary, however, did not declare Tunisia a secular state, as in Turkey. Still, the proclamation of the principle of popular sovereignty and the establishment of the law, issued from an elected parliament, as the most legitimate expression of that sovereignty, in addition to the absence of any reference to sharia as a legal source, was nothing but a recognition of the state as the sole legal source.[4]

The 1967 Law on the Organization of the Judiciary and on the Supreme Judicial Council[5] was the logical outcome of the constitution and its modern open-mindedness, in that it does not contain any discriminatory clauses regarding the recruitment of judges. For example, Article 29 of this law states that 'judges shall be recruited amidst the graduates of the Higher Magistrates' Institute,' with no direct or indirect evocation of gender. Moreover, during the debate on this law by the Committee on General Legislation in the National Assembly, deputies clearly asserted that: 'Since competition is the form of access retained in the draft law as a way to ensure recruitment on the basis of competences, the sole requirement is to fulfil age, nationality, and graduation requirements, which induces the possibility for women to apply for a job in the legal profession.'[6] Later, when this law was reviewed in 2005, it was determined that among all those whose role is determining for judges' careers and promotion should be two women appointed by order on a proposal by the minister of justice.

The recruitment of women into the legal profession started in 1967–1968. This time coincides not only with the enactment of the Law on the Organization of the Judiciary but also with the graduation of the first Tunisian women in law studies from modern schools. From this time onwards, a paradigm shift occurred, and although the number of women judges remained low until the beginning of the 1990s, women's access to the judiciary had become accepted by the law and had, in a way, become irreversible.

Court Structure and Organization

The Tunisian legal system, unlike the French system, is composed of judicial tribunals and administrative tribunals. Here is the repartition of women in the two branches:[7] the jurisdictions of the judiciary are headed by the Court of Cassation. The judicial jurisdictions are organized as follows: 28 lower Courts of First Instance (one in each Governorate, except for Tunis, where there are two), 10 Courts of Appeal, 84 Cantonal Courts, all of them headed by the Court of Cassation. The Property Court has 15 regional offices and a head office located in Tunis.

The number of judges of the judicial order, sitting at the beginning of judicial year 2012–2013 was 1,814, with 44 Presidents of Court. Of these 1,814 judges, 670 are Judges of First Class, 539 of Second Class and 605 of Third Class. According to Article 13 of the 1967 Law on the Organization of the Judiciary, First Class Judges sit in Courts of First Instance and Property Court, along with the deputy public prosecutors. As for the Second Class Judges, they are the Counsellors to the Court of Appeal and Deputy Attorney General to the Court of Appeal. Finally, Third Class Judges are Counsellors to the Court of Cassation and Advocate General to the same court. The number of prosecutors at the beginning of the judicial year 2012–2013 was 34 for the Court of Cassation, 57 for the 10 Courts of Appeal and 120 for the 28 Courts of First Instance. Out of 1,875 judges in 2010–2011, 607 were women, that is to say 32.4%. However, only 15% of those women held senior positions. There are six women in the prosecutor's office, among whom one is a Deputy Attorney General, and 12 women Presidents of Chamber in the Court of Cassation, out of 29. The number of women judges in senior positions in 2014 is presented in Table 6.1.

Table 6.1 Women Judges in Senior Positions in Tunisia, 2014

Total number of judges: 128	*Number of women judges: 63*	*49.21%*
4 Presidents of the Chamber of Cassation	0 Women	0%
2 Presidents of the Advisory Chamber	0 women	0%
6 Presidents of the Appeal Chambers	5 Women	83.33%
5 General State Commissioners	2 Women	40%
13 Presidents of the Trial Chambers	5 Women	38.47%
3 Presidents of the Consultative Section	1 Woman	33.34%
9 State Commissioners	5 Women	55.56%

Gender and Representation

The feminization of the judiciary was, at the beginning, very slow, although there were no administrative obstacles. We should bear in mind that after the 'Tunisianization' of justice and the abolition of the French courts,[8] Tunisia had no judges trained in modern law schools, or there were not enough of them, which forced the country to integrate into the 'secular' courts; Qadhis graduated from the Zitouna school, that is to say the Maliki Islamic law. Those conservative judges did not appreciate the modern state's orientation and the right of women to become judges. Since those conservative judges were sitting on the recruitment boards, they adopted a discriminatory policy towards female candidates. It was only progressively, after the first law schools were established in Tunisia[9] and the first waves of jurists trained in those law schools accessed the judiciary and then the recruitment boards, that women judges started to gain acceptance, though even this was a very slow process.

In 1970, only one woman was recruited to become a judge; in 1975, two women out of 32 judges; in 1980, two women out of 19 judges and in 1985, six women out of 80 judges (Sana, 2007, p. 21). In 2015 the number of women judges is about 600.

What does the future hold for women, working in the judiciary, after the revolution of 2011 and the enactment of the 2014 constitution? As noted before, women are now well established in the judicial branch and it is no longer possible to turn back. The core of the issue is now to know how to reinforce and build upon this accomplishment, in terms of absolute numbers of women judges in courts, but also in senior positions.

In order to answer that question, it is necessary to refer to the text of the new constitution enacted on January 26, 2014, and more precisely, to what has been provided in the chapter relating to rights and liberties and in the chapter on jurisdictional power. Concerning the chapter on rights and liberties, two articles deserve mention: Article 21, which states that: 'All citizens, male and female, have equal rights and duties, and are equal before the law' and Article 46, which was enacted following pressure from civil society, and states that:

> The state commits to protect women's accrued rights and works to strengthen and develop those rights. The state guarantees the equality of opportunities between women and men to have access to all levels of responsibility in all domains. The state works to attain parity between women and men in elected Assemblies. The state shall take all necessary measures in order to eradicate violence against women.

The inclusion of these progressive rules within the text of the 2014 constitution derives from the observation that the prescription of equality between men and women for more than 60 years had not yielded the expected result as regards the place of women in government and particularly in the judicial system. Positive discrimination measures thus had to be taken in order to make equality a reality. The principle of parity in all elected bodies as provided for in Article 46 of the 2014 constitution concerns both political representative bodies, such as the parliament or regional and municipal councils, and professional representative bodies, such as the judiciary. Such interpretation is based on the fact that the term 'elected bodies' is used in absolute terms, without specifying the kind of body concerned, thus extending the scope of meaning to any elected representative body. It is also reinforced by the previous paragraph of the same article on equality of opportunities between men and women to access responsible positions in all domains.

Thus, the law which has to be established concerning the future Supreme Judicial Council[10] and the various sector councils comprised in it will have to take parity into account, or an action may be brought against it for unconstitutionality. This law has yet to be adopted in Tunisia. But what will the feminization of the judiciary bring to the interpretation of law and its enforcement?

Women and the Judiciary

The Tunisian constitution of 2014, as the one of 1959, provides in the first article that: 'Tunisia is a free, independent, sovereign state; its religion is Islam and its regime is republican.' There were stormy debates in the National Constituent Assembly (NCA) in 2011 on the very meaning of this article, even though the issue was supposed to have been resolved in 1959. Still, some members of the NCA interpreted this article as meaning that Islam is the religion of the state and urged the inclusion of an article specifying that sharia will be the source of Tunisian law;[11] other members argued that the article was merely a description of Tunisian society, as mostly of Muslim faith, and that it does not influence the source of Tunisian law, which shall remain, according to the principle of popular sovereignty, an exclusively positive legal system, at least formally, in its elaboration. The latter interpretation eventually prevailed and the reference to sharia was erased from the preamble of the draft constitution. As such, the absence of any explicit reference to sharia as a formal source of law, either in the constitution or in any legal text, implies that sharia can only be referred to as a material source of law, and conservative judges will have no other choice than to use it within this restricted conceptualization.

Family law, better known in Tunisia as 'personal status,' is the most favorable area for the integration of sharia, even in those countries that are willing to move away from sharia. Through some judicial decisions related to family law, we can see the way the Tunisian judge's consciousness, reflecting a collective consciousness, has evolved, even erratically, from the idea that sharia shall legitimately enter the law of a Muslim country, to the idea that Islam is merely a feature of civilization in society, and that there are other political values, elevated to the status of highest judicial rules, that must prevail when dealing with issues of personal status. This particular issue highlights the importance of supporting women's integration into the judiciary, as they are the first to be affected by a conservative interpretation of family law, known to be discriminatory against women and opposed to equality between men and women.

It is now widely agreed that the implementation of law is inevitably a matter of interpreting such law. This operation, which is at the heart of the judge's work, is not merely about enforcing the law, but also about shaping and creating law. Whether judges are conscious or unconscious of their 'creative and normative power' (Belaid, 1974) when performing their work, they are subject to various constraints. Some constraints are judicial, obviously, as judges are part of a hierarchical judicial system forcing them to consider the position of higher jurisdiction, to which they are answerable; and some constraints are political and social and are bound to influence their decision-making and be evident in their argumentation.

Tunisian judges evolve within a set of provisions that some might describe as incoherent and contradictory, and with which they must remain consistent in their interpretative work,[12] by favoring successively, and according to changing social circumstances, a sharia-based or a positivist interpretation. In the first instance, the judge will exploit the ambiguity of legal texts to make sharia the basis for interpreting the Tunisian law and especially the Code of Personal Status (CPS).[13] Sharia is here raised to the position of secondary source of family law. Case law in this area is abundant and almost constant after a case became a landmark and set a precedent for a long time, the famous 'Houria' case.[14]

This case can be summarized as follows: in 1945 a Muslim Tunisian woman married a Frenchman, thus regarded as a non-Muslim. In 1960, when the mother of the so-called 'Houria' died, she was excluded from the inheritance on the ground that her matrimony with a non-Muslim led to her apostasy, and since she was no longer a Muslim she could not inherit from her mother, who was a Muslim. Two articles from the CPS were used: first, Article 5 relating to the causes of impediment of marriage, and Article 88 relating to debarment from inheritance. The text of Article 5(1) states that: 'The two future spouses shall be free from any legal impediment,' considering the fact that the expression 'legal impediment' is the English translation of the Arabic expression '*al mawani' al shar'yya.'* Article 88 states that: 'Voluntary homicide constitutes an impediment to inheritance. The murderer shall not inherit, whether he is a basic author or an accomplice; the false witness whose testimony induced the capital punishment and execution of the *decujus* is equally impeded from inheritance.' Surprisingly, as we can see, in these two articles disparity of worship is not explicitly mentioned as an impediment to marriage or inheritance. However, as Pr. Ali Mezghani claimed: '[This] phenomenon does not live by itself . . . The recent history of Tunisia clearly demonstrated the causal link between law and what calls for it, i.e. social conditions and social specificities.'

In addition to this, the mentality of judges, shaped by their training, makes them aware of their role, namely to interpret legal texts in order to enforce the law, and they are determined to wield this power. For this reason, they interpreted the two articles in a way that would certainly be considered amazing and unjustified today. Indeed, especially with Article 5,[15] relating to marriage impediment, the judges drew the argument that the spouses may not be in a situation of impediment as provided for by the law and the Arabic word for 'legal' (*shar'yya*).

Judges thus took advantage of this ambiguity, especially as the Arabic text is binding, to infer that the present situation was one of those provided for by the sharia and not one of those provided for by the positive law, and concluded with the apostasy of Houria. Furthermore, with regard to Article 88 of the CPS, the Tunisian judge used the Arabic text, which lists voluntary manslaughter among the causes of debarment from inheritance, and concluded that this list was not exhaustive and he had the right to add other causes and to draw on sharia, which was for him the inspiring power of this code. Starting from sharia, which prohibits inheritance between people of a different faith, the judge concluded that the claimant could not inherit from her mother.

The judge of cassation said that:

> On the arguments raised by the Attorney General and drawn from the violation of article 88 of the CPS which stipulates that voluntary manslaughter is one of the causes of the debarment from inheritance and not the sole impediment, whose list is not exhaustive, and that it was thus required to apply Islamic laws, which are the basis of this code, and stipulate that a Muslim woman who marries a non-Muslim is not allowed to inherit from a Muslim.

In light of Article 88: 'It is undeniable that the marriage of a Muslim woman with a non-Muslim is a cardinal sin, considered by the Islamic law as null and void, but does not make the spouse an apostate, unless she willingly adopted her husband's faith.' It must be noted here that the Court of Cassation, even though it rejected the appeal, does not dispute the arguments used, i.e. the difference of faith as an impediment to marriage or the voidness of the marriage between a Muslim woman and a non-Muslim man.

A similar attitude from the Court of Cassation can be observed with another case, Louise's case,[16] where the trial judges, in both First Instance and Appeal, used arguments claiming that, according to the rules of *fiqh*, inheritance is not allowed between persons of different faiths, an argument which was not disputed by the High Court, which rejected the appeal because the claimants could not provide evidence that Louise was not converted to Islam. In the Stambouli[17] case, we can find the same position, as the Court of Cassation claimed that the rule stating that a non-Muslim may not inherit from a Muslim is part of positive Tunisian law, implicitly drawn from *fiqh*, regarded as 'a supplementary source of the CPS.'

The position of these courts clearly illustrates the dependence of positive law on a text whose meaning is not predetermined, but subject to the interpretation of the judge, with no right of objection, when this judge is at the top of the judicial hierarchy. When it comes to defining positive law, to adding elements taken from *fiqh*, or to deciding that there are flaws in the law, and how to fill them, the judge is the only one in command and the political will expressed by the law maker will make no difference. Such has been the state of case law for about four decades, where some trial judges and a number of judges of appeal tended to interpret the legal texts by turning to external sources, favoring the integration of what is called sometimes *fiqh* or sharia in order to find solutions.

But this situation is progressively changing. Indeed, the changes in the composition of the court, notably the growing number of women, combined with the progressive arrival in courts of jurists trained in Tunisian universities, where education focuses on a secular conception of law, have eventually inflected case law relating to family law. The modernist doctrine, which has gained authority, has also played an important role, to the extent that judges have started to draw arguments from it. These judges bring about a transformation in the approach to the texts. The texts will henceforth be interpreted according to the interpretation techniques embodied in the Tunisian positive law itself and in particular by the express provisions of the Code of Obligations and Contracts. They will assume that the text speaks for itself and there is no need to resort to sources which are irrelevant to it.

Furthermore, and concerning the place of Islamic law in the Tunisian legal system, some authors have insisted that the Tunisian legislator 'operated a selection, it established from Muslim Law the part which the legislator deems to be established and makes it a positive law, formally state law. Anything of Islamic law which was not established . . . was implicitly rejected and can not therefore be regarded as positive law' (Kari, 1992, p. 203). Only such an approach is likely to give coherence to the Tunisian legal order based on the idea of sovereignty, which means that the sharia can be directly applied on the legal status of citizens only when they have expressly consented by a positive law.

Hence, the exclusion of the rule of disparity of religion as a cause of unworthiness to inherit was done in two ways: The first is the strict interpretation of Article 88 of the Code of Personal Status. This article, relative to cases of unworthiness to inherit, can only be interpreted restrictively, following the rules of interpretation embodied in the Code of Obligations and Contracts. This is the way in which judges are committed, according to a decree of May 18, 2000 of Tunis First Instance Court.

The case was about a Tunisian widow of foreign origin who had sold her share of the inheritance following the death of her Tunisian husband. The co-heirs had then filed a case for cancellation of the act of sale, on the grounds that the widow was not Muslim and thereby could not inherit from her Muslim husband. The trial judge responded to this request as follows:

> Considering that the exclusion of the widow of the *decujus* of all heirs, on the basis of her confession, contradicts Article 88 of the Code of Personal Status, which determined the cases of unworthiness to inherit, and

> limited them to voluntary homicide, and since by virtue of article 540 of the Code of Obligations and Contracts, extending unworthiness to inherit to other situations is prohibited, and that if the legislator had intended to predict any other impediment case it would have expressly done it. This is particularly that among the editors of the code there was a former member of the editorial board of the Charter of *Shari'a* rules, article 789, but this article has been abandoned in the drafting of the Code of Personal Status.

We can find the same type of arguments with more insistence, used in a Court of Appeal judgment rendered on June 14, 2002, which stated that:

> Considering that when article 88 of the CPS declared that homicide was a cause of unworthiness to inherit, it intended to make it the only cause of impediment, to the extent that it is expressly provided for, which excludes any another cause of impediment. Considering that the interpretation of article 88 of the CPS, aimed at giving practical effect to the disparity of worship as a cause of unworthiness to inherit, is an interpretation which gives the text an additional cause for impediment that the legislator has not provided for neither expressly nor implicitly and thus significantly exceeds the wording of article 88 of the CPS in addition to the fact that it is a distortion of the express intent of the law, which may not be accepted if we want to respect the provisions of article 532 of the Code of Obligations and Contracts.[18]

These recitals clearly show a tendency among Tunisian judges to move from a textual interpretation in the light of *fiqh*, to an interpretation using text tools with a positive method of interpretation. This tendency will be reinforced by another one based on a reconsideration of the structure of the legal system, a system in which the supremacy of the constitution will be claimed. Since the 'Tunisianization' of justice and the abolition of religious courts, it is the choice of nationality as a connecting factor, in matters of personal status, that will lead to ignoring religious differences in order to allow the full effect of the principle of equality between all citizens and the practice of freedom of conscience without fear, from the part of the concerned person, of being subject to a discriminatory legal system. In that respect, the particularity of the work done by the Tunisian judge is not so much due to changes in his interpretation of the sharia, so as to make it compatible with the contemporary constitutionalism. It seems that the Tunisian judge would have denied adopting such an approach. We think that he wanted to go further, and review the very status of the sharia in the Tunisian legal system.

Indeed, if he had undertaken a rereading of *fiqh* rules to adapt them to the requirements of modern political values, he would have implicitly recognized sharia as a source of Tunisian law, but this was not at all the procedure that he undertook.[19] It is clear, in fact, on the basis of the most recent decisions that he just wants to exclude religious data from juridical arguments, and to exclude them from his reference texts. This tendency may be deemed audacious, insofar as these judges basically sit in the Courts of First Instance or Appeal, while the Court of Cassation, which is the Supreme Court, is still dominated by judges that we can describe, without making any value judgment, as conservative.

Young judges move towards considering the supremacy of the constitution even though they know that their decisions can be overturned by the Supreme Court, which has happened in some cases. But they are probably aware that these precedents represent a kind of pressure that the High Court cannot ignore indefinitely, and that it must take into account one day. This is probably what explains the ambiguity of some of the decisions, which we review below.

The same CPS provisions we have seen above, namely Articles 5 and 88, will start to be interpreted in light of the constitutional provisions and the values that they carry, including those of freedom and equality. This approach will lead to widening the scope of the applicable laws with regard to inheritance, paving on one hand the way for the constitutional provisions and international conventions, particularly those related to freedom of conscience and the principle of equal rights, and on the other hand, recalling the principle of hierarchy of norms leading to classifying the constitution and the duly ratified international conventions above the law and therefore above the CPS.

Three arguments can support the reasoning of the judge's decision in this kind of case: the first argument is derived from the theory of law and relates to the principle of hierarchy of norms. The judge, in fact, constantly refers to the position occupied by each rule invoked in this particular case, compared to others, to end in their interpretation as required in a way that ensures consistency and avoids any possible clash between them. The second and the third arguments are derived from the law itself and call upon on the one hand, domestic law, more precisely Articles 5 and 6 of the constitution and, on the other, international law, specifically all the conventions on the rights and freedoms that Tunisia has integrated into its domestic legal system by ratification.

The same judge's position was upheld and developed in an appeal decree rendered on June 14, 2002 in which concern for respecting the principle of supremacy of the constitution again came to the fore. But what is interesting is that the trial judges have, in both cases, expelled sharia from their argumentation with regard to inheritance law. As yet, the reaction of the Court of Cassation towards this jurisprudence is unclear.

The jurisprudence of the Court of Cassation, in this area, can be described as ambiguous for two reasons. First, because the argument on which it is based is ambivalent, it is so in a judgment rendered on January 12, 2006 when the High Court asserted 'that the law does not expressly enshrine any impediment linked to the disparity of worship,' but returned later to this issue, to address the plea concerning the evidence of religious beliefs and stated that 'in the case there is no act of apostasy since the person is born to a Tunisian father and proclaims that she is Muslim.' This last part of the reasoning can be considered as superfluous, but it proves that the High Court succeeded neither in freeing itself from the weight of tradition once and for all, nor from a reading of family law in light of the sharia. Then, it is described as ambiguous because it is not consistent and we should probably wait, in this case, until a judgment is rendered by the joined chambers of the High Court, to find a more consistent attitude on whether to exclude clearly the principles of sharia or to maintain them.

Indeed, after the above-mentioned decree of January 12, 2006 another decision was issued on January 16, 2007, in which the High Court returned to its former interpretation of Article 88 of the CPS, since it stated that 'contrary to what the judge said in the contested decision, the disparity of worship is one of the impediments to inheritance, in the sense that there can be no inheritance between people of different religion, on the basis of established case law (sic) and in accordance with the provisions of article 88 of the CPS (sic).' Thus, the court, when stating that its position is based, on the one hand, on the established case law and, on the other hand, on the very wording of article 88 of the CPS, seems to reject out of hand all trial courts' attempts to establish a possible new reading of family law, consistent with a political will that has decided that the law will be an expression of the will of the sovereign people and has chosen since independence to abandon the system of religious dogma, with the abolition of Sharia Courts and rabbinical courts.

We can even see in this decree a warning addressed by the Court of Cassation to these daring judges, signaling to them that any attempt to continue in the same direction will be sanctioned and that it will continue to block any secularist interpretation of family law. But nothing is yet definitively decided since as we have seen with the January 2006 decision the cassation court itself is beginning to follow a secular reading of articles 5 and 88 of the CPS, even if it is with some hesitation—and we do not have *Ijmaa* any more on the use of the sharia's vocabulary, within the court, on the issue.

Challenges and Obstacles

Even though the new constitution guarantees equality between women and men, women continue to face obstacles regarding their access to the judiciary in particular and public office in general. These obstacles relate mainly to the fact that women have to shoulder most of the family responsibilities (child care, household maintenance, etc.). These responsibilities slow down the development of their careers, and the state has adopted no social policies to assist women in discharging these domestic responsibilities!

Conclusion

Now, beyond the case law in the areas of marriage, inheritance and contracts, and the effect of female judgeship on interpreting the constitution and law in general, and beyond the constitutional guarantees regarding women's opportunities to be represented in the judiciary, we must focus on two new special pools of judges to be created by the Tunisian state. These are, one, in the area of counterterrorism policy and, the other, in the area of anticorruption and bribery policy, two challenges that Tunisia has confronted since 2011. Women must continue to fight to prove they deserve such access and responsibility as men, and to prove that there are no special areas reserved for men.

However, and in order to further explore the issue, in light of the new constitution, which upheld the principles of equality of rights and duties between men and women, and also maintained freedom of conscience and religion, but has above all added to Article 1 on Islam, Article 2 which proclaims the civilian character of Tunisian state,[20] the constitution that confirmed the obligation of the state to protect and strengthen women's gains and her equal representation in senior positions and in elected bodies—all these elements predict the strengthening of jurisprudence with regard to family law towards a greater protection of women's rights, i.e., towards an outright recognition of legal equality between men and women.

Notes

1 After riots broke out in Sidi-Bouzid, following the self-immolation of a young street vendor, demonstrations progressively extended to the whole country and spawned social and political demands. When, on January 14, 2011, the riots reached the capital, the president of the Republic, Zine El Abidine Ben Ali, took flight. His departure marked a breakdown in the regime and from that moment onward, Tunisia entered a phase of transition to democracy.

2 The constitution of June 1, 1959, the first constitution of an independent Tunisia, enshrined in Article 6 the principle of equality of rights for all citizens and their equality before the law. The same applies to the independence of the judiciary, as Article 65 states that: 'In exercising their functions, judges are subject only to the authority of the law.'

3 Malikis regard being a man as a necessary condition for becoming a judge, Hanafis seem more flexible about allowing women to become judges, except when it comes to enforcing corporal punishment as provided in the Quran. For this topic, we can refer to Abu Al Hassan Al Mawardi, Al ahkam Assultanyya.

4 Article 3 of the 1959 constitution: 'Sovereignty belongs to the Tunisian people, who exercise it in accordance with the Constitution.' Article 18 of the 1959 constitution: 'The people shall exercise the legislative power through the Chamber of Deputies, the Chamber of Advisors, or by means of a referendum.'

5 The Supreme Judicial Council is the institution in charge of judges' careers, but it is also the guarantor of their independence. It was chaired by the President of the Republic and the vice-president was the minister of justice; the most important members were the president of the Court of Appeal, the attorney general of the Court of Cassation, the attorney general director of the judicial services, the inspector general of the Ministry of Justice, etc. The composition and the status of the High Council shall be completely revised in accordance with the rules enacted by the new constitution, which gives more power and independence to this institution so that it can ensure the independence of judges and the judiciary in a more general way. This law has not been passed yet and the 2014 constitution provided in Article 148 that it shall be enacted, at the latest, six months after the legislative elections; thus it shall be enacted at the latest in April 2015.

6 Debate of the Chamber of Deputies, 'Mudawalat Majliss Al Umma,' 1967, p. 301 and following.

7 Since the standardization of the judicial system and the enactment of the 1959 constitution, judicial organization in Tunisia consists of two main branches, the judicial order and the administrative order.
8 The abolition of the French courts in Tunisia initiated under the protectorate, was based on the French-Tunisian agreement of March 9, 1957.
9 The first law school in Tunisia was created in 1966 in accordance with Decree 66–249 of 21 June 1966 on the creation of the Graduate School of Law.
10 Article 112 of the Constitution of January 26, 2014: 'The Supreme Judicial Council is composed of four bodies, which are the Judiciary Council, the Administrative Judicial Council, the Financial Judicial Council, and the General Assembly of the three judicial councils. Two-thirds of each of these structures is composed of judges, the majority of whom are elected . . . The majority of the members of these bodies shall be elected **. . .** ' Article 114 of the Constitution of January 26, 2014: 'The Supreme Judicial Council ensures the sound functioning of the justice system and respect for its independence. The General Assembly of the three judicial councils proposes reforms and gives its opinions on draft laws related to the judicial system, and must imperatively be submitted to it. Each of the three councils is responsible for making decisions on the professional careers of judges and on disciplinary measures taken against them.'
11 This is the standpoint of the Islamic party Ennahdha.
12 Article 146 of the Tunisian Constitution of January 26, 2014 states that: 'The Constitution's provisions shall be understood and interpreted in harmony, as an indissoluble whole.'
13 On this topic, see Mezghanni, 1975, p. 53 and following; Sana, 2007. On the inheritance of a non-Muslim spouse, see Sana, 2005, p. 823 and following.
14 'Houria' Case, Civil Chamber, decree no. 3384, January 31, 1966.
15 Article 5 of the Constitution of June 1, 1959, stating that: 'The Republic of Tunisia shall guarantee the inviolability of the human person and freedom of conscience, and defends the free practice of religious beliefs provided this does not disturb public order.'
16 Court of Cassation, case 10616, February 13, 1985.
17 Court of Cassation, case 7662199, April 28, 2000.
18 Article 532 of the Code of Obligations and Contracts Code states that: 'In implementing law one must not give it any meaning other than the one deduced from its wording, based on its grammar, its usual meaning, and the legislator's intent.'
19 This judge's reservation on the use of sharia can also imply something else, namely, that the Tunisian judge thinks that he is not qualified to implement sharia or *Fiqh*, a set of rules he cannot master the content of or have any command over the specificities linked to their method of interpretation. It is indeed surprising that the judges who have previously based their decisions on sharia or *Fiqh* have never provided a definition of what they stand for.
20 Article 2 of the Constitution of January 26, 2014 states that: 'Tunisia is a civil state based on citizenship, popular sovereignty and the rule of law. This article cannot be amended.'

7 Tanzania

Women Judges as Agents of Judicial Education

Mi Yung Yoon

Historical Overview

The United Republic of Tanzania was born in 1964 when Tanganyika (Tanzania mainland) and Zanzibar—which became independent from Britain in 1961 and 1963, respectively—united to create a single country. Zanzibar, however, has had its own judicial system, constitution, president, and parliament. Tanzania had a complex colonial history. Germany colonized Tanzania mainland as part of German East Africa—which also included Rwanda and Burundi—from 1886 until her defeat in World War I and the subsequent renouncement of her overseas possessions in 1919 by the Treaty of Versailles. Britain then administered Tanzania mainland, named as the Tanganyika Territory by the 1920 Tanganyika Order in Council as its mandate under the League of Nations's mandate system until Tanganyika became independent. However, Zanzibar, which had been dominated by Arabs, became an independent sultanate from 1832 until Britain declared it a British protectorate in 1890 (Bierwagen & Peter, 1989, p. 399)

Though Tanzania experienced both German and British colonialism, its legal framework is based on the English common law system (Nyanduga & Manning, 2006). The British brought a body of law to Tanganyika; in addition, the colonial legislative council 'passed local legislation called Ordinances' (Shivji, Majamba, Makaramba, & Peter, 2004, p. 13). However, the British kept the customary and religious laws—which had governed social behaviors in ethnic and religious communities in precolonial times—to regulate such personal and family matters as marriage, inheritance, succession, and land ownership (Ibid.). The postindependence judicial system merely inherited the British legal practice that recognized customary and religious laws as sources of law.

Tanzania has taken great strides to improve women's representation in politics. In June 2015, women accounted for 36% of parliamentary seats and 31% of cabinet positions. How well, then, are women represented in the judiciary? Though there are some studies on female representation in the Tanzanian legislature, no study has systematically looked into descriptive and substantive representation of women in the judiciary. The purpose of this chapter is to examine women's representation in the judiciary in the context of the country's legal tradition and judicial system. Next, I discuss the sources of law in Tanzania. This part discusses the complex merger of traditional, colonial and modern statutory laws into a single body of law. Next is a discussion of the court structure and selection of judges. The following section discusses female representation in the judiciary. Studies on women's political representation in Tanzania (Yoon, 2011; Yoon, 2013) have found that women in politics make a difference in the lives of women. Have women in the judiciary also made a difference in the lives of women? The remaining part of the chapter, therefore, discusses the efforts female judges have made to promote gender equality before the law, by focusing on the judicial education led by women judges.

The Sources of Law

The sources of Tanzanian law include the constitution, statutory law passed by the legislature, case law, received law, customary law, Islamic law, and international law (Shivji et al., 2004, p. 13). Case law consists of past decisions by the High Court and the Court of Appeal in Tanzania (Tanzania human rights jurisprudence, n.d.). Received law includes the British common law, doctrines of equity, and statutes of general application, applicable prior to July 22, 1920 (reception date) (Shivji et al., 2004, p. 16). The common law is derived from 'customs and practices of the English people' (Ibid.). Equity, which intends to supplement the 'deficiencies of the common law,' focuses on fairness that the common law fails to provide (Ingersoll, 1911, p. 59). Doctrines of equity are past decisions in equity that have become rules. The statutes of general application refer to the acts of the British Parliament. 'Received law is applicable in Tanzania only when there is no local written law to address the matter at issue and when local circumstances permit' (Tanzania human rights jurisprudence, n.d.).

Customary law and Islamic law are also established as sources of law by the Judicature and Application of Laws Act of 1961 (Chapter 358 of the laws of Tanzania). Section 11 (1) of the Act states:

> Customary law shall be applicable to, and courts shall exercise jurisdiction in accordance therewith in, matters of a civil nature (a) between members of a community in which rules of customary law relevant to the matter are established and accepted, or between a member of one community and a member of another community if the rules of customary law of both communities make similar provision for the matter;

The same section also allows courts to apply Islamic law to specific personal matters, by stating:

> nothing in this subsection shall preclude any court from applying the rules of Islamic law in matters of marriage, divorce, guardianship, inheritance,

wakf and similar matters in relation to members of a community which follows that law.

Customary law—reflective of cultures and customs—varies across the communities due to their differences in cultures and customs. Thus, Section 11 (3) addresses, 'in any proceedings where the law applicable is customary law, the court shall apply the customary law prevailing within the area of its local jurisdiction. . . .' As a result, 'judgments vary widely, depending on the court's location and the judge' (Ezer, 2006, p. 614). The Local Customary Law (Declaration) Order of 1963 codified customary law on guardianship, inheritance and wills. The Islamic Law (Restatement) Act of 1964 unified principles of Islamic law on marriage, succession and divorce (Juma, 2013, p. 32). However, when customary and Islamic laws are in conflict with statutory law, statutory law takes precedence (Hashim, 2005, p. 450).

The Court Structure of Tanzania

As Figure 7.1 shows, the court system of the United Republic of Tanzania has two parallel systems (one for Tanzania mainland and the other for Zanzibar) with multiple hierarchal tiers, respectively. The Court of Appeal, as the highest

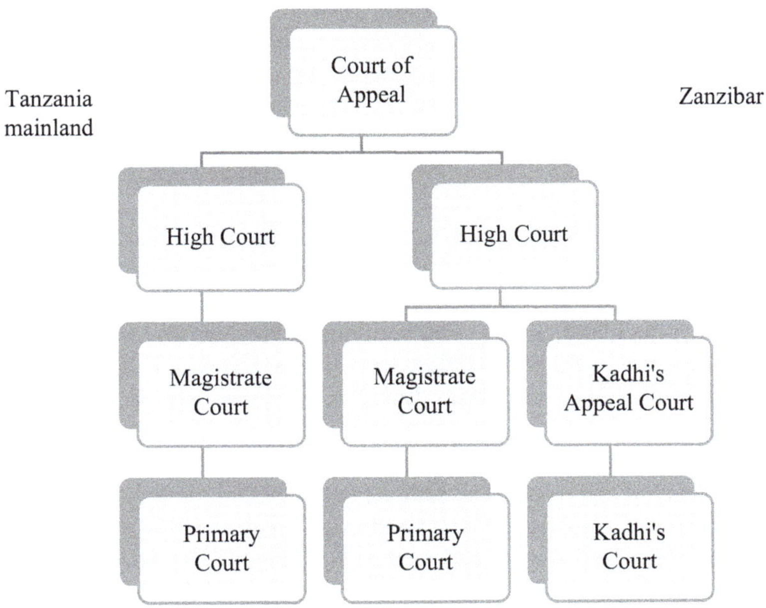

Figure 7.1 The Legal System of the United Republic of Tanzania

Sources: Nyanduga & Manning (2006); Shivji et al. (2004)

court of the country, integrates the two systems. According to Article 117 (3) of the 1977 Constitution of Tanzania mainland, the Court of Appeal hears 'every appeal brought before it arising from the judgment or other decision of the High Court or of a magistrate with extended jurisdiction.' The Court of Appeal also hears appeals from the High Court of Zanzibar, but except for cases concerning (a) interpretation of Zanzibar's constitution; (b) matters of Islamic law which began at the Kahdi's Court; and (c) any other matters mentioned in Zanzibar's constitution or by any other law enacted by the House of Representatives (Constitution of Zanzibar, 2002).

The chief justice is the head of the Court of Appeal and the judiciary. According to Article 118 (1) of the constitution of Tanzania mainland, 'a full bench of the Court of Appeal shall consist of not less than five Justices of Appeal.' 'The quorum at every sitting of the Court of Appeal shall be not less than three Justices of Appeal' (Article 122 [1]). The president appoints the chief justice and other Justices of Appeal 'after consultation with the Chief Justice' (Article 118 [2] & [3]).

The Courts in Tanzania Mainland

During colonial rule, the courts were divided by race (Sawyerr, 1969, p. 31). While non-Africans were subject to 'civil courts applying received law,' Africans (natives) were subject to native courts applying mainly customary law (Sawyerr, 1969, p. 24; Shivji et al., 2004, p. 18). Native courts also contained 'considerable Islamic jurisprudence' (Juma, 2013, p. 35). The British retained this parallel system of jurisdiction by race, first established by the Germans (Bierwagen & Peter, 1989, p. 397). The Magistrates' Courts Act of 1963 abolished the racially divided colonial judicial system, and created a unified 'non-racial' judicial system in Tanzania mainland (Wanitzek, 1990–1991, p. 258).

High Courts: The High Court has full jurisdiction in both civil and criminal matters and hears appeals submitted from the subordinate courts. The High Court also has jurisdiction over matters associated with the constitution of Tanzania mainland and election petitions (Nyanduga & Manning, 2006). It is headed by the Principal Judge, known as the Head of the High Court. The number of High Court judges should not be fewer than 30. The president appoints the Principal Judge and other judges of the High Court 'after consultation with the Judicial Service Commission' (Article 109 [1] of the constitution of Tanzania mainland). The Judicial Service Commission, which plays a significant role in appointing judges and magistrates, consists of

'(a) the Chief Justice who shall be the Chairman; (b) the Attorney General; (c) a Justice of Appeal of Tanzania who shall be appointed in that behalf by the President after consultation with the Chief Justice; (d) the Principal Judge; and (e) two members who shall be appointed by the President.' (Article 112 [2] of the constitution of Tanzania mainland)

Only persons with 'special qualifications' are appointed judges. According to Article 109 (7) of the constitution, a person who meets the special qualifications:

> means a person who holds a degree in law from a University recognized by the accreditation authority in Tanzania and (a) has been a magistrate; (b) has held an office in the public service while possessing qualifications of attorney or has been a private advocate; and (c) possess qualifications for enrolment as an advocate and has possessed those qualifications continuously for a period of not less than ten years.

However, Article 109 (8) allows some flexibility to the special qualifications clause, by stating:

> Where the President is satisfied that a person holding one of the special qualifications has not held that qualification for a period of not less than ten years, but that person has the ability, knowledge and in every respect is suitable for appointment as Judge of the High Court, and there are reasons which make such person deserve to be so appointed, then the President may dispense with the requirement that such person shall have held the special qualifications for a period of not less than ten years, and may after consultation with the Judicial Service Commission, appoint that person Judge of the High Court.

Today, there are 13 High Court centers (Dodoma, Dar es Salaam, Arusha, Moshi, Mwanza, Tabora, Bukoba, Songea, Iringa, Mbeya, Mtwara, Mwanza and Sumbawanga) (Judiciary of Tanzania, n.d.). Each center is 'headed by a Judge-in-Charge' (Shivji et al., 2004, p. 227). 'The Court of Appeal sits in any of those centers when it thinks fit' (Judiciary of Tanzania, n.d.).

Magistrate Courts: Resident Magistrate Courts and District Courts: Right below the High Court, there are the Resident Magistrate Courts and the District Courts, which share concurrent jurisdiction. While the Resident Magistrate Courts are located in major cities, municipalities, and towns, the District Courts are located in districts (Nyanduga & Manning, 2006). Unlike the Resident Magistrate Courts, the District Courts, presided by district magistrates, hear appeals from the Primary Courts (Shivji et al., 2004, p. 225). The Judicial Service Commission appoints both resident and district magistrates (Ibid.). Resident magistrates are university graduates (Bierwagen & Peter, 1989, p. 401). District magistrates are mostly former Primary Court magistrates who have been promoted to their positions after a long term service as Primary Court magistrates (Ibid.).

Primary Courts: The Primary Courts are the lowest courts in the judicial hierarchy. Multiple Primary Courts are located in each district. The Primary Courts are more accessible than the other courts, because they not only can be found at the village level but also use Kiswahili as the official language. Except for the District Courts, which use both Kiswahili and English, the other higher courts use English as the official language (Wanitzek, 1990–1991, p. 260). The Judicial Service Commission appoints Primary Court magistrates (Shivji et al., 2004, p. 223). Though the Primary Courts have jurisdiction on both civil and criminal matters, civil matters applying customary law or Islamic law must start at the Primary Court level (Ibid.). The Primary Courts, therefore, play a unique role of applying three different types of law: customary law, Islamic law, and statutory law (Wanitzek, 1990–1991, p. 259). Instead of establishing separate courts applying customary law or Islamic law, the postindependence legal system designates the Primary Courts also to play the role of such separate courts. The Primary Courts are presided over by Primary Court magistrates who have done 'a short law course . . . to know the basics of the law' (Bierwagen & Peter, 1989, p. 400).

Specialized Courts: Tribunals: Besides the above courts, there are specialized courts, known as tribunals (e.g., administrative tribunals, tax appeals tribunals, fair competition tribunals, land and housing tribunals, etc.), which deal with specific dispute cases (Judiciary of Tanzania, n.d.).

The Courts in Zanzibar

Figure 7.1 shows that Zanzibar, where most people are Muslim, has a dual court system: the common law court system governed by secular law and the Kadhi's Court system applying Islamic law (Legal and Human Rights Centre & Zanzibar Legal Services Centre, 2014, p. 325). The High Court of Zanzibar hears questions concerning interpretation of Zanzibar's constitution, in addition to the appeals from the lower courts. The courts in Zanzibar hear only nonunion matters. The President of Zanzibar appoints the chief justice and other judges of the High Court after consultation with the Judicial Service Commission of Zanzibar, whose composition also includes the Chief Kadhi. Other judges of the High Court should not be fewer than two in number (Article 93 [2] of the constitution of Zanzibar).

The Kadhi's Courts adjudicate such matters as personal status, marriage, divorce and inheritance when 'all the parties profess the Muslim religion' (Kadhis' Courts Act, 1985, Section 6 [1]). The Kadhi's Appeal Court hears appeals from the Kadhi's Courts. The Chief Kadhi and two Senior Kadhis have jurisdiction over appeals from the Kadhi's Courts (Section 4 [4]). Any Senior Kadhis or the Chief Kadhi hear cases alone 'unless the Chief Kadhi directs otherwise' (Section 4 [5]). The Chief Kadhi is appointed by the President of Zanzibar (Section 4 [1]) and other Kadhis are appointed 'by the Judicial Service Commission in consultation with the Chief Kadhi' (Section 5 [1]). A person to become a Kadhi should be knowledgeable of the Islamic law. Each of the 10 districts in Zanzibar has a Kadhi's Court (Section 3 [2]). Like Tanzania mainland, Zanzibar has tribunals to deal with specific legal issues (Legal and Human Rights Centre & Zanzibar Legal Serves Centre, 2014, p. 307).

Gender and Representation

Tanzania—which established the special-seat system for women in the national legislature in 1985—was the first African country to adopt gender quotas to narrow the gender gap in politics (Yoon, 2008, p. 63). Since the first postindependence multiparty elections in 1995, the country has gradually increased the number of parliamentary seats reserved for women to meet its commitment to the targets of the Beijing Platform for Action, the Southern African Development Community, and the African Union. If the draft constitution—which recommends electing one woman and one man in each constituency—had been approved in a referendum scheduled for April 2015, the country would have met the African Union's target of 50% female legislative representation by 2015, during its election in late 2015. However, the referendum has been postponed until after the 2015 election. In Tanzania, a parliamentary seat is a base for a cabinet seat, because the president draws his cabinet members from among parliamentarians. Though female representation in the cabinet has also increased, the percentage of female ministers and deputy ministers has never exceeded the current 31%.

How well, then, have women been represented in the judiciary? Has the country made deliberate efforts to narrow the gender gap in the judiciary as it has to increase female legislative representation? As mentioned above, the president appoints the chief justice and other Justices of Appeal after consultation with the chief justice. He also appoints High Court judges after consultation with the Judicial Service Commission. Magistrates of the Resident, District, and Primary Courts are appointed by the Judicial Service Commission, respectively.

The current president, Jakaya Mrisho Kikwete (2005–2015), has increased women's representation on the bench to a great extent. I ascribe the significant increase to his deliberate effort to narrow the gender gap in the judiciary, the continuous push from women's organizations (e.g., the Tanzania Gender Networking Programme, the Tanzania Media Women Association, the Tanzania Women Lawyers Association, etc.) for more women in decision-making, and the country's commitment to the 50% target of the African Union and the Southern African Development Community set for 2015. When President Kikwete came to office in 2005, of 45 High Court and Court of Appeal judges, 10 were women (President Kikwete's speech, 2014). However, in August 2008, of 56 High Court and Appeal's Court judges, 23 judges were women (Kileo, 2010, p. 166). In 2013, 29 out of 65 judges were women (Chande urges appointment of more women judges, 2013). As of May 2014, 30 of 78 High Court and Appeal's Court judges were women (President Kikwete's speech, 2014). To recognize his effort for gender balance in the judiciary, women judges presented President Kikwete a Human Rights Award at the biennial conference of the International Association of Women Judges held in Arusha, Tanzania in May 2014 (Tanzania: Women judges present Kikwete human rights award, 2014). He appointed more female judges afterwards; as of February 2015, of 97 judges, 39 were women (State losing too many cases, 2015). Table 7.1 summarizes and displays women's representation on the bench over time. As it

Table 7.1 Women's Representation in the High Court and the Court of Appeal in Tanzania

Year	*Number of women (total)*	*Percentage of women*
2005	10 (45)	22.22
2008	23 (56)	41.07
2013	29 (65)	44.62
2014	30 (78)	38.46
2015	39 (97)	40.21

shows, the number of women on the bench has increased with the gradual increase in the number of judges.

Unlike the High Court, the Court of Appeal has had only a few women, due in part to the smaller number of justices. There was no female justice in the Court of Appeal in 2000 (Kileo, 2010, p. 166). However, by 2008, 4 out of 15 justices were women (Ibid.). Of 16 justices in the current Appeal's Court, four (Engela Kileo, Nathalia Kimaro, Sauda Mjasiri, and Katherine Oriyo) are women (Judiciary of Tanzania, n.d.). The chief justice, however, has always been a man. According to Article 110 (1) and (3) of the constitution, High Court judges may serve until they reach the age of 60, but the president may extend their terms if deemed as necessary for the public interest. The age limit for justices of the Appeal's Court is 65 (Article 120 [1]), but it may also be extended by the president for the public interest (Article 120 [3]).

In Zanzibar, of six High Court judges today, two (Fatma Hamid Mahmoud and Rabia Hussein Mohamed) are women (Judiciary of Zanzibar, n.d.). However, all of the Kadhis are males, and women are not represented in the Kadhi's Courts (Majamba, n.d.).

As aforementioned, Article 109 (7) of the constitution specifies special qualifications for presidential appointment of judges. Article 109 (8), however, allows the president to appoint a person who he or she believes 'has the ability, knowledge, and in every respect if suitable for appointment as Judge of the High Court, and there are reasons which make such person deserve to be so appointed. . . . . ' even if the person does not meet all of the qualifications. As such, Article 109 (8) has helped the president draw men and women from diverse backgrounds (e.g., public service, Primary Courts, District or Resident Magistrate Courts, private legal practice, etc.) to the bench (Keregero, 2006). Considering that there is no quota for women's representation in the judiciary, Article 109 (8) might be instrumental in bringing more women onto the bench, though the extent to which the Tanzanian presidents have utilized the Article is yet to be examined with tangible data.

Though women's representation on the bench has improved over time, equal representation has still not been achieved. Chief Justice Othman has identified patriarchy—that denies 'capable women the chance to be appointed as judges'—as a hindrance to women's entry onto the bench across the continent, including in Tanzania (as cited in Chande urges appointment of more women judges, 2013). This view was seconded by then Justice Eusebia Munuo (Ibid.). There is a significant presence of women in the magistracy, though the magistracy remains male-dominated (United Nations Democracy Fund, 2011, p. 9). Tanzania has set a goal to achieve 40% representation of female magistrates by 2013 (Ibid.). However, due to the paucity of data, it is difficult to assess the current level of women's representation in the magistracy. As mentioned earlier, the Judicial Service Commission plays a significant role in appointing judges and magistrates. This begs the question of whether refusing 'capable women the chance to be appointed as judges' results from women's underrepresentation in the Commission, because the male-dominated Judicial Service Commission may not feel compelled to achieve gender equality in the judiciary unless legally mandated. Today, of six members of the Commission (the Chief Justice, the Principal Judge, the Attorney General, a Justice, and two other members appointed by the president), only one (Regina Mulebya) is female (Kapama, 2015). The underrepresentation of women in both the Judicial Service Commission and the courts suggests that to materialize gender equality in the courts, women's representation in the Commission should improve first.

Women and the Judiciary

Do female judges promote gender equality before the law? According to the Chief Justice of the Supreme Court of Canada, Beverley McLachlin, the courts need women judges to ensure that courts are representative of the societies they serve and, hence, preserve their legitimacy, to reflect the society's commitment to equality, to best use available human resources, and to bring new perspectives and rout clichéd stereotypes (as cited in Hedlund, Glazebrook, Pacht, & Wainwright, 2010, p. 3).

The key arguments for bringing women to the bench have been made based on the presumed difference women judges make in the courts, as well as the legitimacy of the judiciary as a democratic institution (Malleson, 2003a, pp. 1–2). The first view suggests that women bring different perspectives and experiences to the judicial process and are more likely to promote gender equality, by making gender-sensitive judgments. Therefore, women's legal status improves with more women on the bench (Feenan, 2008, pp. 491–492). The second view, however, ties gender balance in the judiciary to the question of institutional legitimacy. The same arguments also have been made for women's representation in the legislature.

There are multiple ways to promote gender equality before the law. The most noticeable work of women judges in Tanzania is judicial education. The Tanzania Women Judges Association (TAWJA), in partnership with the International Association of Women Judges (IAWJ), has spearheaded this effort. TAWJA, founded in 2000, is 'a professional association of women judges and magistrates of all levels' in the Tanzanian judiciary (TAWJA, 2012). Its main objectives include advancing women's rights to equal justice, promoting women's access to the courts, advocating for the increase of the number of women judges at all levels, developing judicial leadership, conducting legal research on gender equality and human rights, exchanging information on issues of critical concern to women and uprooting gender bias from the judicial system and the community (Kileo, 2010, p. 165). Of these goals, equal justice and access to the courts and uprooting gender bias from the judicial system and the community appear to have been the focus of the organization. TAWJA has utilized judicial education as a channel to achieving those goals. However, unlike the Tanzania Women Parliamentary Group, which has made a steady effort to improve women's descriptive and substantive representation in parliament, TAWJA's effort to increase women's representation in the judiciary has been unnoticeable, other than recognizing President Kikwete with the aforementioned Human Rights Award in 2014.

Women in Tanzania lack access to justice, due to the lack of knowledge of their legal rights and court procedures (Wanitzek, 1990–1991, p. 263). Legal and paralegal services that would help women are also in short supply (United Nations Development Programme in Tanzania, 2014). Furthermore, many women do not seek justice because of 'intimidation at the police level, extortion at the court level, and sextortion of women and children at many levels' (Ibid.). TAWJA's judicial education, therefore, is twofold: enhancement of women's understanding of the court system and training of judicial officers on women's legal rights. Specifically, women judges have sensitized women on gender-sensitive laws and the court system to enhance women's access to the courts; they have also provided training to judges and magistrates to promote gender-sensitive court proceedings and judgments, based on international and regional human rights laws (UN Women, 2013b; United Republic of Tanzania, 2014). Women judges' judicial education has focused on civil matters affecting women most, such as marriage, divorce, property rights, child custody, domestic violence and inheritance.

President Kikwete, at the biennial conference of IAWJ in May 2014, commended women judges for helping the government address 'human rights issues and domestic violence, including sexual abuse, and mainstream gender issues in planning and budgeting at all levels' (President Kikwete's speech, 2014). Women judges, he also stated, have played a significant role in the Legal Sector Reform Programme, by 'speeding up court cases, improving the quality of court decisions, increasing the pace of reviewing outdated laws and capacity building at all levels across the legal sector institutions' (Speech by president, 2012). Among TAWJA's judicial education efforts, the Jurisprudence of Equality Program (2001–2003), the Jurisprudence on the Ground (2008–2010), and the Sextortion project (2009–2011) are most notable. The targeted audiences of these education programs included a range of individuals from judges to women in rural villages. These programs were initiated by IAWJ, and were not uniquely Tanzanian. Small numbers of other countries have also implemented one or more of these programs.

Under the Jurisprudence of Equality Program (JEP), funded by UN Women (formerly UNIFEM) through a grant to IAWJ, TAWJA began its legal education with seminars and workshops in 2001 (Kileo, 2010, p. 166). It also sent six Tanzanian women judges to IAWJ's Training of Trainers Workshop in Entebbe, Uganda (TAWJA, 2012). 'The goal of the JEP training [was] to equip judges and magistrates with knowledge and skills needed in resolving cases involving discrimination and/or violence against women in accordance with the principles enshrined in domestic, international, and regional human rights treaties' (TAWJA, Stopping the abuse, n.d.). The training capacity of TAWJA has improved, with the increase in the number of trainers to 20 (TAWJA, Background history, n.d.). To sustain the JEP training after its expiration in 2003, the Tanzanian judiciary funded four seminars between 2005 and 2007 (TAWJA, Jurisprudence of equality project, n.d.).

JEP was succeeded by the Jurisprudence on the Ground (JOG) project, which was funded by the United Nations Democracy Fund through IAWJ (TAWJA, 2012). JOG, like JEP, trained dozens of judges and magistrates on women's rights based on human rights laws. It also trained leaders of the Society for Women and AIDS in Africa-Tanzania (SWAA-T) to help rural women and women with HIV/AIDS understand and defend their rights (IAWJ, Judicial training program, n.d.). The SWAA-T leaders 'have used drama, music, brochures, pamphlets, and community meetings' to disseminate the information (Ibid.). Brochures and pamphlets were printed in simple language in both English and Kiswahili to reach broader audiences (United Nations Democracy Fund, 2011, p. 15).

Gender-based violence (e.g., spousal battery, rape, female genital mutilation, sexual harassment at work, trafficking of women, etc.) is epidemic in Tanzania (Legal and Human Rights Centre & Zanzibar Legal Services Centre, 2014, p. 166). Nonetheless, it is 'causally dismissed by the police, judicial authorities, and the community at large' (United Nations Democracy Fund, 2011, p. 8). Tanzania is one of the three countries (i.e., Bosnia-Herzegovina, the Philippines and Tanzania) that implemented the Stopping the Abuse of Power for Purposes of Sexual Exploitation: Naming, Shaming, and Ending Sextortion program—funded by the Ministry of Foreign Affairs of the Netherlands through IAWJ. The objective of the program, Justice Engela Kileo states, is to improve the capacity to deal with gender-based violence cases (as cited in Jacob, 2014). IAWJ coined the term sextortion, which means 'sexual exploitation by authority' in various contexts (TAWJA, 2012). The sextortion program included seminars and workshops for judges, magistrates, nonjudicial personnel in the judiciary, and law enforcement officers; it also disseminated brochures for communities throughout the country to sensitize people on sexual exploitation (TAWJA, Stopping the abuse, n.d.; UN Women, 2013a).

Justice Engela Kileo states that the years of training 'started to bear fruit as seen from the judgments ruled' (as cited in Tambwe, 2013). The IAWJ (Judicial training programs, n.d.) also reports that 'Judges and magistrates who participated in the training seminars are issuing cases that reflect their training on issues ranging from economic discrimination, property rights, custody, inheritance to sexual assault and other forms of violence against women.' Some reported court decisions support their positive assessments of the training. For example, Devotha Christopher, a District Court magistrate in Arusha who received training under JEP, granted a share of matrimonial property to a woman whose marriage was denied by her husband on the grounds that their marriage was never legalized (as cited in UN Women, 2013b). She stated that the knowledge she gained from the training has influenced her handling of cases ever since (Ibid.). A male magistrate in Arusha stated that as a result of the training, he got to know 'why it is so difficult to find witnesses' with respect to violence against women, and he now asks the prosecutor to hide the names of witnesses (Ibid.). Concerning the Mohamed v. Makamo case in 2001, the High Court judge at Dar es Salaam overturned the District Court decision that had awarded the wife 5% of the marital property and the husband 95% upon their divorce, by awarding the wife 50% of their matrimonial assets (International Association of Women Judges, Jurisprudence of equality program decision, n.d.). The Resident magistrate, concerning the Marandu v. Marandu case in 2003, awarded the burial rights to the wife who was in dispute with her in-laws (Ibid.). In Tanzania, most administrators of the estate of the deceased are men. In the Ndossi v. Ndossi case in 2002, which sought to restore the Primary Court decision that had granted a brother of the deceased the right to administer the estate, the High Court judge in Dar es Salaam awarded the widow the right to administer her husband's estate (Ibid.). In the Dotto v. Jilasa child custody case in 2009, the District Court magistrate who received the JOG training granted the child custody to the mother on the ground of best interest of the child (United Nations Democracy Fund, 2011, p. 19). These judges used the Tanzanian constitution and the human rights treaties Tanzania has ratified, including the Convention on the Elimination of All Forms of Discrimination against Women, as the basis for their judicial decisions.

The above gender-sensitive court rulings are indicative of a certain degree of success of TAWJA's judicial education. However, there are no systematic data with respect to gender- sensitive decisions by the trained judges and magistrates since the launch of JEP in 2001. Though IAWJ has solicited reports of decisions made by trained judges and magistrates to post on its website, the number of cases posted is small. For Tanzania, only nine cases are posted on IAWJ's website. United Nations Democracy Fund (2011, p. 17), which sponsored JOG in Tanzania, also suggests that collecting the data on gender-sensitive judgments has not been as effective as hoped due to the lack of reporting. All of the aforementioned court decisions were made by female judges. This begs the question of how the training has affected male judges. It is also unclear whether more women have brought their cases to the courts as a result of the judicial education they received. Various media sources report that TAWJA's training sessions were well attended. SWAA-T's community meetings drew 3,300 people (United Nations Democracy Fund, 2011, p. 1).

However, there is little information on the feedback from the trainees. Though the available data are insufficient to assess the effectiveness of the judicial education accurately, conducting judicial education itself is an important first step in improving the awareness of women's legal rights and bringing equal justice for women.

Challenges and Obstacles

There are multiple challenges undermining the potential positive impact of the judicial education. First, there is no steady flow of funding for legal education, despite the need for continuing education. Former Justice Eusebia Munuo (2014) addresses that 'to expand the capacities of judges and magistrates for better performance of their duties, particularly determining cases,' legal education should continue. TAWJA's judicial education, however, appears to be contingent upon the availability of external funding. As discussed above, all of its judicial education projects were sponsored by multilateral or bilateral donors through IAWJ. The donor-sponsored programs were also short term, lasting only for a few years—which casts doubts on their long-term effects. Considering the complexity of the Tanzanian judicial system and women's disadvantaged status, such short-term programs may not gain much traction if they are ephemeral.

Second, the Tanzanian judicial system does not offer an environment conducive to equal justice for women. The 1996 legal sector review report by the task force headed by former Attorney General Mark Boman pointed out the following challenges of the Tanzanian judiciary: inordinate delays in resolving disputes, limited access to justice and legal services for the majority of the people, corruption in the legal system, low levels of public trust in the legal system, low levels of competence and poor morale amongst public sector legal personnel, inadequate numbers of professionally trained personnel, and poor provision and maintenance of the work environment (as cited in Ministry of Justice and Constitutional Affairs, 2008).

The Tanzanian judiciary today faces the same challenges undermining its efficacy. It still experiences the shortage of judges and magistrates due to budget constraints, the low level of computer literacy among judges and magistrates, the shortage of court rooms, significant corruption in the lower courts, the lack of Internet access, and others (United Nations Democracy Fund, 2011, p. 7). According to the current chief justice, Mohamed Chande Othman, the High Court requires 120 judges (as cited in Robi, 2014). As of February, 2015, however, there were only 81 High Court judges. In 2013, Angela Kairuki, then the Deputy Minister of Justice and Constitutional Affairs, stated that the country is short of '1,600 Primary and District Court magistrates' (as cited in Judiciary short of 1,600 magistrates, 2013). She added that 'there is also a shortage of 751 Primary Courts, 62 District Courts and 13 Resident Magistrate Courts across the country' (Ibid.). 'Proceedings and judgments are still handwritten,' states former chief justice Augustino Ramadhani (as cited in African Union,

2008). These challenges have caused judicial delays and a backlog of cases (United Nations Democracy Fund, 2011, p. 7). Judicial delays have become 'a breeding ground for corruption to the judiciary; [as] court clerks exploited the delays to demand money from clients on behalf of the magistrates to have the judgments written and delivered,' says Prime Minister Mizengo Pinda (as cited in Philemon, 2012).

Due to the shortage of courts, people, particularly in rural areas, have to travel long distances to reach a court. The 2011 United Nations Democracy Fund report on JOG—based on its interviews with TAWJA and SWAA-T members, NGO representatives, and the chief justice in Tanzania—stated that 'it is not uncommon for a person going to the court to be able to dedicate three days—two for travel and one for proceedings' (p. 7). The time required for going to court is a critical factor for women—who need community and family approval to leave their work and families—to decide not to file their claims (Ibid.). According to former Justice Eusebia Munuo (2014), 'delay of cases and unjustified adjournment of cases have made litigation more costly and inaccessible to poor persons especially women.' Judicial corruption also makes litigation more expensive. Women lack resources for fees, transportation, and lodging associated with the access to the legal system (United Nations Democracy Fund, 2011, p. 13). In addition, the lack of English proficiency can become one of the factors hindering women's access to justice (Wanitzek, 2002, p. 10). Considering that the dominant legal language is English, women who lack English proficiency are disadvantaged, because they experience difficulties in presenting their cases effectively (Ibid., p. 9). Therefore, even if women gained knowledge of their rights and the court procedures as a result of legal education, the shortcomings of the legal system make courts still inaccessible to female beneficiaries of the education.

Conclusion

This chapter examined women's descriptive and substantive representation in the Tanzanian judiciary. The evidence suggests that the country for the past 10 years has made steady progress in improving women's representation in the courts, by appointing more women as judges. The percentage of women on the bench is in fact higher than the percentage of women in the legislature, which currently reserves 102 of 357 seats for women. According to former Justice Eusebia Munuo (2014), female representation in the judiciary has encouraged other women to study law and join the legal profession. Her remark suggests that the pool of qualified women for judicial positions is expanding, and female representation in the judiciary is likely to rise in the future if the current trend continues. The aforementioned court decisions by female judges also suggest that women judges promote gender equality before the law.

Discriminatory customary and Islamic laws, the court system reflective of the patriarchal culture outside of it, and women's lack of knowledge of their legal rights and the judicial system have hindered equal justice for women in

Tanzania. In this regard, the legal education TAWJA has implemented is an important first step toward equal justice for women. Though TAWJA's legal education programs have been ephemeral and have reached only limited numbers of judges, magistrates, law enforcement officers and women, they have brought equal justice for women to the forefront. The awareness-raising efforts of women judges in Tanzania were recognized and commended by such organizations as UN Women and IAWJ. However, for their legal education to have a broader and profound impact, it should be continuous, without intervals, and the shortcomings of the country's judicial system should be dealt with. Women's representation in the judiciary in general and in Tanzania in particular has been under-researched, and there should be more studies in the future concerning the factors fostering or hindering women's entry into the judiciary and the effects of a critical mass of women in the judiciary to broaden our understanding of the role of women in government institutions.

8 Benin

Women Judges Promoting Women's Rights

Alice Kang

Perhaps more than in any other country in Francophone West Africa, female judges in Benin have held significant positions of authority. This chapter focuses on the number and impact of women in Benin's judiciary in the democratic era. Since 1990, the Republic of Benin has seen the peaceful alternation of presidential power and regularly holds local and national elections. Benin is an intriguing country for students of judicial politics and women and politics because women's numerical representation in the judiciary has consistently been higher than that of women in the legislature. For instance, in 2007, approximately 21% of active magistrates were women (magistrates include judges and public prosecutors) (Houngan Ayémonna, 2008, p. 11). By contrast, women constituted 8% of the national assembly (IPU, 2008). While I follow Sally Kenney (2012) and seek to avoid stereotyping what women judges are like and what men judges are like, this chapter shows that female judges in and outside the courts have made a perceptible impact on Benin's national laws concerning women's rights and have made decisions that promote equality between men and women.

Historical Overview

What we now know as Benin was once a geographic area consisting of various and dynamic kinds of political entities. The most centralized and powerful polity during the period of the Atlantic slave trade was the kingdom of Dahomey. The French captured the seat of the kingdom, Abomey, in 1893. Dahomey subsequently became part of French West Africa in 1904.

During the colonial period, French administrators established a dualist judicial system that differentiated between citizens (*citoyens*) and subjects (*indigènes*). French legal codes ostensibly were applied for citizens. For subjects, who constituted the majority of the population, two bodies of law were used. A particularly harsh penal code (the *Indigénat*) was in force until 1946. For matters pertaining to family and land, colonial authorities created a customary code, the *Coutumier du Dahomey* (1933), a written document that was ostensibly based on oral custom or tradition.

A product of the colonial period, the customary code, it is important to emphasize, is not an objective account of norms or practices surrounding marriage, divorce, child custody, inheritance, and the management of land. The *Coutumier du Dahomey* does, however, institutionalize patriarchy in colonial jurisprudence. Article 16 of the customary code states that across all customs, the male head of household is the central figure of authority. The code stipulates that the wife must obey her husband and be faithful to him; a husband must treat his wife well but fidelity to her is not required (Article 122). Male heads of household, as stated in the code, enjoy full authority over their children, including the right to punish them (Article 17). The code declares that polygamy is legal, including polyandry among certain groups (Articles 33 and 34), and first wives, with the exceptions of those from two ethnic groups, oversee their co-wives (Article 35). Further, according to the code, 'Women do not have any judicial power' and a woman 'is her husband's property and his inheritance' (Article 127).[1]

After Benin gained independence on August 1, 1960, new leaders retained the colonial system of legal dualism. Judges used the *Coutumier du Dahomey* to help render decisions relating to the family and land. The law of December 9, 1964 created eight Courts of First Instance that, when the conflict dealt with so-called traditional law, called upon customary assessors and the customary code. Over time, however, legal dualism, as least on paper, has slowly eroded. In 1981, under a socialist dictatorship, popular courts were not to use assessors but rather elected, nonprofessional judges. In 1996, the Constitutional Court decided that the *Coutumier du Dahomey* is not a body of law and has no executory power (C.C. 26 septembre 1996, N° 96–063).[2] More recently, in 2004, Benin unified the two legal systems in the domain of family law by adopting a unified *Code des personnes et de la famille* (which I discuss in greater detail below). Yet one must be careful not to overstate the ascendance of so-called modern law in Benin. As Jacques Mayaba (2013), a senior-ranking judge in Benin, writes, legal dualism is eroding in principle but not in practice. In sum, Benin is a civil law country that partially relies on customary law.

Court Structure and Organization

Like many countries in Francophone West Africa, Benin's court structure has significantly changed over time. In this section and the rest of the chapter, I focus on the organization of the judiciary following the December 11, 1990 referendum on a constitution that established Benin as a democratic country (*La Constitution de la République du Bénin*; hereafter, Constitution of 1990). Other key documents or updates to which I refer are the 2002 law on the organization of the judiciary (Loi n° 2001–37), the 2003 law on the magistrature (Loi n° 2001–35), and the 2007 law on the composition and organization of the Supreme Court (Loi n° 2004–07).[3]

Broadly, there are three levels of courts. At the apex are three High Courts. The Constitutional Court, which sits in Cotonou (Benin's economic capital), is the country's highest court on constitutional matters. The court reviews the constitutionality of laws and other regulatory acts. It is also responsible for safeguarding human rights. Noted legal scholars find that Benin's Constitutional Court is an effective and productive institution that 'enjoys great authority' (Gbaguidi & Kodjoh-Kpakpassou, 2009; see also Bourgi, 2002). The Supreme Court, which sits in Porto-Novo (Benin's administrative capital), is the highest court on administrative, judicial and public accounting matters and has three corresponding chambers and a general prosecutor's office. The Supreme Court also hears disputes over local elections. The third type of High Court in Benin is the High Court of Justice, which sits in Porto-Novo. The High Court of Justice is a specialized court that addresses allegations of treason by top officials and, in contrast to the Constitutional Court, is generally looked upon as an ineffectual institution (Gbaguidi & Kodjoh-Kpakpassou, 2009).

At the second level, under the Supreme Court, are the Courts of Appeals and Courts of First Instance (i.e., ordinary courts). There are three Courts of Appeal, in Cotonou, Abomey, and Parakou. A Court of Appeals has a criminal chamber, an indictments chamber, a so-called modern civil and social law chamber, a so-called traditional law chamber, a commercial chamber, an administrative chamber (not yet in place as of 2012), and a chamber of public accounts (not yet in place as of 2012). Each Court of Appeal is composed of a first president, the presidents of the chambers, counselors, and a general prosecutor's office, along with other staff. Below the Courts of Appeal are the courts of first instance. In 2012, there were 14 courts of first instance. (According to the 2002 reform, there will be 28 courts of first instance.) This second level of courts is marked by 'extreme overloading,' which helps fuel corruption and inefficiency at this level of the judiciary (Bierschenk, 2008, p. 105; see also Bako Arifari, 2006 and Tidjani Alou, 2006).

The third level of courts consists of reconciliation boards (*tribunaux de conciliation*). Reconciliation boards are not staffed by professional judges and do not render decisions. As indicated by their name, they were created to bring about conciliation, principally concerning disputes over land. Such disagreements are not infrequent in Benin and may be referred to the traditional law chamber at a Court of First Instance.

Women in the Rank and File of the Courts

Benin has had a woman judge since 1965, only five years after the country gained independence. Since then, what are the numbers in terms of women judges? This section provides information on where and when women first rose to key positions in the judiciary, snapshots of the percentage of women in the judiciary, and the percentage of women on the Constitutional Court and the High Court of Justice since their first mandate. But before continuing, it is important for readers unfamiliar with civil law systems to note that in Benin and in other civil law countries, judges form part of a corpus of magistrates (*corps de la magistrature*; hereafter, the magistrature). Magistrates may serve on the courts or in the ministry of justice or be seconded to other bodies (Article 1 of the 2003 law on the magistrature). In the courts, furthermore, magistrates may be appointed to be judges or public prosecutors, and it is not uncommon for a magistrate to move between the two. Thus, in this section, I will talk about judges as well as public prosecutors, who all fall under the umbrella category of magistrates.

Elisabeth Ekoué Pognon is Benin's first female judge. She was born in 1937. Pognon joined the magistrature in 1965, after obtaining a master's degree in law in 1962 in France. In her first decade of judicial service in Benin, Pognon presided over the Court of First Instance at Cotonou and served as a counselor on the Court of Appeal. In the 1970s, she was appointed counselor to the administrative chamber of the Supreme Court. In 1993, Pognon was appointed to the newly created Constitutional Court and elected by her peers on the bench to be its president. In other words, Pognon was Benin's first female judge, first woman on the Supreme Court and first female president of the Constitutional Court (Houngan Ayémonna, 2008, p. 59). Pognon now is retired from the magistrature.

Benin's first female prosecutor (*procureur de la république*) is Victoire Agbanrin-Elisha. She held that position from 1981 to 1986. Agbanrin-Elisha was born in 1944. Before entering into the office of prosecutor, Agbanrin-Elisha served as a judge on various courts. Her first judicial appointment, in 1970, was to Cotonou's Court of First Instance. Agbanrin-Elisha served on and off as a counselor on the Court of Appeal in the 1970s and 1980s. In 1988, Agbanrin-Elisha was appointed to the judicial chamber of the Supreme Court. She retired from the magistrature later that year and joined the bar (Houngan Ayémonna, 2008, pp. 80–83; International Criminal Court, 2009).

Women have risen to other leadership positions in the judiciary in Benin. Between 1993 and 2013, a woman was the president or vice president of the Constitutional Court. The High Court of Justice has had two female presidents: Clotilde Medegan-Nougbode between 2003 and 2009 and Marcelline Claire A. Gbèha Afouda since 2013. At least one woman has served as a president of a chamber in the Supreme Court; Edwige Boussari in the Supreme Court's judiciary chamber (Houngan Ayémonna, 2008, pp. 93–95). A woman has served as a president of a Court of Appeals (at Cotonou) (Attanasso, 2012, p. 120). Héloise Hessouh has been president of a Court of First Instance (at Ouidah) (Houngan Ayémonna, 2008, p. 120). The office of the public prosecutor at the Court of Appeals has been led by a woman (Attanasso, 2012, p. 120).

Complete, historical information on the percentage of women in the rank and file of the judiciary could not be obtained, but some studies provide a snapshot in time. These snapshots suggest that the percentage of women in the judiciary grew between the 1960s and 1990s but has been stable since the 1990s. One source suggests that the ratio of new female judges to new male judges has been on the decline (Houngan Ayémonna 2008, p. 77, 94, 102). In

August 1990, six or more of the 21 counselors on the Court of Appeals were women (Zantou, 2000–1, p. 112). At the end of 2007, there were four female judges on the Court of Appeals (this includes one president of a chamber) and 13 female magistrates on the courts of first instance (Houngan Ayémonna, 2008, p. 119–121).

In the High Courts, women have served as judges, but it also seems that the percentage of women has been relatively stable over the course of the 2000s and 2010s. In 2002–2003, 10 women served on the Supreme Court, making up approximately 32% of the Supreme Court (Attanasso, 2012, p. 120). That figure was reported to be eight as of the end of 2007 (Houngan Ayémonna, 2008, pp. 119–121). On the High Court of Justice, as shown in Table 8.1, there was one woman out of 13 members; that number has increased to two (Attanasso, 2012, p. 118).

Benin's first Constitutional Court also had one woman (the aforementioned Pognon) out of a total of seven counselors (see Table 8.2). Since then, every Constitutional Court has had two female counselors, making up 28.6% of the country's highest constitutional authority.

The presence of women in other positions relating to the judiciary is worth quickly reviewing. Three women have served as minister of justice in Benin. Grâce d'Almeida Adamon, a lawyer and noted women's activist, was the first woman to hold the post of minister of justice in 1995 and 1996 (Attanasso, 2012, pp. 126, 200). Marie-Elise Gbedo, also a lawyer by training, served as minister of justice and government spokesperson from 2011 to 2013. (Gbedo has also run, unsuccessfully, for president of the republic.) Gbedo was succeeded by a woman, Reckya Madougou, whose has a background in business

Table 8.1 Women on Benin's High Court of Justice, 1999–2014

Years	*Number women*	*Total*	*Percent women*
1999–2003	1	13	7.7
2004–2008	1	13	7.7
2009–2014	2	13	15.4

Source: Attanasso (2012, p. 118).

Table 8.2 Women on Benin's Constitutional Court, 1993–2014

Mandate	*Years*	*Number women*	*Total*	*Percent women*
1st	1993–1998	1	7	14.3
2nd	1998–2003	2	7	28.6
3rd	2003–2008	2	7	28.6
4th	2008–2013	2	7	28.6
5th	2013-present	2	7	28.6

Sources: Attanasso (2012, p. 118); Escobar-Lemmon, Hoekstra, Kang, & Kittilson (2015).

and served as minister of justice in 2013 (Government of Benin, February 11, 2013; Passation de charges, August 13, 2013). Geneviève Boko Nadjo, who is a member of the magistrature, served as chief of staff for two ministers of justice (Attanasso, 2012, pp. 150). The available data show that there certainly are female lawyers in Benin. In 1992, 11 out of 63 lawyers (17%) were women (Djossou-Segla, 1997, p. 13). A 2010 study reports that there were 21 women lawyers out of a total 155 (14%) (Djogbenou, 2010, p. 65). In 1992, two out of every five bailiffs were women, and one out of every six notaries was a woman (Djossou-Segla, 1997, p. 13).

In sum, information about women in the rank and file of the judiciary in Benin is limited, but we can say with confidence that women have long served as judges on the ordinary courts and sit on all three High Courts.

Gender and Representation: The Appointment Process

Broadly, Benin's appointment process uses a combination of a career (or civil service) model and an appointment model. Judges are civil servants and placed on a hierarchy of magistrates. Advancement to higher-level courts is ostensibly based on a combination of one's highest level of education and years of experience.

There are two ways of becoming a judge on the ordinary courts (I will discuss the appointment process to High Courts specifically below). The most common path is by becoming a judge in training (*auditeur de justice*, alternatively translated in English as a student judge or trainee judge). To become a judge in training, one must have a master's degree (a *maîtrise* lies somewhere between a bachelor's and a master's degree in the US) in judicial sciences or an equivalent degree and pass a national entrance exam. One must also be older than 21 but younger than 35 years of age (with exceptions granted on one's military service or number of children). Once the exam is passed, trainee judges take coursework at the *École nationale d'administration et de magistrature* (ENAM), followed by two years of judicial internship for practical training. Upon the conclusion of their internship, trainees are ranked by merit. Those trainees deemed ready for judicial service enter into the magistrature, starting at the bottom of a judicial hierarchy.

An alternative path to becoming a judge in the ordinary courts is by gaining a combination of higher education and experience in the profession (*recrutment sur titre*). Judicial officers and court clerks with a master's degree in law and more than five years of relevant experience may be qualified to move into judgeship. Ministry officials with a master's degree in law and more than five years of experience may also become judges. So may professors of judicial sciences who have taught for five or more years at a law school and lawyers with five or more years of experience. A maximum of 10% of judicial vacancies may be filled through this path.

Once they are accepted into the body of magistrates, magistrates are appointed to be judges (*juges du siège*) or public prosecutors (*magistrats du parquet*). To enhance the independence of the judiciary, judges and public prosecutors are irremovable. That is, judges are not appointed for fixed terms in the Courts of First Instance and Courts of Appeal, and they may not be transferred to another court without his or her consent (Articles 23 and 24, the 2003 law on the magistrature).

To be appointed as a counselor on the Supreme Court, one must be a magistrate or high-level jurist with 15 years or more of professional experience. The same qualifications are required to become a president of a chamber. The president of the Supreme Court who proposes names to the ministry of justice, after having consulted with the *Conseil supérieur de la magistrature* (Article 134, Constitution of 1990). Like their counterparts on the lower courts, counselors of the Supreme Court do not serve fixed terms (Article 7, 2007 law on the Supreme Court). The president of the Supreme Court is nominated for a five year term by the president of the republic after having consulted with the president of the national assembly. The president of the Supreme Court's term may be renewed once.

The appointment process in the Constitutional Court is more decentralized than that of the ordinary courts and Supreme Court. Four counselors are appointed by the office of the national assembly. Three counselors are appointed by the president of the republic. All members are appointed for a term of five years, which can be renewed once. Three members must be magistrates with a minimum 15 years of experience, two appointed by the office of the national assembly and one by the president of the republic. Two members must be high-ranking jurists, professors, or practicing lawyers with at least 15 years of experience, one appointed by the office of the national assembly and one by the president. Two members must be individuals who have an outstanding professional reputation, one appointed by the office of the national assembly and one by the president. In contrast to other positions in Benin's judiciary, the president of the Constitutional Court is elected by his or her peers for a term of five years (Article 116, Constitution of 1990). The president of the court must be either a magistrate or a high-level jurist.

The High Court of Justice is composed of the judges of the Constitutional Court (except its president), six parliamentarians, and the president of the Supreme Court. Members of the conciliation boards are nominated for two years by the ministry of justice on the proposal of the president of the Court of First Instance, after consultation with the mayor (Article 22, 2002 law on the judiciary). They must be selected among notables, retired civil servants, or citizens in the area who can read and write in French. Assessors to the conciliation boards are nominated for two years by an ordinance of the president of the Court of First Instance from the mayor's list of 12 persons.

Scholars of gender and the judiciary find that civil law countries generally favor the appointment and promotion of women judges over that of common law countries (Schultz & Shaw, 2013a, pp. 2–3). This phenomenon, at least among wealthy, stable democracies, is believed to be due to several factors. In civil law countries, an individual may become a judge at 25 years of age. If there is no sex inequality among students obtaining a master's degree in judicial sciences and passing the judicial entrance exam, then ostensibly an equal number of women and men may become judges in training. By contrast, in a common law system, judges tend to be appointed or elected only after having obtained significant experience, and many factors may prevent women from acquiring such experience. Thus, scholars expect to see a more even sex distribution of entry-level judges in civil law countries than in common law countries.

Second, scholars of gender and the judiciary suggest that promotion within the judiciary is more rational and transparent in civil law systems than in common law systems. In civil law systems, judges are civil servants and rise up the ranks through a point system that is partly based on the number of years one has served. Thus, civil law systems could be less prone to discrimination against women's advancement in the judiciary. If this were the case, the proportion of women to men in the Courts of Appeal and High Courts, should be more balanced in civil law countries than in common law countries.

Women and the Judiciary: Judges Promoting Women's Rights

While it is important not to essentialize women or men, specific women have worked to promote women's rights in Benin in and outside the courts. Female judges ruled in favor of women's property rights in the 1980s, and in their role in unifying family law under the *Code des personnes et de la famille*,[4] sought to promote equality between men and women within the household in the 1990s and 2000s.

Women's Property Rights

Before the democratic transition and under the socialist regime, female judges interpreted Article 124 of the basic law (*Loi fondamentale*),[5] which recognized equality between men and women, to mean that women could inherit property. Previously, judges were to follow so-called custom, which generally did not recognize women's property rights. As Clotilde Medegan Nougbode, mentioned above as having been president of the High Court of Justice, said in a study of women leaders (Ministère de la famille, 2011, p. 203):

> I felt that I had to break the taboo that women do not inherit land and to give women the enjoyment of a fundamental right: the right of inheritance. And yet it was the revolutionary period!

In an August 10, 1982 decision, Medegan Nougbode ruled that women had the right to inherit under Article 124 of the *Loi fondamentale*. Quoting her decision in an interview published in Houngan Ayémonna (2008, p. 70): 'the observance of these customary provisions [that only men can inherit property], which are manifestly unjust toward women, shall fall into disuse to ensure the proper administration of justice and in conformation with Article 124 of the basic law.'

Medegan Nougbode was not the only woman judge who ruled in favor of allowing women to own land. Supreme court justice Jeanne-Agnès Ayadokoun, in an interview for a book on female judges in Benin, recalled that when she was on the Court of First Instance in the 1980s, she applied Article 124 in line with Medegan Nougbode: "It is on that basis that I always allowed women, in my decisions, to inherit property" (Houngan Ayémonna, 2008, p. 98).

Women's Equality in the Family

In 2004, Benin's national assembly (for a second time) approved the *Code des personnes et de la famille*. The code stipulates that monogamy is the only recognized form of marriage. The code increases the minimum age of marriage for girls from 16 to 18. It also guarantees that girls and widows have a right to inherit and assures rights for children born out of wedlock. After having accumulated years of experience ruling on family-related disputes in the 1980s and 1990s, noted female magistrates advocated for the improvement of women's equality (as well as children's equality) in the creation of a unified family code. (For a more complete overview of the law and its adoption, see Bolle, 2004.)

When Benin transitioned to a democratic regime in 1990, leaders pledged to unify the customary code and the civil code into a unified body of laws governing the family unit. In September 1995, the executive cabinet approved a family code bill, and the bill arrived at the national assembly for its consideration and vote (Fondation Regard d'Amour, 1998, pp. 22–24). At the national assembly, however, the draft family code languished for several years. Female judges, lawyers and officials mobilized to bring the code back to life.

For example, Claire Houngan Ayémonna, who served as a judge and public prosecutor from 1990 to 2001, also led a pro-children and pro-family nongovernmental organization, Fondation Regard d'Amour (FRA). Founded in 1994, FRA strongly advocated for family law reform to promote children's rights in the family. In 1998, FRA, in partnership with UNICEF-Benin and the ministry of social protection and the condition of women (as the ministry was called at the time), organized a seminar on children's rights in the draft family code. At that time, Houngan Ayémonna was a judge on the Court of First Instance in Cotonou (Fondation Regard d'Amour, 1998, p. 9). At the seminar, participants made a point of explaining that the draft code was not only intended to help women and should not be seen as a feminist project (Fondation Regard d'Amour, 1998, pp. 9, 21, 39). Houngan Ayémonna later served as minister of the family, social protection, and solidarity, between 2001 and 2003, the period in which the family code was finally adopted by the national assembly. (As minister of the family, Houngan Ayémonna also advocated for the adoption of a law against female genital cutting and a law on reproductive health.)

On April 12, 2002, hundreds of women and men marched on the national assembly on the opening day of a new session to demand that the draft family code be considered for vote. A national branch of Women in Law and Development in Africa (WILDAF), whose coordinator was also a magistrate, organized the march with support from the United Nations Population Fund (UNFPA). Members of other women's organizations, human rights organizations, and unions as well as the ministry of family, social protection and solidarity participated. Wearing T-shirts that said, 'Finally vote on the family code,' demonstrators reached the gates of the assembly, which were closed (WILDAF, 2002, p. 8). One women's leader fainted under the heat of the sun. The plan to read their demands to the president of the assembly, Adrien Hougbedji, failed, but the activists were able to hold a press conference, and the march was covered in the news.

On June 7, 2002, the national assembly voted and approved the draft family code. The version that was approved by parliament required that spouses, before the celebration of their marriage, must choose whether to live in a polygamous or monogamous regime. In the absence of such an explicit agreement, monogamy was to be the default form of marriage. The Constitutional Court, which was led by a woman president, Conceptia Ouinsou, however, ruled that the clause on polygamy was unconstitutional (C.C. 23 décembre 2002, N° 02–144).[6] Citing Article 26 of the constitution, which provides that women and men are equal, the court decided that allowing only men to contract polygamous marriages violated the principle of equality. The court sent their decision to the national assembly, which revised the family code to eliminate the recognition of polygamy as a state-sanctioned form of marriage.

In sum, women judges in the ministry of family, in civil society and as members of the Constitutional Court played a critical role in revising Benin's family laws to promote women's and children's rights.

Challenges and Obstacles

Is Benin likely to see parity in the number of women and men in the judiciary in the near future? As stated earlier, women have occupied positions of substantial power in the judiciary in the 1990s and first half of the 2000s in Benin, but the percentage of women judges may have plateaued, or, according to Houngan Ayemonna (2008), has been on the decline. In this section, I identify three possible explanations for why the proportion of women in the judiciary appears to have stabilized or seen a downturn.

The first potential explanation concerns the pool of potential judges in training. Because the selection of judges in training is limited to those who hold a master's degrees in judicial sciences or in law, unequal numbers of women and men that meet this requirement limit opportunities for parity in the magistrature. I could not obtain information on the ratio of women to men obtaining master's degrees in judicial sciences, but in general, men have and continue to outnumber women in postsecondary education in Benin (see Figure 8.1). In 1976, there were approximately 18 women per 100 men enrolled in tertiary schools (i.e., men outnumbered women about five to one) (World Bank, 2015). In 1986, the ratio was similar, about 18 women for every 100 men. In 1996, the figure increased to 22 women per 100 men. In 2011, for every 100 men enrolled in tertiary schools in Benin, approximately 27 were women (i.e., men outnumbered women in higher education by more than three to one). If the balance of women and men obtaining master's degrees in judicial sciences mirrors that of women and men in tertiary schools, then this slow increase may help explain sex imbalances in the judiciary.

A second and related potential factor affecting the entry of women into the judiciary is gendered norms in marriage. While married women certainly work in the formal and informal sectors in Benin, women are more likely not to attend or leave school in order to marry than are men. In a nationally representative survey of people aged 15 to 29 conducted in 2011, approximately 46% of female respondents were married compared to 16% of male respondents (INSAE, 2013). About 31% of female respondents married before 18, while approximately 8% of male respondents married before 18. For respondents who quit school, women were more likely to report that they left school in order to marry than were men (5.2% versus 0.7%) (INSAE, 2013, p. 18). Having children may delay the decision to pursue a tertiary degree or take the national judges' entrance exam, and the window for becoming a judge in training opens at 21 and closes at 35, during a woman's childbearing years. Forty-four percent of female respondents had at least one child compared to 16% of male respondents. These gender gaps may help account for the relatively smaller presence of women in tertiary education than that of men.

Third, it is plausible women were or felt encouraged to join the judiciary during Benin's socialist period, which begin in the mid-1970s and lasted until

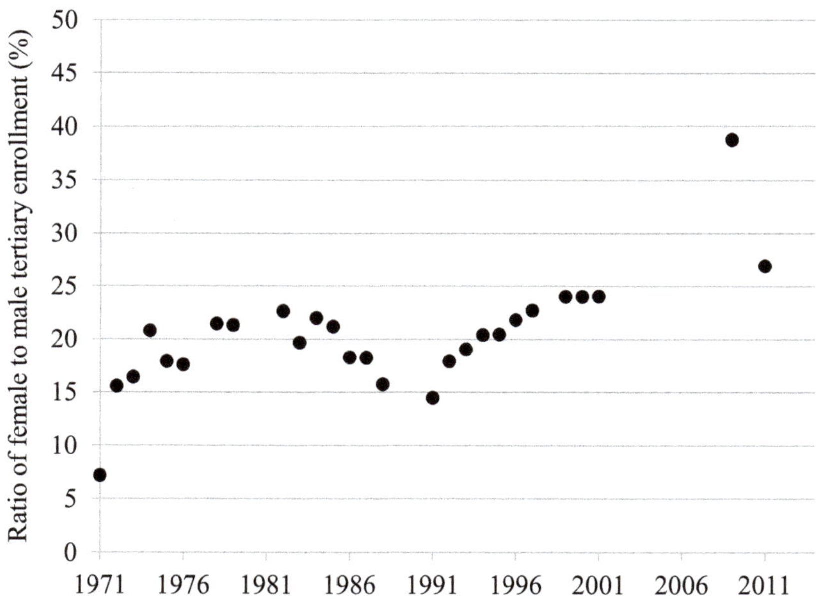

Figure 8.1 Percentage of Women to Men Enrolled at Tertiary Level Schools in Benin, 1971–2011

Notes: Gaps indicate missing data.
Source: World Bank (2015).

the democratic transition. As Attanasso (2012, p. 21) writes: 'from 1972 to 1989, one sees that women made the most significant gains in the political sphere and at different levels of public life.' The 1977 constitutional reform stated, for the first time, that 'women in the Popular Republic of Benin are legally equal to men in all aspects of political, economic, cultural, social, and family life' (*Loi fondamentale*, Article 124). This is not to say that socialist governments are always or necessarily more supportive of sex equality in state institutions. A party-level gender quota was installed at the beginning the socialist regime but eliminated in the 1980s. Nevertheless, the rise of women in the judiciary during Benin's socialist period, as compared to that of the democratic period, demands further exploration.

Conclusion

This chapter has outlined the presence of women in the judiciary in Benin. It finds that women have been active members of the magistrature since 1965. Female judges are not confined to serving in the ordinary courts; two women have served as president of Benin's Constitutional Court and women have held high-level positions within the Supreme Court and High Court of Justice. Women judges have fought for women's equality by invoking and interpreting sex equality clauses in the basic law (during the socialist authoritarian era) and in the constitution (in the democratic era). Furthermore, women who have been trained as judges (and lawyers) have also fought for women's equality outside of the courts in civil society. Nonetheless, there currently is not enough information to provide a full historical account of women in the rank and file of the judiciary. Having a clearer picture of the history of women in the judiciary is necessary for understanding whether and how women enter into and promote women's rights.

Notes

1 Translations from French to English are by the author.
2 C. C. (26 septembre 1996). N° 96–063. Retrieved from www.cour-constitutionnelle-benin.org/doss_decisions/960963.pdf
3 Loi n° 2001–37 du 27 août 2002 portant organisation judiciaire en République du Bénin, J.O. 116è année N° 2001–37 du 16 août 2005, pages 785 et suivants; Loi n° 2001–35 du 21 février 2003 portant statut de la magistrature en République du Bénin, J.O. 115è année N° 6 du 15 mars 2004, pages 171 et suivants. Retrieved from www.gouv.bj/sites/default/files/Loi_Num_2001_35_du_21_Fevrier_2003.pdf; Loi n° 2004–07 du 23 octobre 2007 portant composition, organisation, fonctionnement, et attributions de la Cour Suprême. Retrieved from www.aahjf.org/images/stories/Tous%20les%20liens/Loi_2004–07_portant_composition_organisation_fonctionnement_et_attributions_de_la_Cour_Supreme.pdf
4 Loi n° 2002–07 du 24 août 2002 portant Code des personnes et de la famille. Retrieved from www.law.yale.edu/rcw/rcw/jurisdictions/afw/benin/Benin_Family_Code.htm
5 *Loi fondamentale de la République populaire du Bénin.* (1977, amended 1984). Loi n° 84–003 du 6 mars 1984.
6 C.C. (23 décembre 2002). N° 02–144. Retrieved from www.cour-constitutionnelle-benin.org/doss_decisions/0212144.pdf

9 Ghana

The Paradox of Judicial Stagnation

Josephine Dawuni

In 2007, Justice Georgina Wood was appointed the first female chief justice of Ghana. Her rise to the top-most position of the Ghanaian judiciary was not an easy achievement, considering the enduring challenges women face in the legal and judicial professions in Ghana. Justice Wood's achievement is preceded by women 'firsts' such as Justice Annie Jiagge, the first female to be appointed as a judge (at the magistrate level) in 1954 (Dawuni, 2011). Justice Wood's ascent to the position of chief justice signaled some major changes that have been taking place within the judiciary in Ghana. Within the last couple of decades, the number of women who have joined the judiciary in Ghana has been growing; data available as of 2014 indicate women represent 23% of judges, compared to 5% in 1970. While these numbers may be taken as evidence of some positive developments in the feminization of the judiciary, there is still a long way to go to achieve gender parity for women in the judiciary in Ghana.

The goal of this chapter is to examine the presence of women judges in Ghana's judicial branch of government. Furthermore, it seeks to examine the effects of women's representation on justice delivery and on women's rights in Ghana. To this end, the chapter examines the trajectory of women joining the judiciary in Ghana. It lays out the historical challenges to women joining the judiciary and offers some explanations as to why we are seeing gradual changes in the number of women serving as judges. In this chapter, I argue that the case of Ghana presents a paradox: one of a stagnation of women in the judiciary overall in that the gender composition of women in the inferior courts is less than that of women in the superior courts. This paradox is due to the limited upward mobility of women within the rank and file of the judiciary, a scenario that has the effect of limiting, if not derailing, the attempts at achieving gender parity within the judiciary. I posit that attempts to achieve gender parity must be matched with both upward mobility of women (in terms of promotions) and inward mobility of women (in terms of more women joining the bench at all levels of the courts, especially at the lower levels).

The chapter proceeds by first tracing the historical development of women in the judiciary in Ghana and drawing linkages to existing studies on gender and judging. Next is a description of the judicial structure of Ghana, which sets the context for situating the position of women within each court rank.

A discussion on the representation of women on the bench is then presented, which ties into the perceived contributions of women judges. The concluding section engages in a discussion of ongoing challenges confronting female judges and provides a summary of some strategies to help move from stagnation to growth in the number of women judges in Ghana.

Historical Overview of Women on the Bench

Ghana's legal system derives from the British common law, a leftover effect of colonization. Understanding the current trajectory of Ghana's judicial composition requires a foray into the impact of colonial education policies which still reverberate across Africa, producing mixed results, some of which include documented adverse effects on the legal structures of these countries (Cobbah, 1987).

For one, under British colonialism, existing customary practices that sought to empower women were subjected to the British 'repugnancy' clause. All customary laws found inapplicable, especially to the extent that they were seen as incompatible with the British role of women, were struck down (Akpamgbo, 1977). Ghana gained independence from Britain in 1957, and though political freedom was attained, the legal, bureaucratic and educational systems put in place by the British were continued, and some exist to date. The common law tradition was inherited and the judicial system established reflected courts under the British system. This meant that the deleterious practice under the British whereby the legal profession was and still is to a large extent viewed as the primary domain of men to the exclusion of women was also inherited (Joireman, 2001).

The educational systems set up by the British aimed at educating a handful—often, males—in the basic administration of the bureaucracy. Of the few females who received education from the missionaries, they were usually educated in fields which were seen as necessary for housekeeping such as sewing, cooking and crafts, thus limiting their upward mobility into institutions of higher learning such as the university and law school (Kamau, 2013). Unlike other Western jurisdictions such as the United States, where women were legally barred from joining the law profession, there were no legal bars to women joining the profession in Ghana. However, the Faculty of Law at the University of Ghana and the Ghana School of Law maintained a monopoly over the training of lawyers in Ghana for decades, resulting in entry into law school becoming a very competitive endeavor. Thus the pool of females entering law school initially was very limited, considering that women had been subjected to discriminatory modes of education, which emphasized masculine ability over the feminine. This phenomenon gradually changed as more females made it through the secondary education system, thus allowing for more women to apply to university and specifically to the hitherto male-dominated law school.

The challenges barring women from rising to occupy judicial positions in Ghana were closely tied to socioeconomic and cultural factors as well.

Cultural practices that placed an emphasis on the education of the male child tended to direct girls into professions such as teaching and nursing. The mounting cost of primary and secondary education further complicated the choices parents had to make when deciding which child to enroll in school. Gradual cultural changes in understanding the right of girls to education have increased opportunities for women to acquire a college degree, thus resulting in equal opportunities for women to gain a law degree and be positioned to take up positions in the judiciary. The traditional notion that a highly educated woman will have problems finding a marriage partner has gradually declined, thus allowing women to enter professions which were hitherto considered the domain of men.

The political development in most African countries and the resulting dominance of centralized executives further complicated the opportunity for women to pursue the judiciary as a career path. In the early 1960s, most African countries gained independence from their colonial masters. However, before the new nation-states could begin to build upon their new institutional and educational systems, the continent was plunged into military coups d'état, resulting in military dictatorships that swept the continent between the mid-1960s and the early 1990s. In Ghana, for instance, military dictatorships suspended constitutions and threatened judges who made decisions that were viewed as unfavorable to the military junta (Harvey, 1966). The open threats to the judiciary culminated in the deaths of three judges of the High Court in 1982—two men and a woman.[1] The judiciary was thus seen as an unsafe profession—for both men and women. The constant fear of intimidation and intrusions into the works of judges made the profession one that was not very welcoming for women. Even though the constitution provided for judicial independence, the salaries and benefits of judges were still subject to the control of the executive branch. As VonDoepp (2005; 2006) has argued, across many African countries, the power of presidents to staff the courts with sympathetic members often resulted in 'court packing,' typically with men sympathetic to the ruling party.

The advent of democratic governance in Ghana in 1992 paved the way for the beginning of judicial independence and a gradual development of the legitimacy of the judiciary. However the structural problems within the government after years of military rule were further compounded by the austerity measures set in place by the World Bank in the 1980s. Economic hardships meant that government workers were often not paid on time. The conditions of service of judges were dismal, often characterized by minimal pay, lack of benefits and no allowances for housing and transportation. Thus, many lawyers chose to join private practice rather than the judicial service as judges. These economic factors combined made judges highly susceptible to bribery and corruption, hence reducing the prestige of the profession (Judicial corruption in Ghana, 2011).

A combination of the above challenges posed by colonial education legacies, gender-based discriminatory sociocultural practices, military dictatorship, economic austerity and low public perceptions of the judiciary contributed to make the judiciary a weak institution. The above-mentioned variables combined to create a perception of the judiciary as dangerous and unstable employment where job tenure was not guaranteed. The intrusions of the dominant executive into the appointment and removal of judges resulted in the judiciary being viewed as an institution that had lost its prestige as independent and impartial.

The result was a judiciary that came to be seen as a women-hostile institution due to the high male presence, with limited opportunities for women's entry or upward mobility. A cumulation of these factors contributed enormously to steering women away from the judiciary and into other areas of legal practice.

Court Structure and Organization

The judiciary in Ghana is two-tiered; Article 126 of the constitution establishes the first tier, which consists of the Superior Courts of Judicature comprising the Supreme Court of Ghana, the Courts of Appeal, the High Court and Regional Tribunals. Article 126 establishes the second tier of courts, classified as the Inferior Courts, which consist of the Magistrates' Courts, Circuit Courts, Customary Courts and other tribunals as may be set up by parliament. Figure 9.1 provides a diagrammatic representation of the court structure in Ghana.

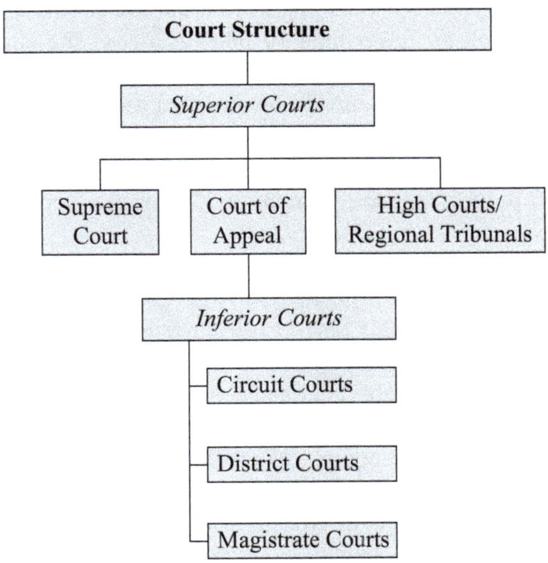

Figure 9.1 The Court Structure in Ghana

The Superior Courts of Judicature

The 1992 constitution of Ghana provides in Chapter Eleven, Articles 125–162 for the structure of the judiciary. There is only one Supreme Court and one Court of Appeal, both located in the capital city of Accra. Each of the 10 district capitals in the country has at least one High Court. In 1972, under the ruling dictatorship of the National Liberation Council, a decree was passed abolishing the Supreme Court and making the Court of Appeal the highest court in the land. The constitution of the Third Republic reversed this in 1979 and re-established the court system as it existed under the 1969 constitution. The 1992 constitution subsequently maintained the two-tier system, with a few modifications (Ghana Judicial Service, 2014). As provided in Articles 129–135, the Supreme Court is the final Court of Appeal in all matters and has original, appellate and supervisory jurisdiction in cases.

The Supreme Court is comprised of the chief justice and no fewer than nine justices. The fact that there is no limit on the number of judges who may serve on the Supreme Court allows for presidents to nominate as many people to sit on the court as they deem necessary. Currently, there are 13 judges on the Supreme Court, of whom five are women, including the chief justice. This brings the female representation to 38%, the highest proportion of women judges within one court ever. By Article 128(4) a candidate for the Supreme Court must have served at least 15 years as a lawyer in good standing and be of a high moral character and proven integrity.

The second highest court is the Court of Appeal. It enjoys only appellate jurisdiction and appeals can be brought from the lower courts. It consists of the chief justice and no fewer than 10 other justices. The chief justice has the power to appoint a Supreme Court judge to sit as an additional Court of Appeal judge for a specified time. To be qualified as a justice on the Court of Appeal, a person must have at least 12 years as a standing lawyer and be of high moral character and proven integrity (Article 136(3)). In mid-2015, out of a total of 27 judges, nine are women, or 33% women judges on the Court of Appeal.

The third court within this tier is the High Court. The High Court consists of the chief justice and no fewer than 20 High Court judges. By Article 140 of the constitution, the High Court has original jurisdiction in all civil and criminal matters. Specialized High Courts such as the fast track courts, commercial courts and human rights courts may be established by the chief justice. In addition, the High Court also has appellate jurisdiction and is bound by the decisions of the two higher courts. Of profound importance is the fact that by Article 140(2), the High Court has the power to enforce the principles of the fundamental human rights of citizens contained in the constitution. High Court judges, in addition to showing good moral character and high integrity, need to have 10 years of experience as a lawyer (Article 139(4)). The appointment of the chief justice and other justices of the Superior Courts are vested in the president, subject to the approval of parliament, acting on the advice of the Judicial Council of Ghana. Currently, women constitute 19% of the judges on the High Court.

The Inferior Courts

The qualifications of candidates and the jurisdiction and the functions of the inferior courts are subject to the Judicial Service Act of 1960, Courts Act of 1993, as amended in 2002, and other legislative instruments. Candidates must have high moral character, proven integrity and at least five years standing as a lawyer. In order to help deal with the backlog of cases facing the courts, in 2008, another stream of magistrates was formed, known as the career magistrates, consisting of individuals who have no law degree but have received two years of training through the Ghana School of Law to sit as judges. Efforts have been made to provide continuing education through the Judicial Training Institute and also provide paid leave for these magistrates to receive a law degree. With the acquisition of a law degree, these judges can then be promoted up the ranks of the judicial ladder. Based on available data gathered during fieldwork for this project in 2013, out of a total of 117 career magistrates, 23 are women, representing 19% of the total number of career magistrates in Ghana.

The inferior courts are normally the Courts of First Instance, though the higher courts have original jurisdiction in some cases. The decisions of the lower courts can be appealed to the higher courts. The lower courts, notably the District and Circuit Courts, are interestingly where fewer women judges are to be found, with women comprising only 23% of all judges in the three lower courts, once again based on data gathered in 2013. Interestingly, these are also the courts where most female litigants approach the Courts of First Instance in matters such as domestic violence, divorce, spousal support and minor civil and criminal offences.

Gender and Representation

Ghana maintained the British common law tradition after attaining independence in 1957. Like other common law countries, judges are not regarded as career or civil servants. However, unlike other common law countries, Ghana does not use elections or appointment commissions when it comes to appointing judges. Ghana, though a common law country, has a judicial appointment process which appears to involve a clever marriage between the common law and civil law systems. The first step involves acquiring a law degree and pupillage served after graduation from law school. The next step is somewhat analogous to the civil law system, where entry into the legal profession is based on taking a competitive exam, though there is no requirement for going to a special judgeship school.

The requirements for judicial appointments in Ghana and the rules on qualifications and the process for the different types of courts are contained in a number of laws, including the 1992 constitution of Ghana and other legislation such as the Judicial Service Act (1960), and Courts Act (1993, as amended in 2002). Overall, the evidence suggests that female judges in Ghana have not faced any specific gender-based discrimination in being appointed to the bench. While Ghana has no instiutionalized affirmative action policy for increasing the number of female judges, no tacit attempts have been made for a fair gender representation on the bench as contained in the Rome Statute, Article 36(8)(a)(iii) for the International Criminal Court.

Table 9.1 shows the number of female judges at the different courts from 1970 to 2013 in Ghana. As of 2013, while there has been no exponential growth in the percentage of female judges, there has been a steady growth in the number of women joining the bench when compared to earlier periods from 1970.[2]

The data presented in Table 9.1 show that since 1996, there has been a consistent, albeit slow, growth in the number of women taking a career in the judiciary. For instance, between 1970 and 1979, we saw a stagnation at 6%; despite the missing data for the years 1979–1996, we see that beginning in 2003, 11 years after the advent of democracy, the number had risen to 23% in 2013.

A person can become a judge after meeting the minimum years of legal experience required by the particular court one is applying to. The process is similar for most candidates who wish to be judges; it starts with filling out the application packet, taking an exam and attending an interview by a selection panel. Once the candidate is successful, he or she is assigned to a judge to shadow for a few weeks and is then assigned a court. In some cases, applicants may be assigned to a court without a period of shadowing a senior judge if there is an urgent need to staff the court. The Judicial Training Institute, which was established in 1965, provides orientation for newly appointed judges and ongoing legal education for judges and magistrates on an ad hoc basis.

Table 9.1 Gender Distribution of Judges in All Courts in Ghana, 1970–2013

Year	*Men*	*%*	*Women*	*%*	*Total*
1970	166	92	10	5	176
1972	170	94	9	5	179
1973	149*	93	11	6	160
1974	187*	93	13	6	200
1979	185*	93	12	6	197
1996	131	85	22	14	153
2003	191	86	31	13	222
2011	250	77	74	22	324
2012	262	75	80	22	348
2013	256	76	78	23	334

*No data available on the Supreme Court.

The Judicial Council (JC) plays a critical role in the appointment of judges. The constitution mandates that in the appointment of judges, the chief justice shall act upon the advice of the Judicial Council. The Judicial Council consists of lawyers, judges from each rank of the courts, four people who are not lawyers and are appointed by the president, a representative of the judicial service staff and a chief, amongst others (Article 153). The gendered composition of the JC is not very encouraging. Out of the 18 members, only five are women. Yet, while there is no record of their proceedings to be analyzed, the mere fact that women represent only 27% of the Judicial Council should be a cause for concern when vetting of female candidates is taking place.

It is worth noting that female candidates who have met all the qualifications and skills needed for the job have not had any difficulties gaining the consent of the Judicial Council. In general, once judges are appointed they are guaranteed tenure until the legal age of retirement or if accused of professional misconduct. The chief justice, acting upon a resolution passed by two-thirds of the Judicial Council, can remove a judge on grounds of sickness or other stated misconduct. Constitutional guarantees of equality under the law, coupled with legislative provisions in the Courts Act (as amended) aimed at making entry into the judiciary one based on merit, have paved the way for engendering the judiciary.

Based on data gathered from the judicial service of Ghana available at the end of 2013, Ghana presents an interesting paradox and challenges any trickle-up hypothesis. Female judges in Ghana have risen to the top in terms of percentage of women within the two High Courts—the Supreme Court and the Court of Appeal, coming in at 38% and 33%, respectively. However, the lower courts show dismal numbers of women judges—19% at the High Court and 23% at the inferior courts. Consequently, I argue that when it comes to increasing the gender composition of the bench in Ghana, progress is yet to be achieved. The percentage of women on the Supreme Court outnumbers those of the lower courts. These women are not token women. They have risen to the top of the court, having served on the lower courts; thus their years of service, combined with their proven integrity and moral character have landed them a place on the highest court in the country.

The evidence unequivocally suggests that the growth of women in the judiciary in Ghana has stagnated at the lower courts, with the higher courts having more gender representation than the lower courts. While extant studies have fully debunked the 'trickle-up' approach to feminizing the judiciary (Malleson, 2003a), Ghana's experience presents a new model—what I choose to call the paradox of stagnation—demonstrating that the few gains that have been made in feminizing the upper echelons of the judiciary in Ghana have not been met with an equal feminization at the lower ranks. By observing the case of Ghana, I hypothesize that in the long run, as the women at the lower courts 'trickle-up' to the top, and more women join the bench, there will be a more uniform distribution of women on the bench.

This hypothesis falls outside the ambit of this chapter and forms the basis of another ongoing research project.

Women and the Judiciary: Contributions

The foregoing discussion has sought to provide an overview of the general pathways women take to the bench in Ghana. But what we might also want to understand in the case of Ghana is why should we be concerned about the presence of women on the bench? For feminist legal scholars, the questions of why the judiciary should have a good representation of women judges and whether women judges make a difference are still relevant. The arguments and findings reached, though still largely inconclusive, are generally applicable to the context of Ghana. In the following discussion, I offer some observations on how female judges in Ghana have made contributions to the judiciary as an institution and to the administration of justice as a whole.

Since the appointment of Justice Annie Jiagge as the first female magistrate in Ghana and the whole British Commonwealth in 1954 (Dawuni, 2011), female judges in Ghana have slowly contributed in diversifying the gender composition of the bench. Though the numbers remain low, the presence of women at all levels of the court structure lends a minuscule sense of legitimacy to the court as an inclusive institution. A representative judiciary—in terms of gender composition—is critical to promoting the legitimacy of the judiciary in the eyes of citizens, and especially women, who access the courts seeking justice.

Women judges have contributed to making a difference. Based on the seminal work of Gilligan (1982), proponents of the difference argument have sought to make the case that men and women think and act differently and thus such differences do and can find their way into the courtroom and decisions made by judges. Critics, however, contend that an unqualified fascination with the theory of difference can lead to the essentializing of women and the possibility of charges of judicial bias (Malleson, 2006). Still, a recurring theme among some of the judges interviewed for this project was that the presence of women on the bench has helped to make a difference for women's lives.[3] A Supreme Court judge, in response to the question, do female judges make a difference, noted thus:

> Judges cannot be promoters of women's rights, because you cannot enforce it through the judgments we make. The constitution grants equality under the law, hence men and women should be accorded the same equality. Having said that, you cannot deny the fact that a female judge who is faced with a life experience of, for example, an unfaithful marriage, will not empathize more with a woman in the court going through the same thing, in the same way a male judge who is being unfaithful may not be harsh on a man accused of infidelity. Nonetheless one can thus make the argument

> that through the enforcement and interpretation of the laws female judges do promote the rights of women.[4]

Other judges were, however, quick to qualify their response by noting that women judges should not be expected to make a difference in the lives of other women merely because they share the same gender. A High Court judge noted the danger of female judges applying a different lens stating:

> I do not see myself as a woman, I am human and it is difficult for me to understand gender constructs. I did not grow up thinking that way. We should see every human for who they are and help them whichever way they need.[5]

Though the difference argument has galvanized much of the debate on gender and judging, some female judges did point out that femininity allows female judges to understand better the whole context under which a woman may be seeking justice. The lived experiences and socialization of individual women allow them to understand what female litigants may be going through. Unsurprisingly, all the judges were quick to point to the need for judicial impartiality and holding the oath of their office to be fair to all parties in a case.

Some judges noted that they have the mandate to use their judicial discretion to settle matters quickly and effectively to ensure that justice is done. For instance, in an effort to promote and protect the rights of women victims in domestic violence cases, advocates argue for the use of judicial power to respond by adjudicating domestic violence cases quickly and working closely with others concerned such as the police and health services to protect the identity of victims and to give them the needed support services such as medical and counseling services (Tetteh-Charway, 2012).

I argue based on the responses that women judges in Ghana are indeed making a difference not only in the lives of women, but also in subtly changing the legal norms and traditions within the judiciary. Female judges are challenging patriarchal norms, for instance, by insisting that they are called 'my lady' instead of the traditional 'my lord' which was inherited from the British. Some judges are also making a difference by ensuring that their courtrooms are conducive to hearing cases involving minors and victims of rape by providing protective screens to shield the victims during court hearings. Through these actions and initiatives, women judges are contributing to gradually changing the judicial culture both within courtrooms and between judges and lawyers and among judges. None of the respondents openly admitted to their conscious roles in making a difference in the lives of female litigants. Though there were some responses that indicated that women judges felt it was a natural inclination or one based on their socialization to protect women litigants. Most interviewees were quick to point out that judges have a primary duty to remain impartial. As one Supreme Court judge noted, in response to the question, do you think women judges bring a different perspective to their roles as judges? 'I do not think so. In writing my judgments my concern is to get it right, emotions do not play a part, if it does it is very negligible.'[6] The fact that the judge recognizes that her emotions as a woman may play a 'negligible' role is quite telling of the difficulty in separating the socialization of women and how they decide their cases. This is in consonance with the inconclusive findings of existing research.

These responses do indicate that female judges appear to have unspoken restrictions on their ability to represent the interests of women. These restrictions appear to be both self-imposed and also ones that may be imposed by the institutional norms of impartiality and nonbias. The responses given have also been indicative of the fact that while women judges do not think that their decisions made a difference in the lives of other women, the fact that they do recognize that their lived experiences can and do impact their decisions is an indicator, albeit minimal, that women judges can and do make a difference. It is not the expectation of this study that female judges must necessarily be advocates for women's rights. However, the fact that the presence of women in the judiciary is making the institution representative, legitimate and diversified is a good starting point. Further studies will need to be conducted to ascertain the extent to which women judges may actually be promoting women's rights through a comparison of the judicial reasoning of male and female judges in similar cases. For now, that project is beyond the ambit of this study.

Female judges in Ghana are perceived to contribute to caseload and courtroom management through strategies aimed at paying closer attention to detail. Some scholars, however, argue that the perception that women pay closer attention to detail may be in response to the need for women who make it to the bench not only to work as hard as their male counterparts, but to work even harder in order to break down any stereotypes that women are less productive than men. In her study of women in the Brazilian judiciary, Junqueira (2003, 447) points out that 'attention to detail and meticulous argumentation, always backing up decisions with reference to case history, then represents a conscious female strategy, in contrast to greater self-confidence among male judges that allows them to make decisions more independently.'

One of my respondents recounted a story of a petition that was made before her by a man who wanted to take a young girl out of the jurisdiction. She noted during the court proceedings that the girl did not seem to know the man; by reading the body language of the child, she could tell that the man was no relation of hers. She goes on to state:

> women by nature are observant, that quality adds up to the female judges and makes us more meticulous in the way we handle cases, I do not think that femininity comes in our decisions, but it may help you arrive at a conclusion of the case, but it will not be the main factor.[7]

Though this argument of women's attention to detail as compared to their male counterparts remains highly subjective, the totality of the argument that women judges are often subjected to higher standards of scrutiny than men may indeed end up being productive.

Women judges in Ghana, it seems, are contributing to changing the societal perception of the judiciary as a corrupt institution. Women judges are generally perceived as being less corruptible than their male counterparts. The judiciary, though insulated from the public discourse and pressures through the principle of judicial independence, is still not free from high levels of corruption in society. Cardinal (2013) in her study of Syrian judges notes that women judges are viewed as having 'clean hands,' meaning they do not accept bribes and are not easily susceptible to corruption.

Women judges in Ghana are also contributing to changing norms on gender representation. This can be viewed in two ways. First, the idea that more women joining the upper ranks of the judicial ladder is contributing to creating a perception of the judiciary as reflective of the society it represents (Hunter, 2008; Rackley, 2013). Second, the idea that more women judges are bringing peer mentoring to the profession. As one respondent noted:

> there are many opportunities for women to decide what to do with a legal career, now from law school your options are many. In the past we did not have many women on the bench so the judiciary was not seen as a place for women, there were very few role models and it was not easy to get in touch with them.[8]

A reasonable number of respondents noted that their decision to join the bench was based on listening to and observing women judges in courtroom. The growing presence of women on the bench has also invariably served to encourage young women to join the bench, even if at a slower pace than would be preferred by feminist legal scholars.

The presence of women on the bench can arguably be viewed as contributing to the development of the democratic legitimacy of the judiciary. The courts exist to represent the needs of all citizens through principles of fairness, equity and impartiality. However, women who access the courts have often felt the composition of the courts, with mostly male judges, meant that they might not be accorded a fair and equitable hearing based on their gender. It can thus be argued that the growth in the number of women judges is contributing to changing the institutional climate of the profession by fostering the creation of a gender-responsive environment within the courts. Changes in institutional culture can and do gradually transform into policy outcomes that can have wider impacts on society at large. As O'Connor and Yanus (2010) have argued, courtroom environments conducive to the work of female judges, such as the respect and collegiality a female judge enjoys from her male colleagues, may also translate into a courtroom where litigants are treated with respect; this can further translate into the language used in the reasoning of the court's decisions.

Other ways in which women judges are contributing to the judiciary is through nonjudicial functions and strategies to advance the rights of women both within the profession and outside. The extrajudicial roles judges play in addressing gendered challenges in the work place need to be recognized (Feenan, 2009). One such strategy has been through associations aimed at equipping women judges to fight for women's rights. The Ghana chapter of the International Association of Women Judges (GHIAWJ) was inaugurated in 2010 as a local chapter of the parent organization which was established in 1991 in the United States. In addressing the group of women judges, Chief Justice Wood noted thus: 'It is intended to equip us so that we can help to eliminate these stereotypical ideas, beliefs and values that could promote gender discrimination and remove obstacles to women and children's access to justice'(Ghana News Agency, 2010).

The chief justice was also quick to stress that the association's membership should not be seen as excluding male judges, rather that men were welcome to form partnerships with women to achieve the goals of the association. The then president of the association, a justice of the Supreme Court, Justice Rose Owusu, also pointed out the centrality of addressing women's issues; she opined: 'Our aims and objectives are to ensure gender equality in accessing justice, ensuring fairness and equality in our various courts while making the judicial systems and procedures accessible to all; in particular women' (Ghana News Agency, 2010).

Since its inauguration, the GHIAWJ has undertaken programs aimed at strengthening the capacity of female judges not only in Ghana but across other African countries. In a Global Leadership Program organized by the GHIAWJ for female judges, the chief justice again reiterated the purpose of having more female judges for promoting equity, fairness and justice which together increase the legitimacy of judicial institutions and contribute to the democratic development and growth of the nation (CJ solicit[s] support, 2013). As part of their efforts to address gender issues, the GHIAWJ has held meetings with female chiefs to educate them on domestic violence, rape and human trafficking. In these meetings, the goal of GHIAWJ has been to sensitize female chiefs to educate their constituents not to settle domestic violence and rape cases out of court.

The current chief justice of Ghana and the first woman to be appointed to that position has also been a key proponent of women's rights. As part of her efforts to reform the judicial service, she has undertaken the establishment of two courts specifically focused on prosecuting cases of domestic violence. In addition, the construction of the Gender Justice Center is underway to provide a comprehensive one-stop shop for cases concerning women and juveniles; it will also host a play-room and temporary shelter for women subjected to violence. The center is also supposed to provide training programs to help women seek economic ventures as channels of empowerment.

The foregoing discussion has sought to draw some general observations on how women judges are contributing to transforming the judiciary in Ghana. These contributions include diversifying the gender composition of the judiciary, introducing a gendered voice to court procedures and case management, changing societal perceptions of judicial corruption, advancing the symbolic and substantive representation of women, increasing the democratic legitimacy of the courts and advancing the rights of women through judicial interpretation and other nonjudicial functions.

It is worth sounding a word of caution that the analyses contained herein are based on the responses of interviewees and may be subject to their self-identified inputs only. However, what I have sought to do is to focus not only on the responses but also to highlight some of the ways in which judges have both consciously and unconsciously contributed to engendering the profession through their extrajudicial activities such as mentoring of junior judges and enforcing the rights of women through associations such as GHIAWJ.

Challenges and Obstacles

From the foregoing discussion, the future looks bright for increasing the number of women on the bench in Ghana. Through an in-depth analysis of interview responses, I have demonstrated some of the contributions women judges are making. Nonetheless, the judiciary as a whole in Ghana faces many challenges that need to be addressed and some of these challenges remain gender specific. The general restraints include the absence and inadequacy of physical resources such as well-equipped courtrooms, well-trained court clerks, adequate and safe housing for judges and provision of security personnel for all judges.

Some of these challenges manifest in a particularly gendered way and it is to this discussion I now turn. First, female judges, despite the high levels of collegiality they enjoy with their male counterparts, still have to negotiate gendered boundaries on a daily basis in their courtrooms. Some of these challenges manifest in the form of male lawyers who come to the courtroom with stereotypical notions of the female judge as being rude or ill-prepared to handle the case. To forestall some of these challenges, some judges have adopted strategies that ensure that their courtroom management skills cannot be faulted. These are done by ensuring that they are firm yet respectful to lawyers and their clients, and that they are punctual and do not adjourn cases without merit. Respondents noted that once they laid down the ground rules, they were respected. Though this solves a problem of attempts to test the authority of the female judge, it is problematic that women judges have to take extra steps to assert their authority in the courtroom. Why do women judges have to resist perceptions of timidity and ill-preparedness and being portrayed as hostile and disrespectful more so than their male counterparts?

Infrastructural challenges are a common problem in all courts in Ghana, but these also affect women disproportionately in some courts. For instance due to the lack of facilities to accommodate all the courts, some courts are housed in temporary buildings with no restrooms for judges and litigants. For instance one Circuit Court judge had to leave her courtroom and travel to another office location in order to use the restroom. Female judges, especially those in the lower courts, also face issues with security because judges in the lower courts do not have security detail in the form of police officers protecting them at work, as is given to all judges in the superior courts.

Another commonly cited challenge was the issue of transfers to other regions of the country that, though expected, had the effect of disrupting family life, especially for female judges, who are often the primary caregivers for children and older family members. Through such transfers, women judges are confronted with making a choice whether to leave the profession and save their family or stay in the profession and lose out on their children and husband.

There is the added burden and social expectations by feminist scholars and women's organizations, on female judges to make a 'difference' in the lives of women. Scholars such as Hunter (2008), drawing on Gilligan (1982), have argued that women judges can, and in some cases, do make a difference both in their judicial decisions and in other modes of representation. To this, other scholars (Malleson, 2003a) have counterargued that an unqualified fixation on the difference female judges make can be real or imagined. The chief justice of Ghana, in swearing in new judges, commended them to be firm in their courtrooms to both litigants and unruly lawyers, but also to listen attentively to the case in order to make the 'best' decision. While this speech was directed at an incoming class of 14 judges (of which six were women), it can be said that female judges do have an undue burden of making their 'best' better than the performance of their male counterparts.

While most of the judges interviewed were divided on the role their gender plays in their decision-making, they were all agreed on one thing—they had to apply the law as it was and not try to address women's issues directly in the courtroom. Junqueria's (2003) analysis of female judges being reduced to 'asexual beings' is confirmed in this study. The situation in Ghana is consistent with existing studies and thus raises the question: why do women judges have to downplay or 'disown' their femininity or pretend to be less gender aware when indeed gender plays a role in the cases that come before them?

Conclusion

Women are gradually beginning to find their niche in the Ghanaian judiciary, demonstrating that women do have the necessary qualifications and merit to fill the positions. The discussion presented here strongly suggests that women are making a contribution to the judiciary through the development of democratic ideals of equity, fairness and representation, values that are highly espoused by the judiciary. The judiciary in Ghana, however, remains a male-dominated institution. While some changes have resulted in an increase in the number of women from 5% in 1970 to 23% in 2013, the numbers are still dismal, considering that more women are joining the legal profession than ever before. With the proliferation of private universities providing degrees in law and improved working conditions and opportunities for the upward mobility of women, it is yet to be seen if more women will join the pool of qualified candidates for the judiciary.

Clearly, female judges in Ghana are not a monolithic group. Female judges realize that there is more yet to be done; the appointment of a female chief justice and the near gender parity on the Supreme Court should not be taken to mean that women are represented enough on the bench. Women still have to face the challenge of working harder to make their judgments stand the test of time and not be overturned on appeal. Women judges will also have to serve as role models for future women judges through a demonstration of ingenuity, creativity and fairness.

In conclusion, I proffer three arguments for the importance of increasing the number and intensity of the pathways for feminizing the judiciary in Ghana. First, the representation of women is a test of democratic principles of equality, inclusiveness and diversity. Second, the continued increase in the number of women will also serve as a test of the judiciary as an independent institution operating on principles of merit. As changes in society take place and patriarchal and sexist norms are challenged and broken down, we expect to see more women fill the top positions in the judiciary—a change that is already taking place. Third, concerted efforts by the judicial council, the executive and women's organizations will attest to the government's commitment to international and regional legal norms aimed at promoting diversity and women's rights to equal employment and nondiscrimination.

The percentage of women in the superior courts is currently higher than the inferior courts—38% at the Supreme Court, 33% at the Court of Appeal, and 19% at the High Court, as compared to 23% at the lower courts. While existing studies have argued either in favor of, or against the 'trickle-up' theory of increasing the number of women in the judiciary, the case of Ghana appears to bear out the trickle-up thesis in the sense that between 1970 and 2015, we have witnessed a higher percentage of women in the Superior Courts of Judicature. Interestingly, the Ghanaian situation presents a new paradox; what we see is a stagnation of women at the upper echelons of the bench with little growth in the number of women in the inferior courts. The result thus accords with Rackley's (2013) argument that women are now 'treading water' and not much growth seems to be happening in creating a critical mass of women on the bench. The current chief justice has been credited with promoting a good number of women to the higher courts (subject to them fulfilling the criteria). It remains to be seen if subsequent chief justices will maintain this trend once Justice Wood retires. More still needs to be done for a total overhaul of the judiciary to achieve near gender parity. With women accounting for a meager 23% presence on the bench, achieving a gender balance in the judiciary will require systematic educational, institutional, cultural and political changes directly aimed at feminizing the judiciary in Ghana.

Notes

1 The death of the three judges was said to have been ordered by the military ruler, Fl. Lt. Jerry John Rawlings. The judges were Mrs. Justice Cecilia Koranteng-Addow, Mr. Justice Kwadwo Agyei Agyepong, and Justice Fred Poku Sarkodie. This act of impunity, and especially one committed against the female judge who was said to be a nursing mother, scared many women from joining the bench. For more on this story see Rawlings ordered killing of judges (2003)

2 This data is derived from the author's coding of the number of male and female judges based on information derived from the human resources unit of the Judicial Service of Ghana in 2013 during fieldwork. Due to the poor data management system employed by the Judicial Service, the author had to manually count and identify judges and their gender based on the names on the list provided by the human resources unit.

3 This study involved interviews with 18 female judges chosen from all levels of the judicial structure. The questions for the interviews were grouped into four main parts. Questions sought to analyze and understand some of the general explanations for the traditional low numbers of women on the bench, the pathways women took to joining the judiciary, the perceived contributions women made on the bench and the continuing challenges faced by female judges.

4 Author interview with a Supreme Court judge.

5 Author interview with a High Court judge.

6 Author interview with a Supreme Court judge.

7 Author interview with a High Court judge.

8 Author interview with Supreme Court Judge.

10 Rwanda

Balancing Gender Quotas and an Independent Judiciary

Jean-Marie Kamatali[1]

Women shall be 'granted a least thirty percent of posts in decision-making organs.'[2] This provision in Rwanda's constitution has been credited with the recent achievements in women's participation in Rwanda's institutions of government. Some of these achievements include bringing the number of women cabinet members in the current government to 50% and bringing the parliament to be ranked first in the world—for many years now—for women's representation in a single or lower house of parliament.

This progress has been the subject of a number of studies trying to explain the policies and outcomes behind it.[3] Most of these studies however, have focused on women in the executive and legislative branches rather than on women in the judiciary. While quotas and affirmative action policies like the ones included in Rwanda's constitution may make sense for increasing the number of women in the executive and legislative branches, their application in the judiciary raises a number of questions, particularly because of the need for judicial independence and for more objective criteria in hiring judges. The extent to which Rwanda has been able to balance this constitutional obligation, on the one hand, and the need for the judiciary's independence, on the other, is the subject of this chapter.

The chapter first presents the history of women's involvement in Rwanda's judiciary; second, it analyzes the current situation of women in the judiciary and explains how Rwanda has tried to combine the objective requirements for an independent judiciary with the need to meet the constitutional quota requirements; finally, the chapter examines whether and how women in the judiciary today have had an impact in promoting women's issues in Rwanda.

Historical Overview: A Long Way Forward for Rwandan Women

Rwanda Women in the Law and Judicial Institutions of the Rwandan Monarchy

Before colonialism, Rwanda was governed by a well-structured and powerful monarchy. The laws and institutions of the monarchy considered a woman as incapable and therefore in permanent male guardianship (Muhayeyezu, 1978, p. 25). When married, a woman was under the authority of her husband, who was the head of the conjugal home. She had no authority over the family property, her children and, to some extent, her own body. They all belonged to her husband (Ibid.). When divorced, she had to return to her father, leaving the children to her husband, and fell back under her father's authority. When widowed, she was under guardianship of her brothers-in-law, who would take over the rights and duties of her deceased husband. A woman had no right to consent to her marriage (Ntampaka, 1992, p. 71). She could be subject to corporal punishment by her husband or any male guardian (Bourgeois, 1957, p. 146). Furthermore, in the event a woman was killed, this did not necessarily induce a vendetta right of her family, a practice that was otherwise customary between families in the case of murder (Paternostre de la Maririeu, 1972, p. 37).

The role of women in the public institutions of the kingdom was also invisible. The only woman with an important position in these institutions was the Queen Mother. She could exercise by regency the responsibilities of king if her son was enthroned at a very young age. As regent, she could be the supreme leader and judge in the country. This was the case, for example, of Queen Mother Nyiratunga, the mother of King Gahindiro, who governed Rwanda by regency for more than 10 years (MINESUPRES, 1984, p. 13). In addition to advising the king, the Queen Mother had some social and economic responsibilities in the kingdom (Kamatali, 2014, p. 157). To show how the public considered her powerful and revered, she was—together with the king—addressed as *Abami* (kings).

Other important institutions of the monarchy, such as the constitutional priests called in Kinyarwanda *Abiru*, the central and territorial administrators called *Abatware*,[4] the sociomilitary institutions called *amatorero*, and the pastoral serfdom institution called *ubuhake*[5] were all exclusively male-dominated. As there was no separation of powers, these institutions usually combined the executive and judicial powers.

Abiru were the depositories of the 'esoteric code' known as *ubwiru*, which was the fundamental law of the dynasty containing all the secrets about different rituals and traditions on how the king was chosen, enthroned, exercised his powers and was removed. Like Supreme Court justices, *Abiru* were also in charge of assessing whether a new rule was compatible with the fundamental charter of the country (Kamatali, 2014, p. 157). No woman in Rwandan history is known to have been part of this constitutional institution.

After the king and *Abiru* were *Abatware* or chiefs. Except in some cases, which may have been mythological,[6] all *Abatware* have been male. Regions were governed concurrently by the *Umutware w'ubutaka* (chief of land) and the *Umutare w'umukenke* (chief of pasture). *Umutware w'ubutaka* was the land administrator and therefore had the responsibility to collect taxes on agriculture and to be the judge in the first instance for cases related to land ownership. *Umutware w'umukenke* was the cattle administrator and therefore had the responsibility to collect taxes on cattle and to decide in the first instance on cases related to pasture. The decisions made by the two chiefs were appealable before the king.

In order for the king, who was the supreme judge in the country, to hear a subject's case, the latter had to be assisted by his military chief, except in cases where the latter was a party to the case (Kagame, 1952, Article 83). Each Rwandan, whatever his condition, had to belong to one or the other social army and had to have a military superior. Every patriarch was required to join a social army known as *itorero* together with his sons, married or not, his brothers and their sons, and his paternal uncles (Maquet, 1961, p. 110). No woman was allowed to join the social army *itorero*. The only case known in Rwanda is that of Ndabaga (D'Hertefelt, 1962, p. 69), who is at the source of the Rwandan saying: 'ibintu byageze iwa Ndabaga.'[7]

Women were also excluded from the conciliation justice known as Gacaca. Senior women (older women, mothers-in-law, aunts) could, however, intervene in Gacaca in cases of family issues involving women. Their role was not, however, to be judges or mediators but rather to provide what is known as *impanuro* (Jyoni wa Karega, 1996, p. 33), which is a combination of advice and warning elders give based on their life experience and sage observations.

Rwandan Women Under Colonial Laws and Judicial Institutions

Colonialism did little to improve the situation of Rwandan women as participants in and beneficiaries of the judicial system. Rwanda was initially colonized by Germany, but then awarded to Belgium when Germany lost its colonies after World War I. Belgium's first ordinance, upon gaining control of Rwanda, was to extend to Rwanda codes and laws applicable in neighboring Belgian Congo.[8] The Belgian Congo codes suffered, however, from two weaknesses that continued to affect women's rights even after Rwanda's independence. First, the Belgian Congo codes were a colonial version of the Belgian civil law system, a system inspired by Roman law with its unfriendly attitude towards women's rights (Gardner, 1986). Second, the codes allowed existing customary rules and institutions that excluded women to remain applicable; while the introduced codes applied to whites, foreigners and matriculated indigenous, customary law continued to be applicable to nonmatriculated indigenous people.

The Codes and Laws of the Belgian Congo (Strouvens & Piron, 1948) contained a number of provisions that treated married women as incapable at the same level as minors.[9] They crowned the husband the head of the household and required obedience and submission from his wife.[10] A woman needed authorization from her husband to enter into a contract or perform any legal act.[11] The Colonial Labor Code[12] forbade a woman from working unless she had express authorization from her husband. In no case could a judge substitute for the authorization of the husband. If the husband had provided authorization for his wife to work, her contract ended automatically when the husband moved far from her place of employment. This was because the wife was obliged to live under the same roof as her husband and to follow him wherever he moved.

Not only did the laws of the colonial legal system limit women's rights, including the right to work, its institutions and particularly the judicial institutions were also exclusively male-dominated. The Rwandan colonial court system was created in 1926.[13] The colonial court system consisted of Customary Courts or *jurisdictions coutumières* that dealt with cases of indigenous Rwandans and Extracustomary Courts or *jurisdictions extra-coutumières* that dealt with cases in which parties were white, foreign or matriculated Rwandans.[14] The colonial administration had already divided the country into nine *territoires* (provinces) and 46 *chefferies* (districts). *Chefferies* were divided into *Sous-Chefferies* (subdistricts). The colonial governor of Rwanda, known as *Commissaire Résident*, governed the country with a power superior to that of the king of Rwanda.[15] This means that with colonization, the king's supreme powers in the judiciary were under the *Commissaire Résident*'s oversight. In 1917, for instance, the king's power to pronounce the death penalty was removed and entrusted exclusively in the hands of the *Commissaire Résident* (Reyntjens, 1985, p. 79).

The *Résident* appointed the *administrateurs du territoire* (governors of provinces) while the king appointed the *Chefs de chefferies* (chiefs of districts) and *Sous-Chefs* (chiefs of subdistricts) after approval by the *Commissaire Résident*. *Administrateurs du territoire* and *Chefs de chefferies* exercised both administrative and judicial powers. The *Tribunal du territoire* (provincial tribunal) had its seat at the provincial capital and was headed by the *Administrateurs du territoire*. The bench of this tribunal was usually made up of one judge selected among chiefs of districts, five associate judges selected among chiefs of subdistricts and a registrar. The resident, his deputy and the administrator of the province were automatically judges of this tribunal, which was competent for all cases that arose between Rwandese or between Rwandese and indigenous people of the neighboring territories. The *Tribunaux de Chefferie* (district tribunals) were established at every *chefferie* and were headed by the *Chef de Chefferie* assisted by associate judges of *chefferie* selected from among the eminent elders of the *chefferie*.[16]

As all *Administrateurs du Territoire*, *Chefs de chefferies*, *Sous-Chefs de chefferies* and eminent elders were male, there was no woman in the colonial judicial system of Rwanda. In a nutshell, during colonialism Rwandan women were excluded from participating in the public life of Rwanda by colonial laws that subjected their participation to their male guardians' authorization. As, however, their male guardians were under customary cultural influence and legal tradition that considered women's role as mother and wife, even a woman who might dream of joining public life would have found herself limited by colonial law, and customary law and traditions.

Women Under Laws and Judicial Institutions of an Independent Rwanda

Like in pre-independence Rwanda, participation of women in the institutions of postcolonial Rwanda, including the judiciary, remained very limited. From Rwanda's independence in 1962 to 1982, only one woman was elected as a member of parliament: Angele Mukakayange, who served only one term, from 1965 to 1969 (Paternostre de la Maririeu, 1972, p. 213). During the 1980s and 1990s the presence of women in parliament remained between 10 and 20%.

In the executive branch, women's representation was even worse. From Rwanda's independence in 1962 to April 1992 only one woman served as minister in the government of Rwanda: Madeleine Ayinkamiye, who was Minister of Social Affairs in 1964. During this period women were not only invisible in the decision-making institutions of Rwanda but this invisibility was not even identified as a problem that needed to be addressed. The awareness of the need for women in Rwandan government institutions started with the beginning of a multiparty political system in 1991 and 1992. Changes started in the leadership of political parties and women moved from being influential in their political parties to becoming influential national political figures. In the April 1992 first transitional government that was shared by major political parties, three out of the four major parties in government appointed one woman each to a government post. With the government reshuffle of July 18, 1993, Agathe Uwilingiyimana became the first woman prime minister in Rwanda (Guichaoua, 2015), a position she held for less than one year before she was assassinated during the 1994 genocide. The number of women in government remained unchanged during the 1990s. In 1995 there were two females and 19 males; in 1997 there were two females and 23 males; in 1999 there were one female and 18 males; in 2000 there were two females and 15 males (Haguruka, 2001, p. 65).

Just like the executive and the legislative branches, Rwanda's postcolonial judiciary remained controlled by men, with little participation by women. The first constitution of an independent Rwanda adopted on November 24, 1962[17] guaranteed equality between men and women (Art. 16). Article 2 abolished the monarchy and stripped the king of all his powers. Article 11 reorganized the territorial administration of the country, replacing the *territoires* by *prefectures* and *chefferies* by *communes*. The same constitution guaranteed that the judiciary was independent, putting an end to the precolonial and colonial practices that allowed administrative authorities to combine executive/administrative and judicial powers (Art. 98). The 1962 constitution created a four-level court system: Canton Tribunals, Tribunals of First Instance, Court of Appeal and the Supreme Court (Art. 99). It divided the Supreme Court into five sections: Department of Courts and Tribunals, Court of Cassation, Constitutional Court, Council of State (*Conseil d'État*) and Court of Audit (*Cour des Comptes*) (Art.103). The constitution also allowed the creation of special courts such as court-martial, military court, magistrate courts and commercial courts (Art. 99). The same constitution provided that the nomination of the president of the Supreme Court is done by the President of the Republic on the list of two candidates established by the parliament and the government meeting jointly. The vice presidents of Supreme Court sections are nominated by the President of the Republic from the list of candidates established by the parliament and the government meeting jointly (Art. 104).

The 1978 constitution kept the same courts system with some modifications. The sections of the Supreme Court: Court of Cassation, Council of State and Constitutional Court, were kept by the 1978 constitution but the Supreme Court as the umbrella under which they operated was dropped. The Constitutional Court ceased to be an independent section and rather became the court composed of joint sessions of Court of Cassation and Counsel of State (Art. 83 and 85). Also the High Council of the Judiciary was created (Art. 82). The same constitution provided also that judges are appointed by the President of the Republic on proposition of the Minister of Justice and after assent of the High Counsel of the Judiciary (Art. 82).

The 1991 constitution kept the same appointment of judges as in the 1978 constitution. It also maintained the same court system but made some modifications on the High Council of the Judiciary. It specified that members of the High Council of the Judiciary are to be elected by their peers, but appointed the minister of justice a member *de jure* of this council (Art. 87). The 2003 constitution made changes in the structure and organization of the judiciary; the old court system was replaced by a new one made of ordinary and specialized courts. Ordinary courts include the Supreme Court, the High Court, Intermediate Courts and Primary Courts. Specialized courts include Gacaca Courts,[18] military courts, commercial courts and any other as may be determined by Organic Law (Art. 143). The Supreme Court is headed by a president assisted by a vice president and 12 other judges (Art. 146). The president, vice president and judges of the Supreme Court and those of the High Court are appointed by the president after consultation with the cabinet and the High Council of the Judiciary, and after approval by the Senate (Art. 147 and 149).

Until the mid-1990s no woman had ever been appointed judge at the Supreme Court. The first woman to be appointed at such a high level of the judiciary was Immaculee Nyirinkwaya in 1995. In 1999 Marie Jose Mukandamage became the first woman to be vice president of the Supreme Court. Before that, other women in top judicial posts had been Agnes Ntamabyariro, who in 1985 became the vice president of the Court of Appeal of Nyabisindu and later became minister of justice; Aurea Mukangabo who in 1985 was vice president of the Tribunal of First Instance of Kigali and then in 1991 became president of the Court of Appeal of Kigali; and Odette Murara who was president of the Court of Appeal of Kigali in 1996.

In 2003 Aloysie Cyanzayire broke the ceiling by becoming the fifth chief justice of Rwanda and the first woman to head the highest court of the country. Until Cyanzayire became chief justice, the overall number of women had remained very small (Haguruka, 2001, p. 73), as illustrated in Table 10.1.

Significant increases in the number of women in the judiciary started in the 2010s. The number of women judges grew from 74 out of 805 judges in 1998 to 110 out of 281 judges in 2014. In other words, the number of women judges moved from 9.1% in 1998 to 39% in 2014 as detailed in Table 10.2.

Gender and Representation: Understanding the Causes of Increases in Women in the Judiciary Since the 2010s

More Women in Law School

Women's increasing access to education, in particular law school, has meant more women available to the judiciary. The situation of women and education in Rwanda today results from how education began and evolved during colonialism. A schooling system started with the arrival of missionaries in Rwanda in 1900. By 1910 Rwanda counted 13 primary schools and by 1915 there were 40 primary schools for 1,500 boys and 500 girls. Between 1949 and 1960 this

Table 10.1 Women Judges in Selected Courts in Rwanda, 1991–2001

Year	*Supreme Court*						*Court of Appeal*						*Tribunal of 1st Instance*						*Tribunal of Canton*			
	Pres.		*V.P.*		*Judge*		*Pres.*		*V.P.*		*Judge*		*Pres.*		*V.P.*		*Judge*		*Pres.*		*Judge*	
	M	*F*	*M*	*F*	*M*	*F*	*M*	*F*	*M*	*F*	*M*	*F*	*M*	*F*	*M*	*F*	*M*	*F*	*M*	*F*	*M*	*F*
1991	3	0	–	–	16	0	4	0	4	0	17	0	10	0	14	1	103	6	143	0	–	–
1998	1	0	4	0	12	0	3	1	4	0	28	0	10	0	16	0	142	17	89	4	417	57
1999	1	0	3	1	15	0	–	–	4	0	20	3	10	0	17	–	142	17	89	4	417	57
2000	1	0	4	2	15	3	–	–	4	0	21	3	6	0	21	0	145	18	80	4	419	55
2001	1	0	4	2	17	3	4	0	6	0	18	3	13	0	23	3	134	13	72	4	394	64

Source: MINIJUST

Table 10.2 Women Judges in Selected Courts in Rwanda, 2008–2014

	2008		*2009*		*2010*		*2011*		*2012*		*2013*		*2014*	
	M	*F*	*M*	*F*	*M*	*F*	*M*	*F*	*M*	*F*	*M*	*F*	*M*	*F*
S.C	6	6	7	7	7	7	7	7	7	7	10	7	10	7
In.C	3	1	3	1	4	1	4	1	4	1	3	2	3	2
H.C	18	8	18	8	18	7	17	8	15	10	17	8	19	10
H.C.C	4	3	4	3	4	3	4	3	4	3	3	3	4	3
I.C	57	30	60	38	62	38	59	37	61	38	58	41	59	35
C.C	11	3	11	3	12	3	12	3	12	3	11	4	15	6
P.C	71	49	72	47	67	45	67	52	73	46	69	50	68	52

S.C: Supreme Court; **In.C**: Inspectors of Courts; **H.C:** High Court, **H.C.C:** High Commercial Court; **I.C:** Intermediate Court; **C.C:** Commercial Court, **P.C:** Primary Court

Source: Supreme Court

number grew from 112,000 to 265,000, of which 31% were girls (Paternostre de la Maririeu, 1972, p. 169). When secondary schools opened in Rwanda, they were boarding schools and admitted only boys. The first secondary school for girls opened in Rwanda in 1939. This school, however, provided only two categories of education: to prepare girls to become nuns or to prepare girls to become the future wives of the Rwandan elite (Mujawamariya & Ship, 2005, p. 26). By the end of the 1950s there were only three nonreligious training secondary schools for girls and they were only training girls to become teachers and nurses (Mujawamariya & Ship, 2005, p. 27).

When the National University of Rwanda (NUR) opened in 1963 as the first higher education institution in Rwanda, it had only 49 students. Although no statistics exist to show when the first woman entered this institution, the statistics on women in secondary schools show that there was not a sufficient number of women to send to university. There were 18 students in the first graduating class at the National University of Rwanda in 1972; 194 in the second completion year 1973–1979, and 786 in the third completion year 1980–1986.[19] By 2012 the number of students who had graduated from the National University of Rwanda was 21,539, 91% of whom had graduated between 1995 and 2012.[20]

The National University of Rwanda opened its law school in 1973 and offered its first law degrees in 1977. The law school did not admit students every year rather, only every second year. By 1994 the law school had graduated fewer than 150 students. Just as 91% of graduates of the NUR, the only university in the country until late 1990s, graduated after 1995, the greatest percentage of law school students graduated after 1995. When I attended law school in late 1980s the number of students was between 100 and 150. When I became dean of the law school in 1998, however, the school counted between 500 and 600 students. The need to train lawyers to deal with genocide cases attracted a significant number of students to law school. During 1999–2000 the law school counted 455 students, 377 men and 78 women.[21] That same year it was observed that the number of students who graduated between 1996 and 1999 was far larger than the number of students who graduated between 1973 and 1994. Since then, the number of law students at the NUR has remained consistently around 500 with the number of female law students ranging between 20 and 30%.

In addition to the law school of the National University of Rwanda, the only public law school, two private law schools have contributed to increasing the number of women lawyers: *Université Libre de Kigali* (ULK), which was created in 1996, and *Institut Laïque Adventiste de Kigali* (INILAK), created in 1997. Unlike the law school of the NUR, located in the Southern Province of Rwanda, these schools are located in Kigali and have evening classes.[22] Women prefer them because most women who go to school live in Kigali and prefer to stay closer to their families and their places of employment. This makes evening classes in Kigali popular among women but also proves the determination of women to succeed professionally while caring for their families.

Thus there has been a significant increase in women law school graduates and women lawyers in Rwanda since 1996. The number of women who graduated from law schools in Rwanda increased from fewer than 100 in 1996 to more than 3,500 in 2013.[23] This has contributed not only to an increase in women in the judiciary but also in law practice. For instance, only four women belonged to the Rwandan Bar Association in 1998, compared to 110 women—around 20% of all bar members—in 2014.[24] This increase has had an impact in terms of generating activism around changing laws that affect women and creating a pool of experienced women from which to recruit women judges into the judiciary. In other words, with this increase the government could not justify a failure to recruit women into the judiciary on the grounds of too few women with law degrees and working experience.

Changes in Law that Limited Women's Participation and the Role of Civil Society

Legal changes and women's activism in civil society have also contributed to their increasing presence on the bench. Although the 1962 constitution and subsequent constitutions guaranteed the principle of equality, it was not until 1988 that the fundamental inequalities between men and women that had been in force since the colonial period began to be addressed. The1895 Belgian Civil Code that had been in force in Rwanda since 1936 was abrogated in 1988.[25]

The 1988 law removed the majority of incapacities that the 1895 Belgian Congo Civil Code had imposed on women due to marriage. Women could therefore exercise parental authority over their children; did not have to follow blindly their husbands; could be parties in court; could exercise any profession, start a business and enter contracts without a legal requirement of consent of their husbands. New labor laws[26] created enabling working conditions for women, for instance, by forbidding direct or indirect sex discrimination in employment or salary; defining the obligations of an employer of a pregnant and breast-feeding woman; protecting against gender violence and harassment in the place of work, and many other changes.

Other limitations on the participation of women in decision-making, in both the public and private spheres, have been removed by a number of laws adopted since 2000. These include the Law on Matrimonial Regimes, Liberalities and Succession that granted women the same rights as men on matrimonial property and in the field of inheritance and succession;[27] the Organic Law on the Organization of Elections to Grassroots Administrative Echelons that granted women a minimum quota of 30% in these echelons;[28] the Land Law that gave women the same rights as men in the use and management of land;[29] and the Law Governing the Registration of the Population and Issuance of the National Identity Card that allowed mothers the same right as fathers to register children.[30] In addition, the Organic Law on Rwandan Nationality allows mothers to transfer their citizenship to their children just as fathers may do;[31] the Law on Prevention and Punishment of Gender-based Violence criminalizes any gender based violence;[32] and the new Penal Code punishes adultery equally for both husband and wife.[33]

The above changes were mainly the result of activism by members of civil society and an increased awareness of the injustices imposed on women by the laws that dated from colonialism. The movement to change laws unfair to women started in 1991 with the creation of Haguruka, one of the oldest and most vibrant advocacy and women's rights organizations in Rwanda. This organization, to which the majority of women leaders in Rwanda in the 1990s and early 2000s belonged, played a significant role in advocating for the adoption of the above-mentioned laws and conducted numerous studies on provisions that still violated the rights of women.[34] Another organization that played a significant role is *Pro-Femme Twese Hamwe*, an umbrella organization of 58 organizations promoting a women's agenda.[35] Unity Club, an organization chaired by the first lady of Rwanda and which brings together present and former members of the Cabinet and their spouses, provided strong political advocacy and financial support for many of the efforts to change the laws that affected women.[36] Also, as more women entered law school and learned the extent to which existing laws treated women unfairly, they contributed to educating politicians and the general population on the need for change.

Enabling Government Policies and Institutions

The increase in women attending law school and the removal of legal barriers to women's participation in decision-making are not enough to guarantee an increase in women in the judiciary, however. After all, in the US it took until 1934—more than 150 years after independence—for the first woman to be appointed to the federal bench and more than 200 years for the first woman to be appointed to the US Supreme Court. Today, although women make up half of all law school graduates in the US, these numbers are not reflected on the bench (Kenney, 2013, pp. 65–67). In Rwanda, removing legal barriers that affected women's access to work unlocked the door to equal opportunities for men and women; the increase in women with a law degree opened the door for women to enter legal professions, including that of judge; but it took enabling government policies and institutions to push women through this door.

Policies to increase the number of women in decision-making structures in Rwanda have existed since the 1990s (Burnet, 2008). While policies such as quotas and political lobbying could facilitate women's access to political and administrative professions, judicial posts presented some challenges that could not be solved by the application of quotas and political lobbying. First, Article 140 of the constitution provides that 'the Judiciary is independent and separate from the legislative and executive branches of government,' branches in which quotas, affirmative action and lobbying can be used to correct past wrongs done to women, but much more difficult to use in the judiciary without compromising its independence principle. Second, and related, the selection and appointment process in the judiciary requires that judges be appointed first and foremost on the basis of objective criteria.[37] In this regard, the law governing the status of judges and judicial personnel contains only objective criteria for the recruitment and promotion of judges; there is no mention of gender or other subjective criteria.[38]

Instead, an insider-outsider collaboration can be identified as the method used to combine the requirements of both a quota and judicial independence. In other words, the judiciary did not just wait for women to apply; it actively sought competent candidates and encouraged them to join. This technique is not unique to Rwanda; indeed it has been credited with allowing President Jimmy Carter to appoint 'more women to the bench than all previous administrations combined' (Kenney, 2013, p., 66).

In the case of Rwanda, the insider-outsider collaboration was facilitated by the fact that both the Minister in the Office of the President whose responsibilities include justice issues and the Chief Justice of the Supreme Court were women for nearly a decade beginning in the mid-2000s. The two women, respectively Soline Nyirahabimana and Aloysie Cyanzayire, are good friends who graduated from law school at the National University of Rwanda at the same time. Cyanzayire's career had been mainly in the judiciary while Nyirahabimana's career was mainly in civil society before joining politics. The two women, who held their respective posts for about eight years from the mid-2000s onward, played a significant role in encouraging and recruiting women into the judiciary.

The President of Rwanda plays a significant role in the appointment of Supreme Court justices and heads of High Courts. According to Articles 147 to 149 of the constitution, the president, the vice president and judges of the Supreme Court, as well as the president and vice presidents of the High Court, are appointed by the president after approval by the Senate. The President selects candidates for such posts after consultation with the cabinet and the High Council of the Judiciary. In order to be appointed to these positions the candidate has

> 1) to be at least twenty one (21) years of age; 2) to be a holder of at least a bachelor degree in law and a certificate issued by a judicial training institution recognized by the Government; 3) to be a person of integrity; 4) to be a person of irreproachable morals and conduct; 5) not to be convicted for ideology of the genocide; 6) not to be characterized by any form of sectarianism; 7) to be impartial; 8) to be independent minded; 9) to have no mental illness that may prevent him/her from performing the judge's duties as attested by a recognized physician; 10) not to have been subject to deprivation of civil and political rights; 11) not to have been sentenced to a six (6) months or more imprisonment; 12) not to have been dismissed or automatically removed from office; 13) not to have committed in service fraudulent acts, desertion of duty or refusal to resume duty after the end of the period of suspension or after request to do so;

> 14) to have successfully gone through the competitive process conducted by the High Council of the Judiciary, except for judges that are appointed by a Presidential Order.'[39]

In addition to the above general conditions, the candidate must have eight years working experience in the legal profession.[40]

The role of chief justice becomes more influential in the appointment of judges of High Court, Intermediate Court and Primary Court. Articles 13 and 14 of the Law Governing the Status of Judges and Judicial Personnel provides that the judges are appointed by the president of the Supreme Court upon approval by the High Council of the Judiciary. As Aloysie Cyanzayire, president of the Supreme Court from 2003 to 2013 was also the chairperson of the High Council of the Judiciary,[41] she was in a good position to recruit women judges. This position was also facilitated by the fact that decisions of the High Council of the Judiciary are mostly made by consensus,[42] making it easier for the chair to influence and persuade council members, even more so because increasing women's participation in government institutions was known to be a national priority.

In a country that had only one law school until early 2000, making it easier for women lawyers to know each other, a couple of organizations promoting women's rights and through which women lawyers could meet and discuss legal issues affecting women, a female chief justice and a female minister in the president's office, and a national policy of encouraging women to join decision-making positions, provided a favorable environment for insider-outsider collaboration in the recruitment of female judges.

Women and the Judiciary: Women Judges and Their Decisions on Legal Issues Affecting Women

Most studies conducted on the legal situation of women in Rwanda have focused on bad legislation or slow change in the patrilineal culture in the face of the new legislation protecting women.[43] No study has been conducted so far assessing the impact of women judges in Rwanda's judiciary. This may be because it is too early to assess this impact. After all, the majority of women in the judiciary in Rwanda have not even been on the bench for five years.

There is no agreement on whether there is a difference in the judgments of women judges compared to those of their male colleagues. Examining whether South Africa's women judges make a difference, Cowan (2013, p. 322) argues that women differed 'from all but one of their male colleagues when cases involved issues clearly related to women's rights or to matters of particular relevance to women's experience.' Dijkesterhuis (2013, p. 281), in examining whether there are gendered–based differences in judges' decision-making in the Netherlands, concluded that 'until now even in the gendered family law a unique female sound in the Dutch Judiciary has not been found.'

Acknowledging that a much broader study is needed on how the debate between Cowan and Dijkesterhuis plays out in Rwanda, in writing this chapter I have tried to examine how this debate is reflected in Rwanda today. I used a small sample of rape and abortion cases to examine whether justices of the Supreme Courts of Rwanda decide on cases differently depending on whether they are men or women. The choice of rape and abortion cases was deliberate, because rape is a crime in which women are victims and abortion is a crime in which women are most of the time the offenders. All the cases I examined are available at the website of the Rwanda Supreme Court.[44] In all these cases, offenders were found guilty at the High Court level (HC) and had received a higher sentence. They had, therefore, appealed before the Supreme Court (SC), asking that their sentences be reduced because they had admitted their offenses in the lower courts. The Supreme Court bench was made up of three judges. I therefore wanted to know whether there was any difference in reducing or not reducing the sentence based on whether the bench was majority male or female. The results are found in Tables 10.3 and 10.4.

In both cases, abortion and rape, there seems to be no difference between male and female justices in deciding whether the person found guilty at the lower court should have his or her sentence reduced or not.

This conclusion corresponds to the results of the discussions I had with a small sample of women judges in Rwanda on whether there is any difference in the way they deal with cases compared to their male colleagues. Most agree that there is a difference in the way they treat people before them, perhaps with more patience and understanding than their male colleagues do, but they did not think that there is any difference in the way they and their male colleagues apply the law.

Table 10.3 Abortion Cases and Sentences by Gender of Justice in Rwanda

Case number	*Female justices*	*Male justices*	*Sentence*	
			HC	*SC*
RPA 0150/09/CS	0	3	Life	10
RPA 0051/08/CS	1	2	Life	5
RPA 0293/08/CS	1	2	7	7
RPA 0200/08/CS	1	2	10	8
			15	0
RPA 0135/08/CS	1	2	20	5
RPA 0021/08/CS	2	1	15	7
RPA 0056/07/CS	2	1	20	20
RPA 0058/06/CS	1	2	Life	10
RPA 0032/06/CS	2	1	Life	Life
RPA 0015/06/CS	1	2	20	0
RPA 0145/05/CS	1	2	Life	10
RPA 0029/06/CS	1	2	Life	8

Table 10.4 Rape Cases and Sentences by Gender of Justice in Rwanda

Case number	Female justices	Male justices	Sentence	
			HC	SC
RPAA 0124/09/CS	1	2	10	5
RPAA 0071/08/CS	2	1	10	6
RPAA 0103/09/CS	2	1	Life	Life
RPAA 0127/09/CS	1	2	20	20
RS/REV/IEN 0067/08/CS	1	2	20	20
RPAA 0156/06/CS	2	1	Life	Life
RPA 0026/07/CS	0	3	Death	Life
RPAA 0143/08/CS	1	2	Life	Life
RPAA 0110/08/CS	1	2	15	8
RPAA0107/07/CS (woman)	1	2	10	10
RPAA 0037/08/CS	1	2	10	7
RPAA 0105/08/CS	1	2	20	6
RPAA 0006/08/CS	1	2	Life	Life
RPAA 0022/08/CS	1	2	20	20
RPAA 0007/08/CS	2	1	Life	Life
RPAA 0120/07/CS	1	2	14	14
RPAA 0062/07/CS	2	1	10	10
RPAA 0150/06/CS	1	2	20	10
RS/REV/PEN 0011/08/CS	2	1	14	14
RPAA 0037/07/CS	1	2	20	20
RPAA 0039/06/CS	2	1	15	15

The fact that the situation of women judges in Rwanda is more similar to that of women judges in the Netherlands than those in South Africa with regard to the existence or lack of a unique female voice on issues affecting women may not be surprising. Rwanda and the Netherlands share the same civil law legal system as opposed to the common law legal system that dominates in South Africa. In the civil law legal system, in contrast to the common law legal system, the role of judges is mainly to apply existing legislation rather than to create law.[45] In Rwanda, then, given that the old laws that were unfavorable to women were changed before the increase in women in the judiciary, it is easier for judges—whether male or female—to decide on issues affecting women.

The presence of women in the judiciary is not, however, without a significant impact. Between 2005 and 2013, out of 30 disciplinary sanctions against judges and court registrars for corruption, only five were against women; this suggests that women judges and registrars may be less prone to bribery and corruption.[46] Also, the role of women judges in inspiring girls to study law and become judges cannot be ignored. These assertions need to be studied with larger samples and better methodologies.

Conclusion

Women's participation in Rwanda's judiciary is both an expression of a broader participation of citizens in politics and a means to promote women's rights. As an expression of broader participation, the increase in women judges is connected to the recent increase in women in decision-making positions across the country. This increase reflects an approach that Rwanda has adopted to respond in a more manageable way to the needs of democracy, in particular citizen participation in government. While previous regimes had adopted ethnic and regional quotas as policies to make Rwandans feel more fully represented in government, the current regime seems to have opted for gender promotion policies to achieve these same objectives.

As a means to promote women's rights, the increase in women's participation in the judiciary is geared more toward giving women equal opportunities as men to become judges, rather than for women judges to promote women's rights. As Rwanda utilizes a civil law legal system, the role of women judges in the promotion of women's rights depends on existing women's rights legislation. Unlike in common law legal systems where judges create law, the role of judges in civil law systems is mainly to interpret existing legislation. The fact that Rwanda adopted laws that assert and protect women's rights before more women joined the judiciary has facilitated the role of judges—male or female—because most women's rights have already been addressed by new legislation.

This does not mean, however, that Rwanda's women judges do not have other challenges. Most of these challenges are related to the patriarchal culture of the country. The speed in adopting new legislation and involving women in the judiciary should not be understood as the result of a similar swift change in the Rwanda's patriarchal society. It is rather a first step toward changing this society. Although both male and female judges now have good legislative tools with which to handle cases of violations of women's rights, only a deep transformation of the society can keep such cases from ever occurring in the first place. This transformation is also needed with respect to women judges, because as much as the judiciary expects them to perform at the same level as their male colleagues, many in Rwandan society expect them to remain traditional Rwandan wives and mothers. This puts a heavy burden on them that still needs to be alleviated.

Notes

1 The author wishes to express gratitude to Justice Therese Mukamulisa of the Supreme Court of Rwanda for her contributions to this chapter.
2 Article 9 paragraphs 4, 76 and 82 of the Rwanda constitution.
3 See Burnet, 2008; Burnet, 2012; Hunt, 2014; Longman, 2006; Newbury & Baldwin, 2001.
4 The kingdom had different kinds of *abatware*. The military institutions had *umutware w'urugo rw'umwami* (the Chief of the Royal Palace) who was the commander of the personal army of the king; and the *umutware w'itorero* (company commander). There were four to five companies each with a special name and commander appointed by the Chief of the Royal Palace. In the administration of territories there was at the head of each district *umutware w'umukenke* or chief of pasture and *umutware w'ubutaka* or the chief of land. Both had equal powers in the

district each in his attributions (land or pasture). Below these chiefs were also other chiefs such as *abatware b'umusozi* or hill-chiefs. See Kamatali, 2014, pp. 158–160.

5 The institution of *ubuhake* was defined as a contract of pastoral servitude by which a person known as *umugaragu* (servant), who had an inferior social status and was less well off, provided cattle to, offered his services to and asked protection from a person called *shebuja* (master), whose status was higher and whose wealth was greater. See Kamatali, 2001, p. 109; Kamatali. 2014, pp. 160–161

6 These include Nyagakecuru, who was the wife of Samukende, who governed the *ibisi bya Huye* in the current Southern Province of Rwanda. See MINESUPRES, 1984.

7 Meaning that the situation is so desperate that even Ndabaga, the woman, had to be sent to the battlefield. This saying is used when a situation is so dire that there is no other solution but calling for desperate means.

8 See Loi du 21 août 1925 sur le Government du Ruanda-Urundi (B. O. 1925, p. 443).

9 See, for example, Article 2 (citizenship) of the Law of 1908 on the Government of Belgian Congo and Articles 58 (domicile) and 29 (registration).

10 Ordonance of May 14, 1886 portant Code Civil de l'Administration Générale au Congo (as modified) Book I (Des Personnes) is the Decret of May 4, 1895. Rendered enforceable in Rwanda and Burundi by O.R.U no 11/82 of June 21, 1949.

11 Article 124.

12 Article 4 of the Decree of March 16, 1922 on the labor contract between indigenous and Civilized Master (Code et Lois du Congo Belge, p. 915).

13 See the regulation of the Resident, letter No. 96/O.R.G. of November 5, 1926.

14 For details see Havugimana, 1989, p. 52.

15 The Colonial Decree of April 6, 1917 provided that 'Sous l'autorité du Commissaire résident, les sultans (Bami) exercent leurs pouvoir politique et judiciaire dans la mesure ou il reste en accord avec les coutumes indigènes et avec les instructions du Commissaire Royal.'

16 For more details see Hagenimana, 1990, p. 30.

17 Rwanda became independent on July 1, 1962 and the first formal constitution of the Republic of Rwanda was adopted on November 24, 1962 by an all-male parliament.

18 In 2012 Gacaca courts were ended by the Organic Law No. 04/2012/OL of 15/06/2012 Terminating Gacaca Courts and Determining Mechanisms for Solving Issues Which Were under Their Jurisdiction.

19 NUR Facts and Figures June 2013. Retrieved from http://archive.wikiwix.com/cache/?url=http://www.nur.ac.rw/spip.php?article808&title=NUR%20Facts%20and%20Figures

20 Ibid.

21 See UNR [NUR], Distribution des étudiants par Facultés et Écoles pour l'année 1999–2000. Retrieved from www.natcomreport.com/rwanda/livre/universite.html

22 INILAK has another campus in the Southern Province of Rwanda and ULK has another campus in the Western Province of Rwanda. Also, the law school of the NUR has evening classes but they are not as widely attended as the ones of ULK and INILAK, mainly because of its location. In September 2015 the government decided to move the Law School that was located in the Southern Province to Kigali.

23 Personal email communication with Ministry of Education.

24 See Roll of Advocates and List of Interns, at http://rwandabar.org.rw/?page_id=199

25 See Law No. 42/88 of October 27th, 1988 Establishing the Preliminary Title and the First Book of the Civil Code, Official Gazette 1989.

26 See Law No. 51/2001 of December 30, 2001 establishing Labor Code (OGRR No5 of 01/01/2002) and Law No.13/2009 of 27/05/2009 OGRR No. Special of 27/05/2009.

27 The Law N° 22/99 of 12/11/1999 to supplement Book One of the Civil Code and to institute Part V regarding matrimonial regimes, liberalities and successions.

28 The Organic Law N° 42/2000 of 15/11/2000 on the organization of elections to grassroots administrative echelons (J.O. n° spécial du 19/12/2000).
29 Organic Law N° 03/2013/OL of 16/06/2013 repealing Organic Law N° 08/2005 of 14/07/2005 determining the use and management of land in Rwanda.
30 Law N° 14/2008 of 04/6/2008 governing legislation of the population and issuance of the national identity card.
31 Organic Law N° 30/2008 OF 25/07/2008 relating to Rwandan nationality.
32 Law No. 59/2008 of 2008 on Prevention and Punishment of Gender-Based Violence of 10 September 2008.
33 See Article 24, of the Organic Law N° 01/2012/OL OF 02/05/2012 Instituting the Penal Code. Even before this law the Supreme Court had ruled in 2008 that adultery had to be punished with six months of imprisonment, whether committed by the husband or wife. (RS/Const/Pen 0001/08/C.S of 26/09/2008. J.O No. 21 bis of 01/11/2008, p. 123)
34 See the list of laws as well as the list of studies conducted by Haguruka at www.haguruka.org.rw.
35 See activities of this organization at http://profemmes-twesehamwe.org.
36 See more details on Unity Club at www.unity-club.org.
37 See American Bar Association, Judicial Reform Index Factors, at www.americanbar.org/advocacy/rule_of_law/publications/assessments/jri/jri_factors.html.
38 For judges appointed before 2013 see Articles 8 to 11 of Law No. 6 bis/2004 on the Status of Judges and other Judicial Personnel (O.G. No. 10 of 15/05/2004), and for judges appointed after 2013 see Article 12 of Law No. 10/2013 of 08/03/2013 governing the Status of Judges and Judicial Personnel, J.O. No. 15 of 15/04/2013.
39 Law No. 10/2013 of 08/03/2013 governing the Status of Judges and Judicial Personnel, Article 12.
40 Article 18 Law No. 10/2013 of 08/03/2013 governing the Status of Judges and Judicial Personnel.
41 See Article 2 of the Organic Law No. 7/2012/OL of 19/09/12 determining the Organization, Powers and Functioning of the High Council of the Judiciary, O.G. No. 45 of 05/11/2012.
42 'The General Assembly of the High Council of the Judiciary shall make decisions by consensus. If not, decisions may be taken by absolute majority votes of members present.' Article 20 of the Organic Law No. 7/2012/OL of 19/09/12 determining the Organization, Powers and Functioning of the High Council of the Judiciary.
43 See, for example, the list of studies conducted by Haguruka at http://haguruka.org.rw.
44 www.judiciary.gov.rw/case_law/judgements/?cat=8
45 See Dutch Civil Law (DCL), Legal System of Civil Law in the Netherlands; www.dutchcivillaw.com/content/legalsystem011.htm. See also Goodman, 2008, p. 11.
46 Data received by the author from the Supreme Court. Statistics on file with the author.

11 Gender and the Judiciary in Africa

Conclusion

Gretchen Bauer

Just as with executives and legislatures across Africa, at a rapid pace and in increasing numbers, women are accessing judiciaries, as judges and justices across a wide range of lower level and upper level courts, including but not limited to Magistrates' Courts, Intermediate Courts, Primary Courts, Courts of First Instance and Tribunals, on the one hand, and High Courts, Courts of Appeal, Supreme Courts and Constitutional Courts, on the other hand. In several African countries in 2015, including Ghana, Lesotho, Malawi, Niger, Nigeria and Sierra Leone, women serve as chief justices or presidents of Constitutional Courts, and other women have done so in other countries in the recent past (Dawuni & Kang, 2015). How women have been able to access judiciaries across Africa depends, in part, on legal traditions in a country, court structures and organization and appointment processes. What African women judges have been able to do once on the bench has also depended on a range of factors. As Prempeh (2006, p. 593) has noted, there is a 'paucity of scholarship and research on courts in Africa'—all the more so on women and the courts in Africa. This book, with case studies from northern, eastern, southern and western Africa, is the first to examine gender and the judiciary in Africa comprehensively. In this chapter we present a summary of the major findings of the book, concluding with remaining challenges and obstacles facing women in the judiciary in Africa today and some thoughts on future research questions.

Historical Overview: Enduring Legal Systems and Diverse Legal Traditions

In the foreword to this book, Judge Agyemang reminds us that across Africa, courts have 'been with us for a long time.' African countries, nearly all the former colonies of one or another European power, 'have had enduring legal systems—often a hybrid of received foreign law: common law, civil law, Roman-Dutch law, and local customary laws.' Indeed, the experience of nearly a century of European colonial rule, imposed upon traditional and religious legal practices, has resulted in a mix of legal traditions across the continent. As Stoeltje, Firmin-Sellers and Ogwang (2002, pp. xi–xii) note and our chapters demonstrate:

> multiple legal systems operate simultaneously in African societies today. In any one location, legal systems and practices reflect the combined influences of indigenous forms of governance, the manipulation of those systems by colonial powers (often known as "indirect rule"), Islam which includes a system of law all Muslims are expected to follow, and the various Western legal systems . . . established by the colonial powers wherever they established domination, plus the policies associated with globalization.

In much of Africa, long before the arrival of European colonial powers and institutions, established judicial systems existed in abundance, some version of which is typically referred to today as 'customary law' or 'Customary Courts.' Today customary law continues to be widely used by rural and urban populations, with many constitutions recognizing the application of customary law without resolving its conflict with human rights provisions (Ndulo, 2011). In South Africa Customary Courts still exist, although a reform process is under way. The early South African state like other colonial states, according to Albertyn and Bonthuys, maintained a clear divide between civil law, for whites, and customary law, for blacks, 'administered by a different and inferior system of customary or traditional courts, presided over by male elders and traditional leaders which left virtually no space for women to preside or indeed act as litigants or witnesses.' In neighboring Botswana, customary law lives on through the institution of the *kgotlas* with women making slight inroads both in terms of their participation and leadership (Bauer, 2014). In Tanzania, according to Yoon, customary law varies across communities, reflecting the differences in cultures and customs, and continues to be utilized under certain circumstances, such as marriage, inheritance, succession and land ownership, although 'statutory law' always takes precedence. In Nigeria and Ghana, Customary Courts continue to exist at local levels—as in other countries—adjudicating matters relating to marriage, custody of children and inheritance, among others.

In other parts of Africa, especially northern and western Africa, we find, as Hamad describes for Egypt, 'the traditional influence' coming from 'the residual weight of a millennium of religious or Shari'a courts' that dominated until the 19th century. As Hamad further notes, 'while Islam has provided women with a plethora of civil and political rights, traditional Islamic practices forbade females from serving as judges,' with courts remaining an exclusive domain for men in most Arab and Muslim countries well after the establishment of modern states. According to Ibrahim, the Islamic law of sharia has always been a part of Nigeria's legal system with a 'New Shariah' introduced in the north in 1999, adding crime to the purview of sharia jurisdiction whereas only matters of a civil nature had been so regulated in the past. This 'New Shariah' legal system raises serious human rights concerns, according to Ibrahim, in that some laws contradict binding international treaties to which the country is a signatory. In Tanzania, Islamic law may be applied in matters of marriage, divorce, guardianship, inheritance and similar matters in communities that follow that law, but with statutory law taking precedence. Tunisia appears to be an exception in terms of courts with religious influences, with sharia and rabbinical courts abolished shortly after independence, in 1956 and 1957, respectively. About a decade later French courts in Tunisia were also abolished; and from around that time the recruitment of women into the legal profession in the country began in earnest.

While customary and Islamic influences must be taken into consideration, there are also important distinctions depending on the use of common law or civil law legal traditions or, in some African countries, both. There are several significant differences in the two types of legal systems. In the chapter on Rwanda, Kamatali addresses the distinction between civil and common law system countries and the respective roles of judges: 'Unlike in common law systems where the judge creates the law, the role of judges in civil law systems is mainly to interpret existing legislation rather than creating new laws.' Thus for Rwanda, which has a civil law system, he continues, the role of judges seeking to advance women's rights, male or female, has been facilitated by the fact that Rwanda first adopted a series of laws that protect women's rights before bringing more women into the judiciary. According to Schultz and Shaw (2012a, p. 2) this distinction between the two systems also means that in common law countries decisions will be more often 'scrutinized and criticized' with a view to the personal characteristics of the judge, including gender. Schultz and Shaw (2012a, p. 2) also suggest that the judiciary commands a higher social status and income in common law countries than in civil law countries. Perhaps in keeping with this, 'it is easier for women to enter the judiciary' in civil law than in common law countries, where 'key access criteria for judicial office . . . are more rational and transparent.' For this reason, they note generally, the increase in the number of women in the judiciary in civil law countries happened about two decades earlier than in common law countries (Schultz and Shaw, 2012a, p. 3). Common law countries among our cases include the former British colonies of Ghana, Nigeria and Tanzania (with Ghana mixed with customary law and Nigeria and Tanzania mixed with customary law and Muslim law), with Botswana and South Africa experiencing a mix of the two systems (and with customary law). Our remaining cases, Benin, Egypt, Rwanda and Tunisia are civil law countries, mixed with customary law in Benin.

While the precolonial and colonial periods contributed the great mix of diverse legal traditions across the continent, the independence era brought silence to many courts. Ellett (2013, p. 32) argues that 'independence governments inherited rather hollow judiciaries, whose role was purely instrumental to promoting the interests of the powerful.' Moreover, she continues, in most African countries, 'a scarcity of local judges and lawyers created a weak base upon which to build a powerful judiciary at independence.' With the rapid concentration of power in executives, courts might be 'co-opted into despotic regimes or simply ignored altogether' (Ellett, 2013, p. 32). Or, as Judge Agyemang states: many judiciaries in Africa 'suffered violence' in the first 30 years of independence when 'a change of government'—typically the turn to single party rule or a military regime—'often meant the overthrow of the constitution and the consequent marginalization of the Judiciary.' As she further notes, it is only with the political transitions of the last few decades that, in 'fledgling democracies,' the rule of law has 'attained prominence as a benchmark of proper governance. Thus have judiciaries been recognized (albeit grudgingly) as pivotal to the attainment of true democratic governance.'

In writing about courts and democracy in postconflict transitions in Africa, Widner (2001b, pp. 72–75) traces the way in which a 'confluence of events' began to develop across Africa from the mid to late 1980s, as 'people started making increasing use of the courts in many countries, filing more cases each year'—in Customary Courts but also in Magistrates Courts. As political transitions unfolded, and influenced by the need to curb corruption, distinguish a new administration from a previous 'arbitrary and abusive' one and respond to donors, governments 'granted judiciaries more autonomy and refrained from actions that visibly interfered with judicial independence,' according to Widner (2001b, p. 73). In addition, Widner argues, 'judicial attitudes began to alter' as increased access to international meetings and new technologies provided more familiarity with international standards, 'helping to diminish an "executive-minded" predisposition to favor the government in disputes' (Ibid). In many political transitions senior judges were part of commissions that drafted new constitutions (VonDoepp, 2009). Thus, as Judge Agyemang indicates and, as Widner (2001b, p. 64) affirms, 'in this new era, law plays a central, visible, yet delicate role. . . . the success of a post-conflict [or other] transition will depend, in part, on the role of courts in sustaining a spirit of liberty and tolerance in their societies.'

Court Structures and Overview

What do we find when we look at court structures and women judges' presence in them for our selection of African countries? As with all of our findings we uncover great diversity in terms of where women judges are found in our nine case studies—both across countries and within countries. Beginning with those with fewer women judges, we note that in Egypt's civilian courts, in those bodies with the power to dispose of cases, women judges are hardly represented at all. In the ordinary courts, composed of the Courts of Cassation, Courts of Appeal and Courts of First Instance, women are 42 judges out of approximately 12,000 judges and prosecutors. In the administrative judiciary (council of state) there are no women judges and on the Supreme Constitutional Court there are also no women, although there was one from 2003 to 2012. Women judges are better represented in those courts in Egypt that have no power to dispose of cases, according to Hamad, the state cases authority (10% women judges) and the administrative prosecution authority (41%).

For Botswana, we find that women have also never served on the apex court, the Court of Appeal, though in 2015, 17% (four of 24) of judges on the High Court are women, so there has been some movement of women into one of the superior courts. This is, however, a fairly recent development with the first woman appointed to the High Court only in 1998 and she served alone until a brief interlude from 2003 to 2005, when she was joined by a second woman judge. Only since 2011 have there been more women on the High Court. On the inferior courts, by contrast, there are many more women—at least in the Magistrates Courts where 56% of judges are women. In the Customary Courts, women are making only very small inroads into the chieftaincy. In South Africa, with the transition to democracy in the early 1990s, a new Constitutional Court was created which was to be the apex court in all constitutional matters, driving the jurisprudence on the Bill of Rights, including on women's rights. Otherwise, South Africa also maintains a two-tiered systems of courts: provincial High Courts and a Supreme Court of Appeal on the higher tier and magistrates and regional courts on the lower tier. In South Africa women, particularly black women, are best represented in the lower tier of the judiciary with 39% of all magistrates being women and almost half of regional court magistrates being women in late 2013. By contrast, 32% of all High Court judges were women (and 63% of all High Court judges were black) in 2014, although women are severely underrepresented in the most senior positions in the High Courts. While these numbers still do not reflect the national demographics of the country they are a vast improvement, and are a direct result of the democratic transition of the early 1990s and the aspiration to dramatically transform the judiciary.

The apex of the judicial hierarchy in Nigeria is the Supreme Court, below which sits a Court of Appeal and below which sit federal High Courts, High Courts of States, High Courts of the Federal Capital Territory (FCT), the National Industrial Court, Sharia Courts of Appeal, and Customary Courts of Appeal of States and FCT. Inferior courts include the Magistrates Courts/District Courts of States and FCT and Sharia Courts/Area Courts and Customary Courts of States/FCT. According to Ibrahim, Nigeria 'prides itself with achieving one of the highest rates of female judges on the African continent,' although on the Supreme Court only 18.75% of judges are women, one of whom is the former first female chief justice. This compares to sub-Saharan African and world averages of about 27% 'women's representation in the judicial system' in 2011–12 (Kalantry, 2012). No women judges or registrars are to be found in Sharia Courts, although there have been women chief judges in some state High Courts in northern states. According to Ibrahim, the 'greatest feats of gender diversity . . . have been attained in southern Nigeria,' with local media reporting in 2014 that 'women currently dominate the Lagos judiciary.'

In Tanzania where the legal tradition is similar to that of Nigeria, the apex of the judicial system is the Court of Appeal, below which are the High Courts, Magistrates Courts and Primary Courts (plus Kadhi's courts in Zanzibar). Currently four of 16 judges on the Court of Appeal, or 25%, are women, though the chief justice has always been a man. As Yoon reports, since President Kikwete came to power in 2005, the number of women judges has steadily increased such that in 2015, 40% of judges on the Court of Appeal and High

Courts (mainland) were women (up from 22% in 2005). Data for the lower courts in Tanzania have been hard to come by, though Yoon suggests a 'significant presence of women in the magistracy.' Tanzania had set a target of 40% women judges in the lower courts by 2013, though whether this has been met is uncertain.

Benin's current court structure dates from the transition to democracy and new constitution in 1990 and some more recent updates in the early 2000s and is marked by three levels of courts. At the apex are three High Courts: a Constitutional Court, a Supreme Court and the High Court of Justice. The second level of courts are Courts of Appeal and Courts of First Instance and the third level consists of reconciliation boards which, however, are not staffed by professional judges and do not render decisions. Kang shows a doubling in the number of women judges (from one to two) from the 1990s to the present on the Constitutional Court and the High Court of Justice (28.6 and 15.4%, respectively in 2014), although the number of women judges on the Courts of Appeal and the Supreme Court has fallen slightly.

Like other common law countries, Ghana has a two-tiered judiciary with the first tier being the Superior Courts of Judicature: Supreme Court, Court of Appeal, the High Court and Regional Tribunals and the second tier or Inferior Courts such as Magistrates Courts, Circuit Courts, Customary Courts and other courts as may be set up by parliament. In Ghana women were much better represented in the first tier than in the second tier of courts in 2013, according to Dawuni: 38% of judges on the Supreme Court were women, 33% of judges on the Court of Appeal, and 19% of judges on the High Court, compared to 19% of judges in the Magistrates Courts and 23% of judges in the District and Circuit Courts. This puts Ghana clearly at the higher end of our cases and for judiciaries generally worldwide.

In Rwanda, where there is a stated commitment, indeed a constitutional obligation, to 30% women in positions of power and decision-making, we find the greatest presence of women in the judiciary. In Rwanda since the new constitution in 2003 there are two tiers of courts: ordinary courts (Supreme Court, High Court, Intermediate Courts and Primary Courts) and specialized courts (Gacaca Courts, Military Courts, Commercial Courts and others as may be established). For five years, from 2008 to 2012 women were 50% of judges on the Supreme Court, falling to 41% in 2013 and 2014 when the number of judges overall on the Supreme Court was increased. In general, Kamatali suggests that the number of women in the judiciary increased significantly beginning in the 2010s in Rwanda. In the intermediate courts in 2014 women were 35 of 94 judges, or 37%; in the primary courts in 2014 women were 52 of 120 judges, or 43%. Overall, according to Kamatali, women are around 39% of judges in ordinary courts in Rwanda today.

It is difficult to draw any conclusions from our sample of countries, except to note, again, the tremendous diversity. Common law countries such as Ghana and Tanzania are at the higher end of countries in terms of women's representation on higher courts, though the highest representation is in a civil law country like Rwanda and another civil law country, Benin, shows a moderate representation of women in two higher courts. In the two common law/civil law mixed systems of Botswana and South Africa, Botswana lags far behind South Africa in terms of women in the higher courts, though in both countries there is a higher percentage of women magistrates than women judges in the higher courts. Ghana presents an interesting puzzle: significantly more women in the upper echelons than in the lower echelons of the courts. Egypt trails the continent, though elsewhere in northern Africa, women in Tunisia have made great strides into the judiciary. Those countries at the higher end in terms of women in the judiciary tend to be those in which strong national, even constitutional, commitments have been made to increasing women's access to positions of power and decision-making and where women can be found in other elected and appointed leadership positions in government (Rwanda, Tanzania, South Africa, Tunisia), though as Egypt demonstrates, such stated commitments are not always realized.

Gender and Representation

Much of the variation in women's presence on benches can be traced to appointment processes—with stark differences between the practices in common law versus civil law countries—mindful also of the role of specific gatekeepers. Other factors are also at play, like access to legal education, which influences the supply of women attorneys and potential women judges, the role of executives such as presidents, political will on the part of executives and others, constitutional and organizational commitments to women in positions of power and decision-making and the role of legal associations and other civil society actors. As noted above, Schultz and Shaw (2012a, p. 2) suggest that the appointment of women is easier in civil law countries than common law countries, in that in the former countries

> key access criteria for judicial office, such as formal qualification and examination results, are more rational and transparent and therefore more easily met by women than those in the common law world, where professional visibility, favourable evaluations of professional achievement, and access to—traditionally male—networks are of crucial weight.

In Egypt, women have made little headway as judges despite the fact that Egypt's judiciary is the oldest in the Arab world and has a reasonable record, by Middle Eastern standards, of advancing gender equality, according to Hamad. While successive Egyptian constitutions guaranteed gender equality, they did not mandate gender equality in the courts; nor did they lead to the realization of gender equality in the public sphere. The 2014 constitution is different in stipulating women's access to judicial appointments. But this stipulation too has not yet been realized. Hamad attributes the ongoing challenge to women in the judiciary in Egypt not to sharia law or religion alone, but rather to the 'conservative nature of the courts themselves.' What will be required, according to Hamad, are time, effort and political will. In Botswana, with very few women in its higher courts, other factors are at play. There, decades of expatriate judges, often white men from South Africa, kept indigenous men and women out of the upper echelons of the courts until well into the 21st century. Indeed the first Motswana judge was not appointed to the High Court until 1992 and the Court of Appeal until 2012. This reflected in part a small indigenous legal community stemming in part from legal education only available outside the country until the late 1980s. At the same time, today, with women about one-third of lawyers in the country and more than half of magistrates, the supply of potential candidates should be sufficient. Other factors beyond a delayed indigenization that may have affected the delayed feminization of the judiciary include an appointment process in which a Judicial Service Commission (JSC) whose members are largely appointed by the president make recommendation to the president for higher court appointments but in the process also facilitate 'executive overreach.' Indeed, even then the president has rejected a woman candidate recommended by the JSC. As in Egypt, lack of political will, in Botswana's case from the executive (and observed also with regard to the legislature), provides another explanation for the lack of women judges.

By contrast, in South Africa, since the transition to black majority rule and democracy in 1994, there has been an explicit commitment to transforming the judiciary and making it more representative of the population and to making the judiciary a 'legitimate and independent guardian of the constitution.' So whereas prior to democracy South Africa 'followed the British convention of a "tap on the shoulder" in appointing judges,' today an open and transparent system makes the procedure for the appointment of judges 'highly visible, often contested and connected to current political debates about race and gender.' Among other things, South Africa teaches us about the value of constitutional reform and of a constitution that provides a new and more open mechanism for judicial appointments and a provision that explicitly requires women in the judiciary. Furthermore, the new process for judicial appointments also provides for a wide array of civil society actors to engage the bodies that appoint judges and to advocate for the appointment of certain judges. In South Africa, the concern has been not only to appoint more women judges but also to consider other factors such as race, religion and cultural background so as to achieve a diversity of opinion and to transform the judiciary.

In Tanzania, Yoon identifies a number of factors as responsible for the high percentages of women in the upper courts in the country. The president appoints justices to the Court of Appeal in consultation with the chief justice and judges of the High Court after consultation with a JSC (on which, Yoon notes, women are grossly underrepresented—as also in Botswana). Magistrates of the lower courts are appointed by the JSC. Yoon credits the current president with increasing representation on the bench, in an effort to narrow the gender gap in the judiciary, and in response to a constant push from women's organizations for more women in decision making as well as the country's commitment to a 50% target for women in positions of decision-making as set by the African Union and Southern African Development Community (SADC). President Kikwete has been able to do this, Yoon argues, because of Article 109(8) of the constitution which allows the president to appoint a person he or she believes 'has the ability, knowledge, and in every respect is suitable for appointment as Judge of the High Court, and there are reasons which such person deserve to be so appointed' even if the person does not meet all of the qualifications. As Yoon further notes, while the numbers of women in the judiciary are growing, they have not yet reached parity which some Tanzanian justices have attributed to 'patriarchy,' that denies 'capable women the chance to be appointed as judges.'

Rwanda has an even more firm commitment to parity in political decision-making positions than Tanzania, or at least until Tanzania's proposed new constitution is adopted. In Rwanda, the president plays a significant role in the appointment of Supreme Court justices and heads of the High Court. Kamatali notes that large increases in the number of women in the judiciary began in the 2010s. He attributes this to a number of factors: first, women's increased access to legal education, in particular to law school (with the establishment of two new Kigali-based law schools in the late 1990s), led to more women lawyers. Second, legal changes removed limitations on women's participation in decision-making, first in 1988 and then again from the 2000s onward; the removal of these legal barriers resulted in large part from pressure from civil society activists. Finally, specific government policies such as quotas, affirmative action and political lobbying have had a big impact on the legislature but cannot be used in the judiciary; rather 'insider-outsider collaboration'—in which the judiciary does not just wait for women to apply, it actively seeks competent candidates and encourages them to join—has made the difference to the judiciary in Rwanda, combining the benefits of a quota with the need for judicial independence. In Rwanda, according to Kamatali, insider-outsider collaboration was facilitated for many years by the fact that both the minister in the office of the president responsible for justice issues and the chief justice of the Supreme Court were women who actively encouraged and recruited women into the judiciary. For Ghana, Dawuni also suggests that the current woman chief justice can be credited with promoting a number of fully qualified women to the higher courts and that more women judges on the bench in general serve as role models to other potential women judges.

In Nigeria, a clear divide exists between the south and the north in terms of women's access to the judiciary, beginning with access to education. The south has a better education system and one that is more inclusive of girls and women; more women read law and they come from families with many generations of educated members. In the north, by contrast, girls may not be encouraged to attend school beyond the elementary level. According to Ibrahim, some states such as Lagos followed deliberate policies from the 1990s onwards to bring more women into the judiciary while in other states in the north that may rely on customary or sharia laws, patrimonial and patriarchal interests prevail. Indeed, Ibrahim reports that in some cases in the south there is even declining interest among men to take judgeships because they are perceived as 'civil service like' jobs—as Schultz and Shaw (2012a, p. 3) have predicted might happen with an increase in the proportion of women in the judiciary—that there could follow a 'lowering of judicial prestige and income.'

Benin follows appointment procedures typical for a civil law legal system, though Kang is not optimistic about a continued upward trend in women's access to the bench in the country. She cites continued low enrollments of women relative to men at university in Benin, as well as gendered norms around marriage and childbearing that may make women far less available to become a judge in training during the eligible years, ages 21 to 35. Finally, she suggests it is possible that a commitment to gender equality during the socialist era, from 1972 to 1989, during which women experienced significant gains in public life, may not have been replicated in the democratic era. For Tunisia, Klibi describes a 'paradigm shift' in the late 1960s once more women began to graduate from law school but also with the passage of a new law in which no 'evocation of gender' was made with reference to the recruitment of judges. Tunisia's 2014 constitution embodies the principle of parity, including in the judiciary, though the law establishing the mechanism for this in the judiciary is yet to be adopted. Klibi notes the pressure from civil society on the new constitution.

Our sample of African cases reveals some different factors at play from other parts of the world, in helping or hindering the recruitment of women into the judiciary. To begin with, the experience of colonialism and in some countries, such as Botswana, the historical legacy of an expatriate-dominated judiciary contributed to a delayed feminization of the judiciary. Regime type—for example a socialist regime with a stated commitment to gender equality in Benin—as well as regime change across the continent have also had significant positive and negative impacts. In particular the transitions to democracy in the early 1990s (or more recent transitions in northern Africa) have had a profound influence in almost all of our cases, with progressive new constitutions being adopted and new laws pertaining to the judiciary (and the rights of women) being adopted. Thus in South Africa there has been a purposeful attempt to transform the judiciary into one that is legitimate, independent, representative and diverse. Similarly, in Rwanda a constitutional commitment to women holding at least 30% of positions of power and decision-making in government is evident in the judiciary. Also in Tanzania, such a commitment exists in the yet to be adopted new constitution (though no specific mention is made of the judiciary in this regard) and in the fulfillment of regional and continental obligations to the African Union and SADC. New constitutions adopted in Egypt and Tunisia in 2014 should be making a difference to the recruitment of women into the judiciary in those countries though not yet as expected, as will be discussed below.

Some of the factors helping or hindering women into the judiciary are similar to other parts of the world, for example, the 'pipeline,' as in women's increased access to education and legal training facilitating women's access to the judiciary in places like Botswana, Rwanda, Tunisia, southern Nigeria and so on. Also we see the role that individual women judges and advocates can make, not just as role models, but in actively encouraging and recruiting other women as has the current chief justice in Ghana or a past chief justice in Rwanda and a minister in the office of the president in Rwanda ('insider-outsider collaboration'). Other officeholders, in particular in the executive, can make a difference; so in Botswana the president can overlook a woman applicant to the High Court, while in Tanzania the president receives an award from the International Association of Women Judges for appointing women to the judiciary—and then appoints more women judges! Judicial service commissions and similar bodies such as judicial councils are pivotal and their gender composition also makes a difference, with fewer women on those bodies negatively influencing women's appointments to the courts. Critical roles are played across Africa, as in other places, by civil society organizations and women's associations, as well as law societies and national chapters of the International Association of Women Judges in exerting pressure for more women in judiciaries. Finally, 'political will' has been identified in a few of our cases, and the lack thereof, and enduring patterns of patriarchy continue to thwart women's access to the judiciary in Africa, as in other places.

Women and the Judiciary

What, if anything, has been the impact on the judiciary and the quality of justice of the increasing presence of women in all levels of courts across the continent? Are women judges more likely to uphold the rights of women litigants and seek to reform patriarchal legal rules and concepts? For more than a decade research has revealed that women members of parliament (MPs) in sub-Saharan Africa have had an impact (Bauer, 2012). Such impacts have been identified as substantive representation effects of more women MPs—how women's interests are represented through women MPs' policy priorities and legislative accomplishments—and symbolic representation effects of more women MPs—how public attitudes towards women in politics are changed and women's own engagement in politics increases (Franceshet, Krook & Piscopo, 2012). What about in judiciaries? Is it possible to discern a similar effect because of more women judges? Is it fair to expect women judges to solve a problem like patriarchy or is this not an issue to be addressed by all judges? Is it realistic to expect women to be able to overcome conservative and male-dominated institutions like the judiciary—and if so, not to experience backlash? Is a 'critical mass' (Dahlerup, 2006) of women judges the key to having an impact or are 'critical actors' or 'critical acts' (Childs & Krook, 2006) all that are required? Also what about impartiality and objectivity as overarching concepts central to judges and judging? Have there been impacts of women judges outside the courtroom?

Again, our cases reveal mixed outcomes. For Botswana, Bauer and Ellett identify two cases of great significance to women in Botswana over the last quarter century—the Citizenship Case of the 1980s and 1990s and the much more recent Mmusi case of the 2010s. Botswana's first woman High Court judge, Unity Dow, was involved in the Citizenship Case, but as plaintiff, not as judge, ultimately winning the case and the right for citizenship to pass from a mother to her children as well as from a father to his children. Botswana's second High Court judge, Athaliah Molokomme, was involved in the Mmusi Case, but as attorney general, not as judge, and weighed in on the losing side of 'custom' in a case in which elderly sisters were allowed to inherit the family homestead rather than a younger nephew. In both cases in Botswana, where only very recently have very few women entered the upper echelons of the courts, progressive male judges have won important rights for women in the country. In neighboring South Africa, Albertyn and Bonthuys note that significant gains for women have been accomplished in the courts, in particular in the areas of customary law, gender-based violence and family law. But they are unable to attribute a 'progressive and gendered jurisprudence in the courts' to women judges. Moreover, in South Africa in particular, multiple identities, such as race, class, sexual orientation, rural origins, religious affiliation and cultural heritage, intervene. Albertyn and Bonthuys cite one preliminary study that suggests that women judges tend to agree with one another and with feminist men more often in cases involving gender, which may be an indication that women judges think differently than men judges. At the same time they also note that all of the groundbreaking judgments in South Africa that have substantially extended the rights of women have come from African male judges, with significant support from other male and female judges.

Dawuni finds from interviews with women judges and justices in Ghana that while some may feel they are better able to empathize with female litigants or they have been able to 'promote the rights of women,' others insist that their gender does not influence their judgments in any way; rather they are bound by powerful norms of impartiality and objectivity. At the same time, Dawuni suggests that women judges may be changing practices/institutional culture in the courtroom in important ways, such as in the manner that female judges are addressed or that cases are heard—being more respectful of minors and victims of gender-based violence and paying more attention to detail. In Nigeria, Ibrahim found from her interviews that women judges are more likely to ensure that cases are filed electronically, thereby ensuring greater transparency. Indeed, in both Ghana and Nigeria, women judges are apparently considered to be less susceptible to corruption. Dawuni raises the important point of the role of women judges outside the courtroom, for example, in the first female chief justice spearheading the establishment of a Gender Justice Center and in the creation of a Ghana chapter of the International Association of Women Judges in 2010 (as women judges did in Botswana in 1999 and Tanzania in 2000) aimed at strengthening the capacity of women judges but also at undertaking education, for example with women chiefs who confront issues of gender-based violence in the Customary Courts.

Kang argues that women judges in Benin have promoted women's rights in the areas of women's property rights and women's equality in the family. Under the socialist regime in Benin, and before the transition to democracy, women judges repeatedly interpreted Article 124 of the basic law to mean that women could inherit property. Similarly, Kang argues that women judges—in the ministry of family, in civil society and as members of the Constitutional Court played a critical role in the late 1990s and early 2000s in revising Benin's family laws to promote women's and children's rights. For those other countries with some of the highest percentages of women judges, it has been just as difficult to discern the impact of more women judges. For Rwanda, Kamatali sought to determine whether justices of the Supreme Court of Rwanda decided rape and abortion cases differently depending on their gender. He found no differences between male and female justices in their decision on whether those found guilty at the lower courts should have their sentences reduced or not. Further, in interviews with a small sample of women judges he found that women judges identified no difference from the way in which they and their male colleagues apply the law, though there may be differences in the way that women judges treat litigants. Indeed Kamatali suggests that in Rwanda, more women in the judiciary may be more about giving women equal opportunities to become judges than it is about women judges promoting women's rights. Kamatali does suggest, as in Ghana and Nigeria, that women judges in Rwanda may be less prone to corruption and, as noted earlier, that they play a pivotal role as role models and mentors in bringing more women into the judiciary.

In Tanzania, Yoon finds that women judges are having a significant impact outside the courtroom. There too a Tanzania chapter of the International Association of Women Judges (TAWJA) formed in 2000 has worked tirelessly to advance women's rights to equal justice, promote women's access to the courts, advocate for more women judges at all levels, develop judicial leadership, conduct legal research on gender equality and human rights, exchange information on issues of importance to women and uproot gender bias from the judicial system and the community, with emphasis on access to the courts and eliminating gender bias from the judicial system. Widner (2001a) has observed the impact in Tanzania and across Africa of the 'international community' as a source of support to African judges. TAWJA's effort to increase women in the judiciary has, however, been 'unnoticeable,' according to Yoon. At the least, Yoon argues, there has been a small degree of success in TAWJA's judicial education efforts.

So, as in other parts of the world (Kenney, 2012) then, we do not find that in Africa women judges judge differently simply because they are women, though it should also be acknowledged that this question has not been thoroughly researched. In Africa too, women judges express concern about abiding by norms of impartiality and objectivity; anecdotal evidence shows that progressive male judges have been responsible for some of the most far-reaching decisions advancing the rights of women in a number of countries. But there are important ways in which women judges and justices in Africa are making a difference, even if only in the last decade or two. This includes mentoring and recruiting future women judges and justices, participating in civil society organizations and in law societies and national chapters of the International Association of Women Judges to educate women, advocate for more judges, and scrutinize appointment processes and decisions. Further, it appears from many of the case studies that women judges, like their legislative counterparts, may be changing courtroom cultures and practices and may be less prone to corruption than their male colleagues.

Challenges and Obstacles

Our case studies reveal a plethora of challenges facing women in the judiciary in Africa today. Just as for women in the other branches of government, in Africa and elsewhere, the obstacles to women seeking appointment to the judiciary and seeking to promote women's rights are many. Nearly every chapter mentions the overarching challenge of patriarchy; this can be the patriarchy manifest in attitudes about women's (lackluster) competencies in Egypt, or the patriarchal culture in which courts are embedded in Tanzania. In a couple of countries, such as Egypt, a conservative understanding of Islam holds the appointment of female judges to be incompatible with sharia, while in several others expectations about marriage and family militate against women judges. In Rwanda, many expect women to remain 'traditional' wives and mothers rather than become judges or justices, and in Tunisia family responsibilities, in the absence of state policies to assist families, slow down women's legal careers; in Benin, Ghana or Nigeria, expectations around age of marriage and childbearing have made women less available for legal careers in the past, though this may be changing. Lack of access to education and the appropriate legal training (for financial and other reasons) can keep women from judicial posts. Across Africa a host of general challenges to the courts can hamper women judges who feel they have to outperform their male colleagues, including poorly equipped courtrooms, poorly trained clerks, shortages of judges that result in backlogs and delays that are the breeding ground for corruption, temporary courtrooms that can mean a lack of appropriate facilities such as restrooms, transfers or assignments far from home and so on. Around the world (male) judges are considered to be traditional and conservative and this can be even more so in some African countries. Women who dare to contravene some of the biased and stereotypical representations of them by others may find themselves abused, as women judges have in Nigeria. In some places like Botswana or Egypt, where despite large numbers of qualified women, gatekeeping in the legal profession and career paths for women lawyers on the one hand and lack of political commitment to feminization of the judiciary on the other hand, have contributed to keeping women off the bench. As noted in the South Africa chapter, dismantling structures of gender oppression should not be a task that falls to women judges alone, but so long as we can assume that this will be a task likely to be embraced by women judges, we need to consider those challenges and obstacles continuing to face them.

Conclusion: Future Research

This volume has brought together nine case studies of women and the judiciary from across the African continent. We have represented all geographic regions on the continent and we have included examples of countries that practice various mixes of the legal traditions dominant on the continent. The cases represent a wide range in terms of women's representation in judiciaries with hardly any women judges in a country like Egypt to approaching parity in a country like Rwanda. It is clear to us that in Africa as elsewhere there is a need for more women judges and justices in order to foster gender balance in positions of power and decision-making in government, achieve greater judicial representativity and diversity and enhance the legitimacy of the courts.

One of the main findings of the book is just how much we do not know about women and the judiciary in Africa today. To begin with, we could find no reliable source of comparable data across countries and courts—so any central source of data on women in the highest court in all African countries, or in the higher courts as a group, or in the lower courts as a group. Even data on women chief justices and presidents of Constitutional Courts in Africa is not readily available. Even within countries it is difficult to find longitudinal data on women on the bench, at almost any level. In addition to generating such data, interesting future research might include profiles of women justices and judges from across Africa, as has been done in the case of women in positions of executive power around the world (less so in Africa). Such profiles would shed some light on the career trajectories that the most accomplished women judges and justices have taken to enter the judiciary—starting with law school and then possibly pursuing private practice, serving as government attorneys or joining the lower courts. It would also be interesting to compare women and men judges on the same court in the same country, to get a sense of how the qualifications of men and women judges compare. A clearer picture of appointment processes to the bench across countries, including the role of specific 'gatekeepers,' would help us to better understand those factors likely to help or hinder women's access to the judiciary. National chapters of the International Association of Women Judges seem to play important advocacy and educational roles and could contribute to studies of women's access to the judiciary in Africa. The question of the influence of civil society and other organizations on women's appointments offers potential avenues for fruitful future research as well.

More in-depth interviews of sitting women judges and justices, some of which were conducted for this volume for Egypt, Nigeria, Ghana and Rwanda, would provide the 'qualitative narratives and oral histories' that Ibrahim recommends to shed light on women judges' roles in enhancing justice and promoting women's rights. The significant diversity of legal systems (and to some extent regime types, even if only historically) across Africa offers an opportunity for informative research on what women judges are able to accomplish in different legal and political contexts. In the meantime, the case studies presented in this volume have provided a compelling narrative of how women have been breaking gender stereotypes and accessing the judiciary as judges and justices in several African countries, what they have been able to accomplish once on the bench despite the many challenges and obstacles, and what aspirations propel them forward.

Contributors

Cathi Albertyn is professor of law at the University of the Witwatersrand, Johannesburg, South Africa, where she teaches undergraduate and postgraduate courses on constitutional law and human rights. Prior to joining the academic staff at the Wits School of Law, she was the Director of the Centre for Applied Legal Studies, a human rights research and advocacy center attached to the Wits School of Law. Albertyn has a BA, LLB from the University of Cape Town and a PhD from Cambridge University, where she wrote a thesis on South African political trials. Albertyn's research interests include equality, gender studies, human rights and constitutional law. She has published extensively on equality and gender, including a chapter on 'Judicial Diversity' in C. Hoexter & M. Olivier's *The South African Judiciary* (2014). She is also an editor of the most cited South African law journal, the *South African Journal on Human Rights*.

Gretchen Bauer is professor in the Department of Political Science and International Relations at the University of Delaware (USA). Her current research focuses on women's political leadership in sub-Saharan Africa. She has published widely on politics in southern Africa and women in politics across sub-Saharan Africa. She is the co-editor with Hannah Britton of *Women in African Parliaments* (Lynne Rienner 2006) and the co-editor with Manon Tremblay of *Women in Executive Power: A Global Overview* (Routledge 2011). Bauer has been a Visiting Researcher at the Institute for Public Policy Research in Namibia in 2002 and at the University of Botswana in 2009, 2011 and 2013, and a Fulbright Scholar at the University of Ghana Legon in 2016.

Elsje Bonthuys obtained her BA, LLB and LLM degrees at Stellenbosch University in South Africa and her PhD at Cambridge University. She is a professor who teaches family law and law of contracts at the University of the Witwatersrand in Johannesburg, South Africa and researches in the areas of gender, sexuality and family law.

Josephine Dawuni is assistant professor of political science at Howard University (USA). She received her PhD from Georgia State University. She is qualified as a Barrister-at-Law before the Superior Courts of Judicature in Ghana. Prior to joining Howard University, she worked at [Georgia Gwinnett College], as a barrister in Ghana and in the banking industry in Manchester, United Kingdom. Dawuni has a certificate in women's studies and much of her research and many of her publications are in the areas of gender and the judiciary, gender and development, and international human rights law. She has conducted extensive fieldwork in Ghana with women's organizations and female judges. Her current research focuses on women in the legal and judicial professions across Africa.

Rachel Ellett is associate professor of political science at Beloit College (USA). Her research is located at the intersection of politics and law. Ellett writes on judicial politics, rule of law and development, and lawyers as political actors in southern and eastern Africa. She has conducted fieldwork in Uganda, Tanzania, Malawi, Botswana, Zambia and Lesotho. She has published in *Comparative Politics*, *Northern Ireland Legal Quarterly*, *Law and Courts* and recently published 'Going off bench: Protecting Judicial Autonomy in Competitive Clientelist Regimes' with Alexei Trochev in the *Journal of Law and Courts*. She is the author of *Pathways to Judicial Power in Transitional States: Perspective from Africa Courts* (Routledge 2013). Ellett has also written a series of reports on judicial independence in southern Africa as a consultant for Freedom House.

Mahmoud Hamad holds a joint appointment as associate professor of political science at Drake University (USA) and Cairo University (Egypt). He received his PhD in political science from the University of Utah and his BA and MA in political science from Cairo University, Egypt. His teaching and research interests focus on Middle East politics, comparative judicial politics, civil-military relations, as well as religion and politics. Prior to coming to Drake, Hamad taught at Cairo University, Brigham Young University, and the University of Utah. Hamad was a Fulbright Scholar twice during his graduate study. He has written extensively in both Arabic and English journals. Mahmoud is the editor of *Elections and Democratization in the Middle East: The Tenacious Search for Freedom, Justice, and Dignity* (Palgrave 2014). He is also the author of *Generals and Judges in the Making of Modern Egypt* (forthcoming).

Hauwa Ibrahim, Esq. is a senior Fellow at the WANA Institute, Majlis El-Hassan in the Hashemite Kingdom of Jordan. Prior to joining the Harvard Divinity School as a Visiting Lecturer, Ibrahim was a jointly appointed fellow at the Radcliffe Institute for Advanced Study at Harvard University and at Harvard Law School's Human Rights Program and Islamic Legal Studies Program. A lawyer, author and mother, Ibrahim built up a unique practice, representing in Sharia Courts women and children condemned to death by stoning or to limb amputation for offenses like adultery and theft, among others. She defended over 150 cases pro bono, helping to save the lives of numerous women, including in the internationally known cases of Amina Lawal, Safiya Hussaini, and Hafsatu Abubakar. In May 2014, President Jonathan appointed her to serve on the presidential committee charged with fact-finding to help rescue the 219 girls kidnapped by the Boko Haram from Chibok, northern Nigeria. Ibrahim has been honored with the European Parliament 2005 Sakharov Prize for Freedom of Thought.

Jean-Marie Kamatali is associate professor of law at Ohio Northern University Pettit College of Law (USA). He teaches in the areas of human rights, transitional justice and law reform. He is former dean of the University of Rwanda Law School. He also participated in the design and implementation of legal and institutional solutions in postgenocide Rwanda including Gacaca, legal training, and justice reforms. Kamatali has taught at the University of Notre Dame Law School, Kent State and Indiana University, and the University of Leuven in Belgium. He has worked as consultant for governmental organizations and institutions including the World Bank, UNICEF, US Department of Justice, USAID and the Office of the UN Special Advisor on Genocide. His media appearance and op-ed contributions include NPR, Voice of America, Democracy Now, C-Span, and the *New York Times*.

Alice Kang is a scholar of women and politics and African politics. Kang is the author of *Bargaining for Women's Rights: Activism in an Aspiring Muslim Democracy* (University of Minnesota Press 2015). She has published articles in *Comparative Political Studies*, *Politics & Gender*, and *Women's Studies International Forum*. Her current work focuses on women on High Courts and is funded by a collaborative research award from the National Science Foundation. Kang is assistant professor of political science and ethnic studies at the University of Nebraska-Lincoln (USA).

Salsabil Klibi is a Tunisian legal expert and assistant professor at the Faculty of Law at the University of Tunis, where she teaches courses in constitutional law, legal theory and election law. She received her law degree and her MA in law from the Faculty of Law, University of Tunis. Klibi holds a number of leading positions in Tunisian and Arab law associations, including being the vice president of the Arab Organization of Constitutional Law. She is the author of a number of research papers in Arabic, French and English. Klibi is a co-author of the *Handbook on Democracy and Human Rights for Tunisian Youth* (UNESCO 2011).

Mi Yung Yoon is professor of international studies at Hanover College (USA). She received her PhD in political science from Florida State University. Her areas of research include women's political representation, democratization, territorial dispute, and foreign aid in Africa. Her research has appeared in the *Journal of Conflict Resolution*, the *Legislative Studies Quarterly*,

Democratization, *Africa Today*, the *Journal of Contemporary African Studies*, *Commonwealth & Comparative Politics*, *Women's Studies International Forum*, and others. She was awarded a Fulbright Scholar grant in 2011 for her research on Korea's bilateral official development assistance to Africa. She published the findings of her Fulbright-funded research in the *Journal of East Asian Studies* (2014). She is an Africanist, and visits Africa every other summer for field research.

Bibliography

14 new judges sworn in. (2013, August 7). *GhanaWeb*. Retrieved from www.ghanaweb.com/GhanaHomePage/NewsArchive/artikel.php?ID=281737

Abdelkader, E. (2014). To judge or not to judge: A comparative analysis of Islamic jurisprudential approaches to female judges in the Muslim World (Indonesia, Egypt and Iran). *Fordham International Law Journal, 37*, 309–372.

Abrahamson, S. (1998). Do women judges really make a difference? The American experience. In Shetreet, S. (Ed.), *Women in law* (pp. 195–216). London, England: Kluwer.

African National Congress. (1989a). Constitutional guidelines for a democratic South Africa. Retrieved from www.anc.org.za/show.php?id=294

African National Congress. (1989b). Harare declaration. Declaration of the OAU Ad-hoc Committee on Southern Africa on the question of South Africa. Retrieved from www.anc.org.za/show.php?id=3856

African National Congress. (1992). Ready to govern: ANC policy guidelines for a democratic South Africa. Retrieved from www.anc.org.za/show.php?id=227

African National Congress (2012, March). Peace and stability. Policy Discussion Document. Retrieved from www.anc.org.za/docs/discus/2012/peacev.pdf

African Union. (2008). Report of the promotion mission to the United Republic of Tanzania. Retrieved from www.achpr.org/states/tanzania/missions/promo-2008/

Aguda, J.A. (1973). Legal development in Botswana from 1885 to 1966. *Botswana Notes and Records*, *5*, 52–63.

Akpamgbo, C. (1977). A 'woman to woman' marriage and the repugnancy clause: A case of putting new wine into old bottles. *The Journal of Legal Pluralism and Unofficial Law, 9*, 87–95.

Albertyn, C. (1994). Women and the transition to democracy in South Africa. *Acta Juridica*. 39–63.

Albertyn, C. (2011). Law, gender and equality in South Africa. *Oxford Development Studies 39*, 139–162.

Albertyn, C. (2014). Judicial diversity. In Hoexter, C. & Olivier, M. (Eds.). *The judiciary in South Africa* (pp. 245–287). Cape Town, South Africa: Juta.

Al-taweel, A. (2012). *Almraah almesria wa wazefet aladaa alam*. Cairo, Egypt: ACIJLP.

Al-wafd. (2012, September 24). Rady. A. (2012, September 24). Interview with Anani AbdelAziz, president of the APA. *Al-Wafd* (p. 8). Retrieved from *http://* alwafd.org/حوارات-وملفات/268917-نظام-«مبارك»-نزع-أنياب-هيئة-النيابة-ال
ادارية-لتجنب-الملاحسقة[1]

Amadiume, I. (1997). *Re-inventing Africa: Matriarchy, religion and culture*. London, England: Zed Books.

Ammar, N. H. (2003). To object or not to object: The question of women judges in Egypt. *International Journal of Comparative and Applied Criminal Justice, 27*, 69–83.

Attanasso, M. O. (2012). *Femmes et pouvoir politique au Bénin: Des origines Dahoméennes à nos jours*. Cotonou, Benin: Friedrich Ebert Stiftung. Retrieved from http://library.fes.de/pdf-files/bueros/benin/10194.pdf

Baaitse, F. (2015, March 30). Lawyers, Khama clash over judicial appointments. *Weekend Post*. Retrieved from www.weekendpost.co.bw/wp-news-details.php?nid=784

Backhouse, C. (2003). The chilly climate for women judges: Reflections from the Ewanchuck case. *Canadian Journal of Women and the Law, 15*, 167–193.

Bako Arifari. N. (2006). La corruption quotidienne au Bénin. *LASDEL Études et Travaux 43*.

Barmes, L., & Malleson, K. (2011). The legal profession as gatekeeper to the judiciary: Design faults in measures to enhance diversity. *Modern Law Review, 74*, 245–271.

Bauer, G. (2010). 'Cows will lead the herd into a precipice:' Where are the women MPs in Botswana? *Botswana Notes and Records, 42*, 56–70.

Bauer, G. (2011). Update on the women's movement in Botswana: Have women stopped talking? *African Studies Review, 54*, 23–46.

Bauer, G. (2012). 'Let there be a balance:' Women in African parliaments. *Political Studies Quarterly, 10*, 370–384.

Bauer, G. (2014). What is wrong with a woman being chief? Women chiefs and symbolic and substantive representation in Botswana. *Journal of Asian and African Studies*, doi: 10.1177/0021909614545700

Bauer, G., and Okpotor, F. (2013). 'Her Excellency:' An exploratory overview of women cabinet ministers in Africa. *Africa Today, 60*, 76–97.

Belaid, S. (1974). *Le pouvoir créateur et normatif du juge*. Paris, France: LGDI.

Bierschenk, T. (2008). The everyday functioning of an African public service: Informalization, privatization, and corruption in Benin's legal system. *Journal of Legal Pluralism, 40*, 101–139.

Bierwagen, R. M., & Peter, C. M. (1989). Administration of justice in Tanzania and Zanzibar: A comparison of two judicial systems in one country. *The International and Comparative Law Quarterly, 38*, 395–412.

Bolle, S. (2004). Le code des personnes et de la famille devant la cour constitutionnelle du Bénin. La décision DCC 02–144 du 26 décembre 2002. *Afrilex, 4*. Retrieved from http://afrilex.u-bordeaux4.fr/sites/afrilex/IMG/pdf/04jur15bolle.pdf

Bonthuys, E. (2008a). The personal and the judicial: Sex, gender and impartiality. *South African Journal on Human Rights, 24*, 239–262.

Bonthuys, E. (2008b). Institutional openness and resistance to feminist arguments: The example of the South African Constitutional Court. *Canadian Journal of Women and Law, 20*, 1–36.

Bonthuys, E. (2013). Gender and the chief justice: Principle or pretext? *Journal of Southern African Studies, 39*, 59–76.

Bonthuys, E. (2014). Commitments to gender equality in South African family law: 'Unpredictable and sporadic?' In Sagade, B., Vedna, J., & Forster, C. (Eds.), *Feminism in the subcontinent and beyond: Challenging laws and changing laws* (pp.193–212). Westbrook, ME: Eastern Book Company.

Bonthuys, E. (2015). Gender and race in South African judicial appointments. *Feminist Legal Studies, 23,* 127–148.

Bourgeois, R. (1957). *Banyarwanda et Barundi*. Brussels, Belgium: Académie Royale des Sciences Coloniales.

Bourgi, A. (2002). L'évolution du constitutionalisme en Afrique: Du formalisme à l'effectivité. *Revue française de droit constitutionnel, 4*, 721–748.

Bratton, M. & Van de Walle, N. (1997). *Democratic experiments in Africa: Regime transitions in comparative perspective*. Cambridge, England: Cambridge University Press.

Brinton, J. Y. (1968). *The mixed courts of Egypt*. New Haven, CT: Yale University Press.

Brown, N. (1997). *The rule of law in the Arab World: Courts in Egypt and the Gulf.* Cambridge, England: Cambridge University Press.

Budlender, G. (2005). Transforming the judiciary: The politics of the judiciary in a democratic South Africa. *South African Law Journal, 122*, 715–724.

Burnet, J.E. (2008). Gender balance and the meanings of women in governance in post-genocide Rwanda. *African Affairs, 107*, 361–386.

Burnet, J.E. (2012). Women's empowerment and cultural change in Rwanda. In Franceschet, S, Krook, M.L., & Piscopo, J. (Eds.). *The impact of gender quotas* (pp. 190–207). Oxford, England: Oxford University Press.

Cardinal, M. (2008). Women and the judiciary in Syria: Appointments process, training and career paths. *International Journal of the Legal Profession, 15*, 127–139.

Cardinal, M. (2013). The impact of women on the administration of justice in Syria and the judicial selection process. In Shultz, U., & Shaw, G. (Eds.), *Gender and judging* (pp. 191–209). Portland, OR: Hart Publishing.

Chande urges appointment of more women judges. (2013, August 14). *Daily News*. Retrieved from http://archive.dailynews.co.tz/index.php/local-news/21090-chande-urges-appointment-of-more-women-judges

Chanock, M. (2001). *The Making of South African Legal Culture 1902-1936: Fear, Favour and Prejudice*. Cambridge, England: Cambridge University Press.

Childs, S., & Krook, M.L. (2006). Should feminists give up on critical mass? A contingent yes. *Politics & Gender, 2*, 522–530.

CJ solicit[s] support for women judges. (2013, September 9). *Modern Ghana*. Retrieved from www.modernghana.com/news/488353/1/cj-solicit-support-for-women-judges.html

Claassens, A., & Weeks, S. (2009). Rural women redefining land rights in the context of a living customary law. *South African Journal on Human Rights, 25*, 491–516.

Cobbah, J. (1987). African values and the human rights debate. An African perspective. *Human Rights Quarterly, 9*, 309–331.

Collins, P.M., Manning, J.R., Kenneth, L., & Carp, R.A. (2010). Gender, critical mass and judicial decision making. *Law & Policy, 32*, 260–281.

Constitution de la République du Bénin. Loi n° 90–32 du 11 décembre 1990 portant constitution de la république.

Constitution of the Federal Republic of Nigeria. (1999). Retrieved from www.icnl.org/research/library/files/Nigeria/constitution2.pdf

Constitution of Tanzania. (1977). Retrieved from www.judiciary.go.tz/downloads/constitution.pdf

Constitution of the Republic of South Africa. (1993). Retrieved from www.constitutionalcourt.org.za/site/constitution/english-web/interim/.

Constitution of the Republic of South Africa. (1996). Retrieved from www.gov.za/documents/constitution-republic-south-africa-1996

Constitution of Zanzibar. (2002). Retrieved from www.wipo.int/edocs/lexdocs/laws/en/tz/tz028en.pdf

Corder, H. (1984). *Judges at work. The role and attitudes of the South African appellate judiciary: 1910–50*. Cape Town, South Africa: Juta.

Coutumier du Dahomey. (1933). Retrieved from http://landwise.landesa.org/record/1815

Cowan, R. (2006). Women's representation on the courts in the Republic of South Africa. *University of Maryland Law Journal of Race, Religion, Gender & Class, 6*, 291–317.

Cowan, R. (2013). Do women on South Africa's courts make a difference? In Schultz, U., & Shaw, G. (Eds.), *Gender and judging* (pp. 317–333). Portland, OR: Hart Publishing.

Cowen, S. (2005). Breaking through glass ceilings. *Advocate, 18*, 47–50.

Cowen, S. (2010). Judicial selection in South Africa. Research report. Cape Town, South Africa: Democratic Governance and Rights Unit, University of Cape Town.

Dahlerup, D. (2006). The story of the theory of critical mass. *Politics & Gender, 2*, 511–522.

Dawuni, J. (2011). Justice Annie Jiagge. In Acheampong, E., & Gates, H.L. (Eds.), *Dictionary of African biography* (pp. 207–208). London, England: Oxford University Press.

Dawuni, J., and Kang, A. (2014). The rise of women chief justices in Africa. Paper presented at the African Studies Association 2014 annual meeting, Indianapolis, IN.

Democratic Governance and Rights Unit. (2009, September 20–22). Summary of JSC interviews for the Constitutional Court vacancies. Cape Town, South Africa: University of Cape Town.

Department of Justice and Constitutional Development. (2015, January). The South African judiciary. Retrieved from www.judiciary.org.za/heads-of-superior-courts.html

D'Hertefelt, A. (1962). Le Rwanda. In D'Hertefelt, A., Trouwborst, A., & Scherer, J. (Eds.*), Les Anciens Royaumes de la zone interlacustre meridionale: Rwanda, Burundi, Buha*. London, England: International African Institute.

Dijksterhuis, B. (2013). Women judges in the Netherlands. In Schultz, U., & Shaw, G. (Eds.). *Gender and judging* (pp. 267–282). Portland, OR: Hart Publishing.

Djogbenou, J. 2010. *Bénin: Le secteur de la justice et l'État de droit*. AfriMAP/Open Society Initiative for West Africa. Retrieved from www.afrimap.org/english/images/report/AfriMAP_Benin_Justice_Principal.pdf

Djossou-Segla, A. (1997). *Promotion de la femme du Bénin: Livre blanc*. Cotonou, Benin: Friedrich Ebert Stiftung.

Dow, U. (Ed.). (1995). *The citizenship case: The Attorney General of the Republic of Botswana vs. Unity Dow. Court documents, judgments, cases and material*. Gaborone, Botswana: Lentswe la Lesedi.

Du Bois, F. (2006). Judicial selection in post-apartheid South Africa. In Malleson, K., & Russell, B.P.H. (Eds.), *Appointing judges in an age of judicial power: Critical perspectives from around the world* (pp. 280–312). Toronto, Ontario: University of Toronto Press.

Du Plessis, C. (2013a, April 21). Women judges still do 'double shift.' *City Press*.

Du Plessis, C. (2013b, July 14). Beware agents of racism. *City Press*.

Dugard, J. (1971). The judicial process, positivism and civil liberty. *South African Law Journal, 88*, 181–200.

Ellett, R. L. (2010). The African lawyer as political insider/outsider. American Political Science Association 2010 annual meeting. Available at SSRN: http://ssrn.com/abstract=1643413

Ellett, R. L. (2013). *Pathways to judicial power in transitional states*. London, England and New York, NY: Routledge.

Ellett, R. L. (2014). *Politics of judicial independence in Malawi*. Report prepared for Freedom House. Retrieved from https://freedomhouse.org/report/special-reports/politics-judicial-independence-malawi#.VS3O1kJxDVI

Ellett, R. L., and Mafukidze, T. (2013). Importing justice? Expatriate appointments in Botswana, Lesotho and Swaziland. Paper presented at the International Political Science Association 2013 annual meeting, Dublin.

Ellis, J. (2012, June 29). Botswana's fearless legal eagle fights male bias. Retrieved from www.cnn.com/2012/06/29/world/africa/unity-dow-botswana-judge/index.html

El-Nahal, G. H. (1979). *The judicial administration of Ottoman Egypt in the seventeenth century*. Minneapolis, MN: Bibliotheca Islamica.

El-Omda. M & R. Abdallah, (2014, January 20). Council of State rejects Talawy's letter. El-Waten. Retrieved from www.elwatannews.com/news/details/400405

Escobar-Lemmon, M., Hoekstra, V., Kang, A., & Kittilson, M. (2015). *Diversity on high courts: International influences on women's appointments*. Paper presented at the American Political Science 2015 annual meeting, San Francisco, CA.

Ezer, T. (2006). Inheritance law in Tanzania: The impoverishment of widows and daughters. *Georgetown Journal of Gender and the Law*, *7*, 599–662.

Feenan, D. (2008). Women judges: Gendering judging, justifying diversity. *Journal of Law and Society*, *35*, 490–519.

Feenan, D. (2009). Editorial introduction: Women and judging. *Feminist Legal Studies*, *17*, 1–9.

Fombad, C. M. (2011). Update: Botswana's legal system and legal research. Retrieved from www.nyulawglobal.org/globalex/Botswana1.htm

Fondation Regard d'Amour. (1998). *Les droits des enfants au regard du projet de code béninois des personnes et de la famille: Document de synthèse*. Abomey-Calavi, Benin: Fondation Regard D'amour; Organisation Non Gouvernementale de Protection des Enfants et de Promotion de la Famille.

Franceshet, S., Krook, M. L., & Piscopo, J. (2012). Contextualizing the impact of quotas. In Franceshet, S., Krook M. L., and Piscopo, J. (Eds.). *The impact of gender quotas* (pp. 3–26). Oxford, England: Oxford University Press.

Gardner, J. F. (1986). *Women in Roman law and society*. Bloomington, IN: Indiana University Press.

Gbaguidi, N., & Kodjoh-Kpakpassou, W. (2009). Introduction au système juriqidue et judiciaire du Bénin. Retrieved from www.nyulawglobal.org/globalex/BENIN.htm

Gender Links. (2013). *SADC Gender Protocol 2013 barometer*. Johannesburg, South Africa: Gender Links.

Ghana Judicial Service. (2014). History of the courts. Retrieved from www.judicial.gov.gh/index.php/history/summary.

Ghana News Agency. (2010, April 15). International Association of Women Judges inaugurated. Retrieved fromwww.ghanaweb.com/GhanaHomePage/NewsArchive/artikel.php?ID=180261

Gilligan, C. (1982). *In a different voice: Psychological theory and women's development*. Cambridge, MA: Harvard University Press.

Glenn, P. (2014). *Legal traditions of the world. Sustainable diversity in law*. Oxford, England: Oxford University Press.

Goodman, C. F. (2008). *The rule of law in Japan: A comparative analysis*. Amsterdam, The Netherlands: Walters Kluwer.

Government of Benin (2013, February 11). *Passation de service au Ministère de la justice: Réckya Madougou Yedo s'installe*. Retrieved from http://news.acotonou.com/h/580.html

Graycar, R. (2008). Gender, race, bias and perspective: Or, how otherness colours your judgment. *International Journal of the Legal Profession, 15*, 73–86.

Grey, S. (2006). Numbers and beyond: The relevance of critical mass in gender research. *Politics & Gender, 2*, 492–502.

Gros, J-G. (Ed.). (1998). *Democratization in late twentieth-century Africa: Coping with uncertainty*. Westport, CT: Greenwood Press.

Guichaoua, A. (2015, January 23). Gouvernement, representation politique, principaux corps d'état, institutions de la societé civile du Rwanda. Retrieved from www.francerwandagenocide.org/documents/guichaoua-annuaire.pdf

Hagenimana, F. X. (1990). *La separation des pouvoirs et histoire constitutionnelle Rwandaise*, Kigali, Rwanda: National University of Rwanda.

Haguruka. (2001). *La femme Rwandaise et l'accès à la justice*. Kigali, Rwanda: The Author. Retrieved from http://repositories.lib.utexas.edu/bitstream/handle/2152/4881/3989.pdf?sequence=1

Hallaq, W. B. (2009). *Sharī'a: Theory, practice, transformations*. New York, NY: Cambridge University Press.

Hallward-Driemeier, M., & Hasan, T. (2013). Empowering women: Legal rights and economic opportunities in Africa. Washington, DC: World Bank.

Harvey, B. (1966). *Law and social change in Ghana*. Princeton, NJ: Princeton University Press.

Hashim, A. (2005). Muslim personal law in Kenya and Tanzania: Tradition and innovation. *Journal of Muslim Minority Affairs, 25*, 449–459.

Hassim, S. (2002). A conspiracy of women? The women's movement in South Africa's transition to democracy. *Social Research, 69*, 693–732.

Havugimana, D. (1989). *La competence d'attribution des juridictions de l'ordre judiciaire en droit rwandais*. (Unpublished doctoral dissertation). Antwerpen: University of Antwerp.

Hedlund, M., Glazebrook, S., Pacht, A., & Wainwright, J. (Eds.). (2010). The IAWJ: Twenty years of judging for equality. Retrieved from www.iawj.org/jubilee_book_iawj_website_final_2_.pdf

Hill, E. (1979). *Mahkama! Studies in the Egyptian legal system: Courts and crimes, law and society*. London, England: Ithaca Press.

Hoexter, C. (2014). The structure of the courts. In Hoexter, C., & Olivier, M. (Eds.), *The judiciary in South Africa* (pp. 1–25). Cape Town, South Africa: Juta.

Holm, J., & Molutsi, P. (Eds.). (1990). *Democracy in Botswana*. Athens, OH: Ohio University Press.

Houngan Ayemonna, C. (2008). *Femmes juges du Bénin: Visages et contribution à l'évolution du droit*. Cotonou, Benin: Association Internationale des Femmes Juges—Section Béninoise.

Hunt, S. (2014, May/June). The rise of Rwanda's women: Rebuilding and reuniting a nation. *Foreign Affairs*. Retrieved from www.foreignaffairs.com/articles/rwanda/2014-03-30/rise-rwandas-women

Hunter, R. (2008). Can feminist judges make a difference? *International Journal of the Legal Profession, 15*, 7–35.

Huntington, S. (1991). Democracy's third wave. *Journal of Democracy, 2*, 12–34.

Ingersoll, H. H. (1911). Confusion of law and equity. *Yale Law Journal, 21*, 58–71.

INSAE (Institut national de la statistique et de l'analyse économique). (2013, December). Transition vers le marché du travail des jeunes femmes et hommes au Bénin. *Work4Youth Série de publication, 7*.

International Association of Women Judges (IAWJ). (n.d.). Jurisprudence of equality program decision. Retrieved from www.iawj.org/JEPcases.html

International Association of Women Judges (IAWJ). (n.d.). Judicial training programs: The jurisprudence of equality programs (JEP): Tanzania. Retrieved from www.iawj.org/JOGProgram1.html

International Criminal Court. (2009). *Agbanrin-Elisha, Victoire Désirée Adétroro*. Retrieved from www.icc-cpi.int/iccdocs/asp_docs/EJ2009/ICC-ASP-EJ2009-BNN-CV-FRA.pdf

Inter-Parliamentary Union (IPU). (2008). Historical archive of parliamentary election results. Retrieved from www.ipu.org/parline-e/reports/2033_arc.htm

Islamic Law (Restatement) Act. (1964). Retrieved from www.saflii.org/tz/legis/num_act/ila1964242.pdf

Jacob, M. (2014, December 18). Tanzania: Mara magistrates attend seminar on gender-based violence. *allAfrica*. Retrieved from http://allafrica.com/stories/201412180615.html

Johnson, R. E. (2014). Women as a sign of the new? Appointments to South Africa's Constitutional Court since 1994. *Politics & Gender, 10*, 595–621.

Johnson, S. W., Songer, D. R., & Jilani, N. A. (2011). Judge gender, critical mass, and decision making in the appellate courts of Canada. *Journal of Women, Politics & Policy, 32*, 237–260.

Joireman, S. (2001). Inherited legal systems and effective rule of law: Africa and the colonial legacy. *The Journal of Modern African Studies, 39*, 571–596.

Jones, K. B. (1993). *Compassionate authority: Democracy and representation of women*. New York, NY: Routledge.

Joseph, R. (1998). Africa: 1990–1997: From abertura to closure. *Journal of Democracy, 9*, 3–17.

Joseph, R. (Ed). (1999). *State, conflict and democracy in Africa*. Boulder, CO: Lynne Rienner.

Judicature and Application of Laws Act. (1961). Retrieved from www.tanzania.go.tz/egov_uploads/documents/JUDICATURE AND APPLICATION OF LAWS ACT.pdf

Judicial corruption in Ghana is not a perception: It is real. (2011, September 16). *GhanaWeb*.. Retrieved from www.ghanaweb.com/GhanaHomePage/NewsArchive/artikel.php?ID=218885

Judiciary of Tanzania. (n.d.). Retrieved from www.judiciary.go.tz

Judiciary of Zanzibar. (n.d.). Retrieved from www.judiciaryzanzibar.go.tz/#.php

Judiciary short of 1,600 magistrates. (2013, May 16). *Guardian*. Retrieved from www.ippmedia.com/frontend/functions/print_article.php?1=54749

Juma, I. H. (2013). Role of law and politics in making a nation and integration. *Law Reform Journal, 4*, 8–38.

Junqueira, E. B. (2003). Women in the judiciary: Perspective from Brazil. In Schultz, U., & Shaw, G. (Eds.), *Women in the world's legal professions* (pp. 437–450). Portland, OR: Hart Publishing.

Jyoni Wa Karega, J. (Ed.). (1996). Gacaca: Le droit coutumier au Rwanda: Rapport final de la première phase d'enquête sur le terrain. Kigali: Haut Commissaire aux Droits de l'Homme des Nations Unies.

Kadhis' Courts Act. (1985). Retrieved from www.judiciaryzanzibar.go.tz/act_1/The%20Kadhis%20Court%20Act%20No%2003%20of%201985.pdf

Kagame, A. (1952). *Le code des institutions politiques du Rwanda precolonial*. Brussels, Belgium: Institut Royal Colonial Belge.

Kakuli, G. (1997). The history and development of the rule-making power in the courts of Botswana and suggested reform. *The Comparative and International Law Journal of Southern Africa*, *30*, 190–198.

Kalantry, S. (2012, summer). Women in robes. *Americas Quarterly*. Retrieved from www.americasquarterly.org/women-in-robes

Kamatali, J-M. (2001). Ethnicity and constitutionalism in post-genocide Rwanda. In Oloka-Onyango, J. (Ed.), *Constitutionalism in Africa: Creating opportunities, facing challenges* (pp. 103–127). Kampala, Uganda: Fountain Publishers.

Kamatali, J-M. (2014). State-building in Rwanda. In Agbese, P., & Kieh, G. (Eds.), *Reconstructing the authoritarian state in Africa* (pp. 154–179). London, England: Routledge.

Kamau, W. (2013). Women judges and magistrates in Kenya: Challenges, opportunities and contributions. In Schultz, U., & Shaw, G. (Eds.), *Gender and judging* (pp. 167–190). Portland, OR: Hart Publishing.

Kapama, F. (2015, February 3). Tanzania: Escrow-tainted judges face JSC action. *allAfrica*. Retrieved from http://allafrica.com/stories/201502030575.html

Kari, M. (1992). Note on ambiguous text, Article 535 of the Code of Obligations and Contracts, *Revue Tunisienne de Droit*, 1, 203–235.

Keddie, N. (1991). Introduction: Deciphering Middle Eastern women's history. In Keddie, N., & Baron, B. (Eds.), *Women in Middle Eastern history* (pp. 1–22). New Haven, CT: Yale University Press.

Kenney, S. (2008). Thinking about gender and judging. *International Journal of the Legal Profession, 15*, 87–110.

Kenney, S. (2010). Critical perspectives on gender and judging. *Politics & Gender, 6*, 433–495.

Kenney, S. (2012). Thinking about gender and judging. In Schultz, U., & Shaw, G. (Eds.), *Women in the judiciary* (pp. 85–108). London, England and New York, NY: Routledge.

Kenney, S. (2013). *Gender and justice. Why women in the judiciary really matters*. London, England: Routledge.

Keregero, K. (2006, December 9). Tanzania: 20 new judges appointed. *Guardian*. Retrieved from www.wluml.org/node/3425

Khan, T. (2013, February 18). Legal notables protest against lack of women on JSC's short list. Business Day (p. 3). Retrieved from www.bdlive.co.za/national/law/2013/02/18/legal-notables-protest-against-lack-of-women-on-jscs-short-list.

Kileo, E. (2010). Tanzania Women's Judges Association. In Hedlund, M., Glazebrook, S., Pacht, A., & Wainwright, J. (Eds.), *The IAWJ: Twenty years of judging for equality* (pp. 165–167). Retrieved from www.iawj.org/jubilee_book_iawj_website_final_2_.pdf

Kimble, S. (2014), Feminist lawyers and legal reform in modern France, 1900–1946. In Schandevy, E. (Ed.), *Women in law and lawmaking in nineteenth and twentieth-century Europe* (pp. 45–74). Surrey, England: Ashgate.

King, K. L., & Greening, M. (2007). Gender justice or just gender? The role of gender in sexual assault decisions at the International Criminal Tribunal for the former Yugoslavia. *Social Science Quarterly, 88*, 1049–1071.

Kirkpatrick. D. D. (2012, July 3). Judge helped Egypt's military to cement power. *The New York Times*, p. A1.

Kosheri, R., & Riad, X. (1995). Egypt. In Cotran, E., & Mallat, C. (Eds.), *Yearbook of Islamic and Middle Eastern law* (pp. 177–185). London, England: Kluwer Law International.

Koyana, D. S., & Bekker, J. C. (1998). *The judicial process in the customary courts of Southern Africa*. Mthatha, South Africa: University of Transkei.

Kumado, K. (1993). The constitutional framework of democracy. In Ninsin, K.A., & Drah, F.K. (Eds.), *Political parties and democracy in Ghana's fourth republic* (pp. 53–62). Accra, Ghana: Woeli Publishing Services.

Laing, A. (2012, October 12). Women can inherit the earth rules Botswana judge. *The Telegraph*. Retrieved from www.telegraph.co.uk/news/worldnews/africaandindianocean/botswana/9605346/Women-can-inherit-the-earth-rules-Botswana-judge.html

Langa, P. (2007). The Bram Fischer memorial lecture: The emperor's new clothes. Bram Fischer and the need for dissent. *South African Journal on Human Rights, 23*, 362–372.

Law Society of Botswana. (2011). *Position paper on the appointment of judges*. Retrieved from www.lawsociety.org.bw/news/Position%20Paper%20on%20Appointment%20of%20Judges%20Final%2014%20june%202012%20'Final'.pdf

Law Society of South Africa. (2013, June). *Legal education and development 2012/2013 statistics*. Retrieved from www.lssalead.org.za/upload/STATS_DOCUMENT_2014.pdf

Law Society of South Africa. (2014, June). *Legal education and development 2013/2014 statistics*. Retrieved from www.lssalead.org.za/upload/STATS_DOCUMENT_2014.pdf

Layish, A. 1989. Shariah, custom and statute law in a 'non-Muslim' state. *Law in Multicultural Societies, 101/102*, 101–109.

Lee, H. (Ed.). (2011). *Judiciaries in comparative perspective*. Cambridge, England: Cambridge University Press.

Lee, R. (2013, September 3). Victory for women's rights in Botswana. Retrieved from www.osisa.org/womens-rights/botswana/victory-womens-rights-botswana

Legal and Human Rights Centre & Zanzibar Legal Services Centre. (2014). *Tanzania human rights report 2013*. Retrieved from www.humanrights.or.tz/tanzania-human-rights-report-2013.pdf

Lekgowe, G., & Motswagole, K. (2011, August 8). Court of Appeal and its foreign judges. *Sunday Standard*. Retrieved from www.sundaystandard.info/article.php?NewsID=11580&GroupID=5

LeVine, V. (1964). *The Cameroons: From mandate to independence*. Berkeley, CA: University of California Press.

L'Heureux-Dube, C. (2001). Outsiders on the bench: The continuing struggle for equality. *Wisconsin Women's Law Journal, 16*, 15–30.

Longman, T. (2006). Rwanda: achieving equality or serving an authoritarian state? In Bauer, G., & Britton, H. (Eds.), *Women in African parliaments* (pp. 133–150). Boulder, CO: Lynne Rienner.

Majamba, H. I. (n.d.). Perspectives on the Kadhis' courts in Zanzibar. Retrieved from http://xa.yimg.com/kg/groups/20674633/390109494/

Malleson, K. (2003a). Justifying gender equality on the bench: Why difference won't do? *Feminist Legal Studies*, *11*, 1–24.

Malleson, K. (2003b). Prospects for parity: The position of women in the judiciary in England and Wales. In Schultz, U., & Shaw, G. (Eds.), *Women in the world's legal professions* (pp. 175–190). Portland, OR: Hart Publishing.

Malleson, K. (2006). Rethinking the merit principle in judicial selection. *Journal of Law and Society, 33*, 126–40.

Malleson, K., & Russell, P. (Eds.). (2006). *Appointing judges in an age of judicial power: Critical perspectives from around the world.* Toronto, Ontario: University of Toronto Press.

Mamdani, M. (1996). *Citizen and subject: Contemporary Africa and the legacy of late colonialism*. Princeton, NJ: Princeton University Press.

Manteaw, S. (2008). Legal education in Africa: What type of lawyer does Africa need? *McGeorge Law Review, 39*, 905–970.

Manyathi, N. (2012). Statistics reflect pace of transformation in the attorneys' profession. *De Rebus, 6*, 3–4.

Maquet, J. (1961). *The premise of inequality in Rwanda*, London, England and New York, NY: Oxford University Press.

Martin, E. (1993). The representative role of women judges. *Judicature, 77*, 166–172.

Masengu, T. (2013). Courting controversy: Is judicial activism the only way to tackle gender inequality in southern Africa? Retrieved from www.osisa.org/sites/default/files/sex_03_tabethmasengu.pdf

Masengu, T., & Tilley, A. (2013, October 8). JSC: Cast the net wider to find more women. *Daily Maverick.* Retrieved from www.dailymaverick.co.za/opinionista/2013–10–08-jsc-cast-the-net-wider-to-find-more-women/

Masire, Q.M.J. (2006). *Very brave or very foolish? Memoirs of an African democrat*. Gaborone, Botswana: Macmillan Botswana.

Mayaba, J. (2013). Le juge béninois à l'heure du déclin (officiel) du dualisme juridique. In Otis, G. (Ed.), *Le juge et le dialogue des cultures juridiques* (pp. 135–50). Paris, France: Karthala.

McCormick, P., & Job, T. (1993). Do women judges make a difference? An analysis of appeal court data. *Canadian Journal of Law and Society*, *8*, 135–148.

Menkel-Meadow, C. (1986). The comparative sociology of women lawyers: The 'feminization' of the legal profession. *Osgoode Hall Law Journal, 24*, 897–918.

Mezghanni, A. (1975). Réflexions sur les relations du code du statut personnel, avec le droit musulman classique. *Revue Tunisienne de Droit*, 2, 53.

Michelson, E. (2013). Women in the legal profession, 1970–2010: A study of the global supply of lawyers. *Indiana Journal of Global Legal Studies, 20*, 1071–1137.

Miller, C. (2012, October 29). Judge as judicial midwife? Justice on Botswana's High Court strikes down customary law rule banning female inheritance. Retrieved from www.feministlawprofessors.com/2012/10/judge-judicial-midwife-justice-botswanas-high-court-strikes-down-customary-law-rule-banning-female-inheritance/

MINESUPRES. (1984). *Situation actuelle du recensement des personnages célèbres et des sites historiques*. Kigali, Rwanda: The Author.

Ministère de la famille, des affaires sociales, de la solidarité nationale, des handicapés et des personnes du troisième age (MFASSNHPTA). (2011, September). *Repertoire des femmes leaders au Bénin.* Retrieved from http://offebenin.org/femme/repertoires-des-femmes-leadercadres/

Ministry of Justice and Constitutional Affairs. (2008). Unblocking the road to timely justice for all: First annual review of the legal sector reform programme of Tanzania. Retrieved from www.tzdpg.or.tz/fileadmin/documents/external/dpg_tanzania/MKUKUTA_and_MKUZA_review_and_drafting/LSRP-FINAL-FULL-DRAFT-REPORT-2008.pdf

Mmusi and Others v Ramantele and Another (2012, October 12). (MAHLB-000836-10) [2012] BWHC 1.

Modise, O. (2011, July 2). Academic decries gender imbalance in the judiciary. *Sunday Standard.* Retrieved from www.sundaystandard.info/article.php?NewsID=9886&GroupID=1

Mokgoro, Y. (2010). Judicial appointments. *Advocate, 23*, 43–48.

Molokomme, A. (1993). The legal situation of women in Botswana. In Procek, E. (Ed.), *Changing roles of women in Botswana* (pp. 7–30). Gaborone, Botswana: Botswana Society.

Mooketsi, L. (2010, February 23). Botswana: Lack of women judges causes concern. *allAfrica*. Retrieved from http://allafrica.com/stories/201002230902.html

Moran, L. (2006). Judicial diversity and the challenge of sexuality: Some preliminary findings. *Sydney Law Review, 28*, 565–598.

Morima, N. A. (2013, November 7). Is Botswana's judiciary independent? *Botswana Gazette*. Retrieved from www.gazettebw.com/?p=5867

Morton, F., Ramsay, J., & Mgadla, P. T. (2008). *Historical dictionary of Botswana*. Lanham, MD: Scarecrow Press.

Mosikare, O. (2015, March 20). LSB to sue Khama over Motumise application. *Mmegi*. Retrieved from www.mmegi.bw/index.php?aid=50062

Moyer, L. (2013). Rethinking critical mass in the federal appellate courts. *Journal of Women, Politics & Policy, 34*, 47–71.

Mudawalat Majliss Al Umma (1967). Retrieved from www.chambre-dep.tn/site/main/AR/index.jsp

Muhayeyezu, A., (1978) *Lacapacité juridique des enfants mineurs dans le droit coutumier et ecrit Rwandais*, Memoire de Licence, UNR. Butare, Rwanda: Faculté de Droit.

Mujawamariya, D., & Ship, S. (2005). La guerre et le génocide de 1994: Impacts et nouveaux espoirs sur l'éducation des jeunes filles au Rwanda. *Canadian and International Education/ Education canadienne et international, 34*, Article 3.

Munuo, E. (2014, May). Reflections on the changing meaning of justice for all. Retrieved from www.iawj.org/Eusebia_Munuo_-_Reflections_on_Justice_for_All_-_Speech_-_IAWJ_Conf_2014.pdf

Nafie, R. (2003, August 14–20). Obituary: An honourable man, Fathi Naguib (1938–2003). *Al-Ahram Weekly*. Retrieved from http://weekly.ahram.org.eg/2003/651/eg2.htm

Ndulo, M. (2011). African customary law, customs, and women's rights. *Indiana Journal of Global Legal Studies, 18*, 87–120.

Newbury, C., & Baldwin, H. (2001). Confronting the aftermath of conflict: women's organizations in post-genocide Rwanda. In Kumar, K. (Ed.), *Women and civil war: Impact, organizations, and action* (pp. 97–128). Boulder, CO: Lynne Rienner.

Ntampaka, C. (1992). *Éléments de droit coutumier*. Butare, Rwanda: National University of Rwanda.

Nyanduga, B., & Manning, C. (2006). Guide to Tanzania legal system and legal research. Retrieved from www.nyulawglobal.org/globalex/Tanzania.htm

Obilade, A. O. (1979). *The Nigerian legal system*. London, England: Sweet & Maxwell.

O'Connor, K., & Yanus, A. B. (2010). Judging alone: Reflections on the importance of women on the court. *Politics & Gender, 6*, 441–452.

O'Connor, S. D. (1991). Portia's progress. *New York University Law Review, 66*, 1546–1558.

Okechukwu, O. (2005). Seeking justice in transitional societies: An analysis of the problems and failures of the judiciary in Nigeria. *Brooklyn Journal of International Law, 31*, 9–82.

Okertchiri, J. (2013). Ghana's women showing their mettle in governance. Retrieved from www.spyghana.com/ghanas-women-showing-their-mettle-in-governance/

Olivier, M. (2014a). The magistracy. In Hoexter, C., & Olivier, M. (Eds.), *The judiciary in South Africa* (pp. 319–354). Cape Town, South Africa: Juta.

Olivier, M. (2014b). The selection and appointment of judges. In Hoexter, C., & Olivier, M. (Eds.), *The judiciary in South Africa* (pp. 116–153). Cape Town, South Africa: Juta.

O'Regan, K. (2012). A pillar of democracy: Reflections on the role and work of the Constitutional Court of South Africa. *Fordham Law Review, 81*, 1169–1186.

Owor, M., and Musoke, H. (2012). The neglect of gender questions in judicial education in Uganda. Paper presented at the 2012 Law and Society International Conference, Honolulu, Hawaii.

Palacio. A., Sage. M., & Woolcock, M. (2006). *Law, equity, and development*. Washington, DC: World Bank.

Passation de charges au ministère de la justice: Madagou Yèdo s'en va et Djènontin s'installe. (2013, August 13). *La Presse du jour*. Retrieved from www.lapressedujour.net/archives/27260

Paternostre de la Maririeu, B. (1972) *Le Rwanda et son effort de development*. Brussels, Belgium: A. de Boeck.

Philemon, L. (2012, November 13). Stop unnecessary judgment delays, judiciary officials told. *Guardian*. Retrieved from www.ippmedia.com/frontend/functions/print_article.php?1=47946

Prempeh, H. K. (1999). A new jurisprudence for Africa. *Journal of Democracy, 10*, 135–149.

Prempeh, H. K. (2006). African judges in their own cause: Reconstituting independent courts in contemporary Africa. *International Journal of Constitutional Law, 4*, 592–605.

Prempeh, H. K. (2007). Africa's 'constitutionalism revival:' False start or new dawn? *International Journal of Constitutional Law, 5*, 469–506.

President Kikwete's speech at International Association of Women Judges conference. (2014, May 5). Retrieved from www.wavuti.com/2014/05/pres-kikwetes-speech-at-international.html

Quansah, E. K., & Fombad, C. M. (n.d.). Judicial activism in Africa: Possible defence against authoritarian resurgence? Retrieved from www.ancl-radc.org.za/sites/default/files/Judicial%20Activism%20in%20Africa.pdf

Rabkin, F. (2011, October 26). Two women judges for labour court. *Business Day*. Retrieved from www.bdlive.co.za/articles/2011/10/26/two-women-judges-for-labour-court

Rabkin, F. (2013, April 11). JSC backs only male candidate for top post. Business Day (p. 3). Retrieved from www.bdlive.co.za/national/law/2013/04/11/jsc-backs-only-male-candidate-for-top-post

Rabkin, F. (2014, April 10). Few magistrates make the grade with JSC. *Business Day*. Retrieved from www.bdlive.co.za/national/law/2014/04/10/few-magistrates-make-the-grade-with-jsc

Rackley, E. (2013). *Women, judging and the judiciary. From difference to diversity*. Cavendish: Routledge.

Rawlings ordered killing of judges—Adabuga. (2003, May 23). *Modern Ghana*. Retrieved from www.modernghana.com/news/35081/1/rawlings-orderd-killing-of-judges-adabuga.html

Redgment, J. (1988). The structure of the courts of appeal in Botswana, Bophutatswana and Zimbabwe. *The Comparative and International Law Journal of Southern Africa, 21*, 105–113.

Republic of Botswana. (n.d.). Administration of justice: About the Court of Appeal. Retrieved from www.justice.gov.bw/about%20us/about-court-appeal

Republic of Botswana. (n.d.). Administration of justice: About the High Court. Retrieved from www.justice.gov.bw/about%20us/about-high-court

Republic of Botswana. (n.d.). Administration of justice: About Magistrate Courts. Retrieved from www.justice.gov.bw/about%20us/about-magistrate-courts

Republic of Botswana. (n.d.). Administration of justice: Background of the judiciary. Retrieved from www.gov.bw/en/Ministries—Authorities/Ministries/Administration-of-Justice-AOJ/Background-Traditions-Court/Background-of-the-Judiciary/

Republic of Botswana. (n.d.). Administration of justice: The hierarchy of the courts. Retrieved from www.gov.bw/en/Ministries—Authorities/Ministries/Administration-of-Justice-AOJ/About-AOJ1/The-Hierarchy-of-the-Courts/

Resnik, J., & Curtis, D. (2011). *Representing justice: Invention, controversy, and rights in city-states and democratic courtrooms*. New Haven, CT: Yale University Press.

Reyntjens, F. (1985). *Pouvoir et droit au Rwanda, droit public et evolution politique, 1916–1974*. Brussels, Belgium; Musée Royale de l'Afrique Centrale.

Rickard, C. (2005, April 10). Women judges tell of struggles for acceptance. *Sunday Times* (p.11). Retrieved from http://allafrica.com/stories/200504120031.html

Rickard, C. (2005, October 23). Judging women harshly. *Sunday Times*. Retrieved from http://business.highbeam.com/3548/article-1G1-137958861/judging-women-harshly

Rickard, C. (2007, September 11). Time to shape the space for women judges! *Legalbrief Today*. Retrieved from www.legalbrief.co.za/article.php?story=20070911084807646

Robi, A. (2014, August 16). 20 new judges sworn in. *allAfrica*. Retrieved from http://allafrica.com/stories/201408181550.html

Roht-Arriaza, N. (2012). Botswana High Court strikes down customary inheritance law as discriminatory against women. Retrieved from www.intlawgrrls.com/2012/10/botswana-high-court-strikes-down.html

Russell, P. (2006). Conclusion. In Malleson, K., & Russell, P. (Eds.), *Appointing judges in an age of judicial power: Critical perspectives from around the world*. Toronto, Ontario: University of Toronto Press.

Saad, A. (2015, February 23). The Supreme Council of the Judiciary: National Council for Women asked for equality between men and women and we responded by appointing female judges. *Shrouk*. Retrieved from www.shorouknews.com/news/view.aspx?cdate=23022015&id=79575524-a0dd-459f-a307-d7d4626ec99a

Sachs, A. (1973). *Justice in South Africa*. London, England: Sussex University Press.

Samatar, A. (1999). *An African miracle: State and class leadership and colonial legacy in Botswana development*. Portsmouth, NH: Heinemann.

Sana, B.A. (2005). Les figures de l'altérité. In Sassi, B.H. (Ed.), *Melanges Sassi Ben Halima*. Tunis, Tunisia: CPU.

Sana, B.A. (2007). La féminisation de la magistrature en Tunisie entre émancipation féminine et autoritarisme politique. *L'année du Maghreb*, *3*, 55–74.

Sawyerr, J.F. (1969). Reflections on the internal conflict of laws in Tanzania: An outline. *African Spectrum*, *4*, 23–36.

Schroeder, F. (2013, October 13). More women poised to join ranks of judges. *Sunday Independent* (p. 8).

Schultz, U., & Shaw, G. (2003a). Introduction. In Schultz, U., & Shaw, G. (Eds.), *Women in the world's legal professions* (pp. xxv-lix). Portland, OR: Hart Publishing.

Schultz, U., & Shaw, G. (Eds.). (2003b). *Women in the world's legal professions*. Portland, OR: Hart Publishing.

Schultz, U., & Shaw, G. (2012a). Introduction. In Schultz, U. & Shaw, G. (Eds.), *Women in the judiciary* (pp. 1–5). London, England and New York, NY: Routledge.

Schultz, U., & Shaw, G. (Eds.). (2012b). *Women in the judiciary*. London, England and New York, NY: Routledge.

Schultz, U., & Shaw, G. (2013a). Introduction: Gender and judging. In Schultz, U., & Shaw, G. (Eds.), *Gender and judging* (pp. 2–50). Portland, OR: Hart Publishing.

Schultz, U., & Shaw, G. (Eds.). (2013b). *Gender and judging*. Portland, OR: Hart Publishing.

Scribner, D., & Lambert, P. (2010). Constitutionalizing difference: A case study analysis of gender provisions in Botswana and South Africa. *Politics & Gender*, *6*, 37–62.

Segwai, K. (2008, November 14). The departure of a nonconformist. *Mmegi*. Retrieved from www.mmegi.bw/index.php?sid=6&aid=38&dir=2008/november/friday14

Serag, M. (2001–2002). Legal education in Egypt. *South Texas Law Review*, *43*, 615–621.

Sharma, K. (2009). *The role of traditional leaders (chiefs) in the administration of justice in Africa: Customary courts in Botswana*. Institute for African Development occasional paper series. Ithaca, NY: Cornell University.

Shivji, I.G., Majamba, H.I., Makaramba, R.V., & Peter, C.M. (2004). *Constitutional and legal system of Tanzania: A civics sourcebook*. Dar es Salaam, Tanzania: Mkuki na Nyota Publishers.

Sika, N., & Khodary, Y. (2012). One step forward, two steps back? Egyptian women within the confines of authoritarianism. *Journal of International Women's Studies*, *13*, 91–100.

Smith, M.G. (1960). *Government in Zazzau, 1800–1950*. London, England: Oxford University Press.

Southern African Development Community (SADC). (2013). *SADC Gender Monitor 2013: Women in politics and decision-making positions*. Gaborone, Botswana and Harare, Zimbabwe: SADC/SARDC.

Speech by President of the United Republic of Tanzania at the opening of the International Association of Women Judges Africa Region, Arusha. (2012). *Journal of the Tanzania Women Judges Association (TAWJA)*, *1*, 65–70. Retrieved from www.tawjatz.org/publications/

State losing too many cases: Kikwete. (2015, February 5). *Citizen*. Retrieved from www.thecitizen.co.tz/News/national/Too-many-cases-are-lost/-/1840392/2613708/-/f8iyxlz/-/index.html

Statistics South Africa. (2013). *Stats in brief 2013*. Pretoria, South Africa: Statistics South Africa.

Steady, F. (2011). *Women and leadership in West Africa: Mothering the nation and humanizing the state*. New York, NY: Palgrave Macmillan.

Stoeltje, B., Firmin-Sellers, K., & Ogwang, O. (2002). Introduction to special issue: Women, language and law in Africa. *Africa Today*, *49*, vii-xx.

Strouvens, L., & Piron, P. (1948). *Codes et lois du Congo Belge: Annotes d'après les rapports du Conseil colonial, les instructions officielles et la jurisprudence des tribunaux*, Brussels, Belgium: F. Larcier; Leopoldville: Édition de Codes et Lois du Congo Belge.

Tambwe, M. (2013, September 1). Tanzania: More women speak out on sexual harassment at the workplace. *allAfrica*. Retrieved from http://allafrica.com/stories/201309010224.html

Tanganyika Order in Council. (1920). Retrieved from www.kituochakatiba.org/sites/default.files/legal-resources/THETANGANYIKAORDERINCOUNCIL1920.pdf

Tanzania human rights jurisprudence. (n.d.). Retrieved from www1.umn.edu/humanrts/research/TanzaniaB.html

Tanzania Women Judges Association (TAWJA). (2012). A short profile of TAWJA activities. Retrieved from www.tawjatz.org/wp-content/uploads/2012/03/TAWJA-PROFILE.pdf

Tanzania Women Judges Association (TAWJA). (n.d.). Background history. Retrieved from www.tawjatz.org/background-history/

Tanzania Women Judges Association (TAWJA). (n.d.). Jurisprudence of equality project (JEP). Retrieved from www.tawjatz.org/jurisprudence-of-equality-project/

Tanzania Women Judges Association (TAWJA). (n.d.). Stopping the abuse of power for purposes of sexual exploitation: Naming, shaming, and ending sextortion. A toolkit. Retrieved from www.tawjatz.org/publications/

Tanzania: Women judges present Kikwete with human rights award. (2014, May 6). *allAfrica*. Retrieved from http://allafrica.com/stories/20140561174.html

Tetteh-Charway, B. (2012). Promoting a victim-centred approach to the adjudication of domestic violence cases. *Journal of the Association of Magistrates and Judges of Ghana*, *52*, 50–54.

Thornton, M. (1996). *Dissonance and distrust: Women in the legal profession*. Melbourne, Australia: Oxford University Press.

Tidjani Alou, M. (2006). Corruption in the legal system. In Blundo, G., & Olivier de Sardan, J. P. (Eds.), *Everyday corruption and the state: Citizens and public officials in Africa* (pp. 137–176). London, England: Zed.

Tobi, N. (1996). *Sources of Nigerian law*. Lagos, Nigeria: MIJ Professional Publishers.

Tolsi, N. (2013, April 12). JSC conflict laid bare by inconsistency. *Mail & Guardian* (p. 16).

Truth and Reconciliation Commission (1998). Report: Volume 5. Cape Town, South Africa: Juta.

UN Women. (2012). Progress of the world's women, 2011–2012: In pursuit of justice. New York, NY: United Nations.

UN Women. (2013a, March 12). Ending abuse of authority for purposes of sexual exploitation (sextortion): The experience of the judiciary in Tanzania. Retrieved from www.unwomen.org/en/news/stories/2013/3/speech-by-john-hendra-on-ending-sextortion-in-tanzania

UN Women (2013b, May 8). Making laws real and accessible underlines efforts by judges in Tanzania. Retrieved from www.unwomen.org/en/news/stories/2013/5/making-laws-real-and-accessible-underlines-efforts-by-judges-in-tanzania

Underhill, G. (2012, August 17). Judiciary: Appointment queried on gender grounds. *Mail & Guardian*. Retrieved from http://mg.co.za/article/2012-08-17-00-judiciary-appointment-queried-on-gender-grounds

United Nations. (2008). *Country reports on human rights 2008*. New York, NY: United Nations.

United Nations Democracy Fund. (2011, February 4). *Jurisprudence on the ground: Evaluation report*. Retrieved from www.un.org/democracyfund/sites/www.un.org.democracyfund/files/UDF-URT-07–155%20Jurisprudence%20on%20the%20Ground%20in%20Tanzania.pdf

United Nations Development Programme in Tanzania. (2014). Women and justice in Tanzania. Retrieved from www.tz.undp.org/content/tanzania/en/home/presscenter/articles/2014/02/14/women-empowerment-justice-in-tanzania.html

United Republic of Tanzania. (2014). Country report on the review and progress made and challenges encountered in implementation of the Beijing declaration and platform for action and outcomes of the twenty third special session of the General Assembly-Beijing +20. Retrieved from www.unwomen.org/~/media/Headquarters/Attachments/Sections/CSW/59/National_reviews/Tanzania_review_Beijing20.pdf

University of Minnesota Human Rights Library. (n.d.). *Tanzania human rights jurisprudence*. Retrieved from www1.umn.edu/humanrts/research/TanzaniaB.html

Villalon, L., and VonDoepp, P. (Eds.). (2005). *The fate of Africa's democratic experiments*. Bloomington, IN: Indiana University Press.

VonDoepp, P. (2005). The problem of judicial control in Africa's neo-patrimonial democracies: Malawi and Zambia. *Political Science Quarterly, 120*, 275–301.

VonDoepp, P. (2006). Politics and judicial assertiveness in emerging democracies: High Court behavior in Malawi and Zambia. *Political Research Quarterly*. *59*, 389–399.

VonDoepp, P. (2009). *Judicial politics in new democracies: Cases from southern Africa*. Boulder, CO: Lynne Rienner.

Walker, T. G., & Barrow, D. (1985). The diversification of the federal bench: Policy and process ramifications. *Journal of Politics*, *47*, 596–617.

Wanitzek, U. (1990–1991). Legally unrepresented women petitioners in the lower courts of Tanzania: A case of justice denied? *Journal of Legal Pluralism*, *30–31*, 255–271.

Wanitzek, U. (2002). The power of language in the discourse on women's rights: Some examples from Tanzania. *Africa Today*, *49*, 3–19.

Wesson, M., and Du Plessis, M. (2008). The transformation of the judiciary. Fifteen year policy review for the South African presidency. Retrieved from www.thepresidency.gov.za/docs/reports/15year_review/jcps/transformation_judiciary.pdf

Westergren, S. (2004). Gender effects in the Court of Appeals revisited: The data since 1994. *Georgetown Law Journal, 92*, 689–708.

Widner, J. (2001a). *Building the rule of law: Francis Nyalali and the road to judicial independence in Africa*. New York, NY: Norton.

Widner, J. (2001b). Courts and democracy in post-conflict transitions: A social scientist's perspective on the African case. *The American Journal of International Law, 95*, 64–75.

WILDAF. (2002, July). La marche du WILDAF/BENIN sur l'Assemblée nationale. *WILDAF Newsletter, 11*, 8, 10.

Williams, M. (2006). In a different path: The process of becoming a judge for women and men. *Judicature, 90*, 104–113.

Williams, M., & Thames, F. (2008). Women's representation on high courts in advanced industrialized countries. *Politics and Gender, 4*, 451–471.

World Bank. (2015). Ratio of female to male tertiary enrollment. Retrieved from http://databank.worldbank.org/data/views/variableselection/selectvariables.aspx#

Yoon, M. Y. (2008). Special seats for women in the national legislature: The case of Tanzania. *Africa Today*, *55*, 60–86.

Yoon, M. Y. (2011). More women in the Tanzania legislature: Do numbers matter? *Journal of Contemporary African Studies*, *29*, 83–98.

Yoon, M. Y. (2013). Special seats for women in parliament and democratization: The case of Tanzania. *Women's Studies International Forum*, *41*, 143–149.

Youm 7. (2013, September 26). Nermine Suliman, Presidential Decree for the Promotion of SCA members. Retrieved from www.youm7.com/story/2013/9/26/ارق-رشنن ر-رئيس-الجمهورية-بترقية-أعضاء-هيئة-قضايا-الدولة/1268880#.Vcf5SosyBUQ[3]

Zantou, P.A. (2000–1). *Les femmes dans la vie politique au Bénin (1960–1990)* (Mémoire de maîtrise [Unpublished master's thesis]). Université Nationale du Bénin, Cotonou.

Index

Note: Page numbers with *f* indicate figures; those with *t* indicate tables.

For Product Safety Concerns and Information please contact our EU
representative GPSR@taylorandfrancis.com
Taylor & Francis Verlag GmbH, Kaufingerstraße 24, 80331 München, Germany

www.ingramcontent.com/pod-product-compliance
Ingram Content Group UK Ltd.
Pitfield, Milton Keynes, MK11 3LW, UK
UKHW022119190926
475702UK00013B/1529
9780815370550